# MAKHNO **AND** MEMORY

ANARCHIST AND MENNONITE NARRATIVES OF UKRAINE'S CIVIL WAR, 1917–1921

# MAKHNO AND MEMORY

SEAN PATTERSON

UNIVERSITY OF MANITOBA PRESS

Makhno and Memory: Anarchist and Mennonite Narratives of Ukraine's Civil War, 1917–1921


24 23 22 21 20 1 2 3 4 5



University of Manitoba Press
Winnipeg, Manitoba, Canada
Treaty 1 Territory
uofmpress.ca

*Cataloguing data available from Library and Archives Canada*
ISBN 978-0-88755-838-2 (PAPER)
ISBN 978-0-88755-580-0 (PDF)
ISBN 978-0-88755-878-7 (EPUB)
ISBN 978-0-88755-878-8 (BOUND)

Cover image: *Pavel Dybenko and Nestor Makhno.*
Alamy.com, ID E8FCYB.
Cover design by Frank Reimer
Interior design by Jess Koroscil
Map design by Weldon Hiebert

Printed in Canada

The University of Manitoba Press acknowledges the financial support for its publication program provided by the Government of Canada through the Canada Book Fund, the Canada Council for the Arts, the Manitoba Department of Sport, Culture, and Heritage, the Manitoba Arts Council, and the Manitoba Book Publishing Tax Credit.

Published with the generous support of the Canadian Foundation for Ukrainian Studies Scholarly Publication Support Program.

Канадська фундація українських студій
Canadian Foundation for Ukrainian Studies
Fondation canadienne des etudes ukrainiennes

Funded by the Government of Canada | Canada

# CONTENTS

A NOTE ON THE TEXT VII

LIST OF ILLUSTRATIONS IX

MAPS XIII

**INTRODUCTION** 1

**CHAPTER 1**
**THROUGH MAKHNOVIST EYES** 19

**CHAPTER 2**
**THROUGH MENNONITE EYES** 73

**CHAPTER 3**
**THE EICHENFELD MASSACRE** 109

**CONCLUSION** 145

ACKNOWLEDGEMENTS 155

NOTES 157

BIBLIOGRAPHY 181

INDEX 193

# A NOTE ON THE TEXT

Throughout this book, where an English version of a source is available I reference it. In all possible cases, I have checked these translations against the original language sources to ensure accuracy. I take full responsibility for all translations made by myself and any potential errors in this regard. Ukrainian toponyms are used in this book for all place names within Ukraine's current borders. German spellings are used for Mennonite and German colonies. Russian toponyms have been retained only when they appear in the original source being quoted. A simplified Library of Congress system is used to transliterate Russian and Ukrainian. Soft signs, indicated by an apostrophe, have been removed in some cases. For example, Kuz'menko is rendered as Kuzmenko and Oleksandrivs'k as Oleksandrivsk. I have also simplified Zaporizhzhia as Zaporizhia.

I use the word Ukraine throughout this book in a territorial sense. This is done to help orient the reader but does not imply Ukraine existed prior to the civil war period as an organized nation-state. However, the term was employed in a geographical sense as early as the twelfth century and regularly used from the fifteenth to eighteenth centuries by various powers in the region to describe the territories around the Dnipro River including those inhabited by the Zaporizhian Cossacks.[1] In the late eighteenth century, Imperial Russia annexed the lands of the Zaporizhian Cossacks and the Crimean Khanate to the south. The official imperial title for these territories became *Novorossiia* (New Russia), and its Ukrainian-speaking inhabitants were regularly referred to and often self-identified as *malorossy* (Little Russians) or southern Russians. Mennonite sources consistently employ this lexicon. By contrast, Makhnovist sources exclusively use the terms Ukraine and Ukrainian. During the nineteenth century the latter terms increasingly gained currency and the appelation Little Russian was rejected by more ethnically conscious

Ukrainian-speakers.[2] At the same time, it is important to recognize that "Ukrainian" identity and Ukraine's territorial boundaries were in a process of negotiation and were defined in a variety of ways by those who employed these terms. During the civil war, Ukraine existed as an organized state in the form of the Ukrainian People's Republic—declared independent by the nationalist Central *Rada* in Kyiv in January 1918. The latter was briefly supplanted by a coup in April 1918, which led to the formation of the Ukrainian State, often referred to as the Hetmanate. A rival Kharkiv-based Ukrainian Soviet Republic was also declared in 1917 and served as a predecessor to the Ukrainian Soviet Socialist Republic.

# LIST OF ILLUSTRATIONS


1. Peter Kropotkin, c. 1890. https://commons.wikimedia.org/wiki/File:Kropotkin_Portrait.jpg. *p. 5*

2. Vsevolod Eichenbaum (Volin). Paris, August 1927. Alexander Berkman Papers, International Institute of Social History, BG A14/659. *p. 29*

3. A young Halyna Kuzmenko, c. 1917. Gosudarstvennyi tsentral'nyi muzei sovremennoi istorii Rossii (State Central Museum of the Contemporary History of Russia), 4923877. *p. 35*

4. Makhno and his daughter Elena in Paris, c. 1928. Published in *Ogonek* no. 22, 1928. *p. 37*

5. Silberfeld estate, c. 1910. Janzen Family Collection. Permission granted by Margie Koop. *p. 47*

6. Wintergruen estate (formerly part of Silberfeld), 1900. Mennonite Archival Image Database, CA MHC 578-10.0. *p. 47*

7. Huliaipole Peasant Union, 1909. Makhno is seated on the far left in the front row. Voldemar Antoni is seated next to him. Gosudarstvennyi tsentral'nyi muzei sovremennoi istorii Rossii (State Central Museum of the Contemporary History of Russia), 4921265. *p. 49*

8. A group of released Butyrka prison inmates after the February Revolution, March 1917. Prison shackles lay at their feet. Nestor Makhno is seated first from the left in the front row. Unknown source; image available at http://www.makhno.ru. *p. 51*

9. Nestor Makhno and Feodir Shchus. Huliaipole, 1919. Gosudarstvennyi tsentral'nyi muzei sovremennoi istorii Rossii (State Central Museum of the Contemporary History of Russia), 4922217. *p. 57*

10. Makhnovist unit near Huliaipole, March 1919. Gosudarstvennyi tsentral'nyi muzei sovremennoi istorii Rossii (State Central Museum of the Contemporary History of Russia), 4921823. *p. 61*

11. Nestor Makhno in Romania, 1921. Senya Fléchine Papers, International Institute of Social History, BG A8/730. *p. 61*

12. Group of Makhnovists, c. 1920. Published in *Ogonek* no. 12, 1926. *p. 67*

13. Makhnovist Army Staff. Huliaipole, 1919. In the back row, Viktor Belash is seated second from the left and Feodir Shchus is fifth from the left. Gosudarstvennyi tsentral'nyi muzei sovremennoi istorii Rossii (State Central Museum of the Contemporary History of Russia), 4913568. *p. 69*

14. Peasant field workers on the Wintergruen estate, 1900. Mennonite Archival Image Database, CA MHC 578-2.0. *p. 83*

15. Mennonite homestead displaying flags of Imperial Germany. Ohrloff, Molotschna colony, 1918. Mennonite Archival Image Database, CA MHC 044-159.0 *p. 93*

16. Mennonite *Selbstschutz* unit from the villages of Blumenort, Tiege, and Ohrloff. Molotschna colony, 1918. Mennonite Archival Image Database, CA MHC 135-1.0 *p. 95*

17. Abram and Maria Janzen. Janzen Family Collection. Permission granted by Margie Koop. *p. 103*

18. Worker with horse in front of the Silberfeld estate. Janzen Family Collection. Permission granted by Margie Koop. *p. 103*

19. Mennonite homestead in Franzfeld, Jasykowo colony. Mennonite Archival Image Database, CA MHC 044-275.0 *p. 115*

20. The Heinrichs Family in Eichenfeld. A young Heinrich H. Heinrichs and Cornelius H. Heinrichs. Janzen Family Collection, published in *Kornelius Heinrichs and His Descendants.* Permission granted by Marianne Janzen. *p. 117*

21. Jasykowo *Selbstschutz* leader Peter van Kampen, 1913. Mennonite Archival Image Database, CA MHC 680-3.0 *p. 119*

22. Eichenfeld *Selbstschutz* leader Heinrich Heinrich Heinrichs. Janzen Family Collection, published in *Kornelius Heinrichs and His Descendants.* Permission granted by Marianne Janzen. *p. 119*

23. Makhnovist unit entering Oleksandrivsk, 20 October 1919. Gosudarstvennyi tsentral'nyi muzei sovremennoi istorii Rossii (State Central Museum of the Contemporary History of Russia), 4924718. *p. 127*

24. The Stundist Tent Mission that lost five members in the Eichenfeld massacre, c. 1918–19. Mennonite Archival Image Database, CA MHC 044-332.0. *p. 131*

25. Mennonite survivors mourning victims of the Sagradowka massacre in front of a mass grave. Tiege, Sagradowka colony, 1919. Mennonite Archival Image Database, CA CMBS NP145-6-12. *p. 141*

26. Memorial to the Eichenfeld Massacre in Novopetrivka, Ukraine, 2011. Photo by Sean Patterson. *p. 152*

27. Memorial statue of Nestor Makhno in Huliaipole, Ukraine, 2011. Photo by Sean Patterson. *p. 153*

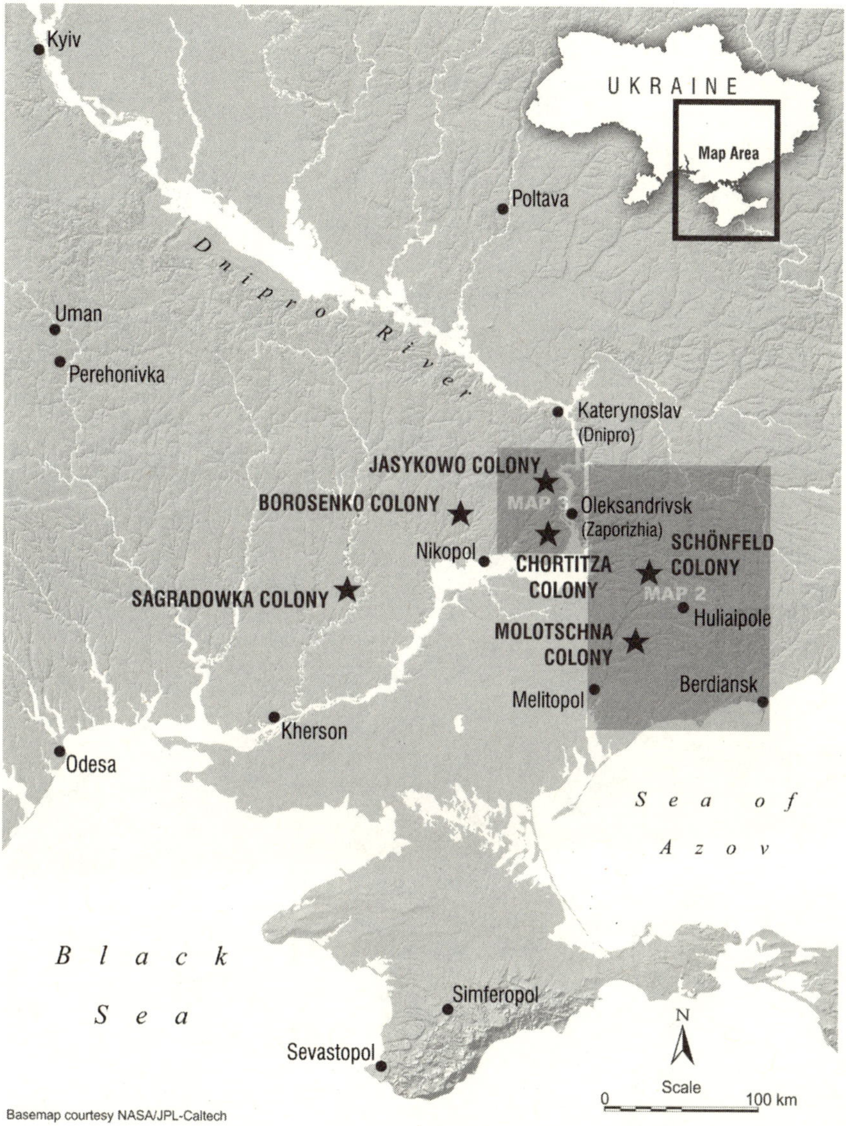


Map 1. Southern Ukraine in 1919.

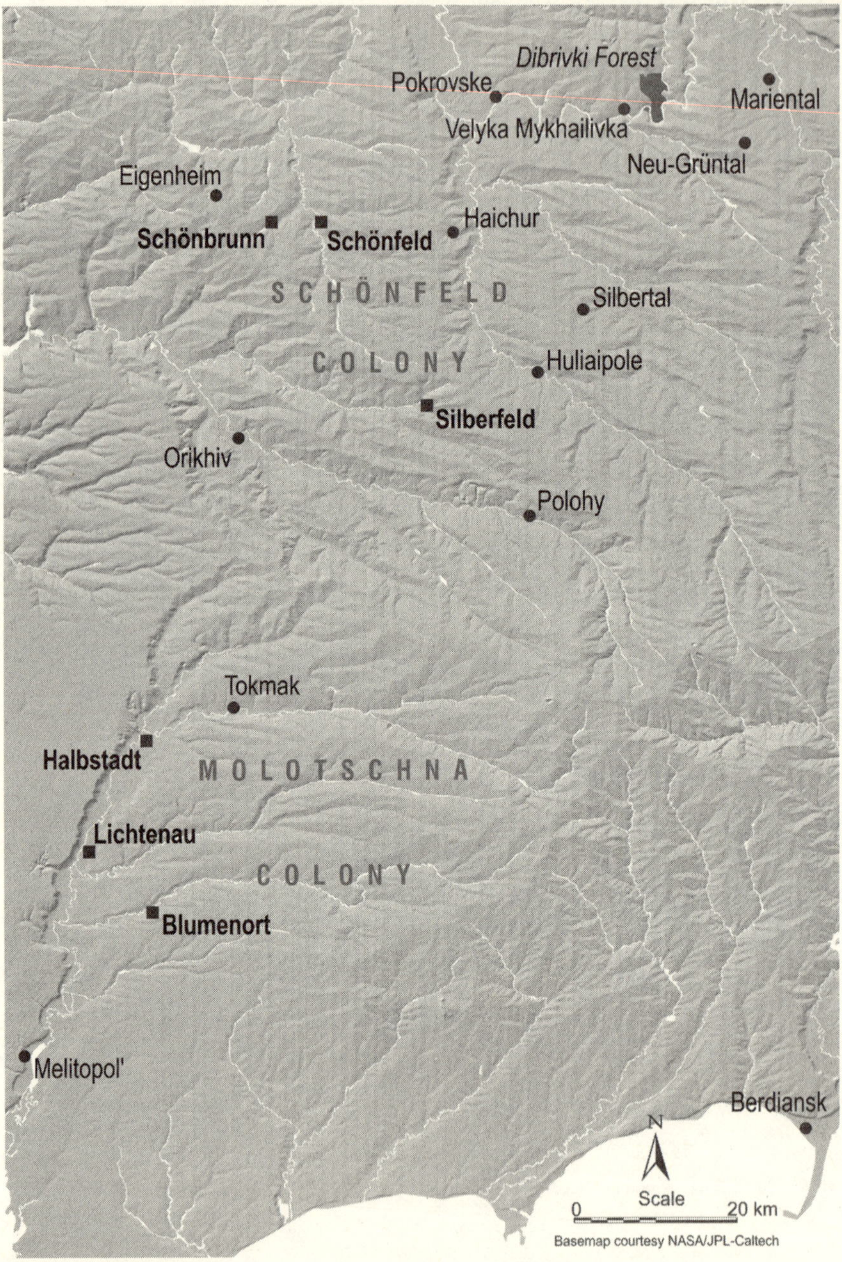


Map 2. Huliaipole and surrounding area.

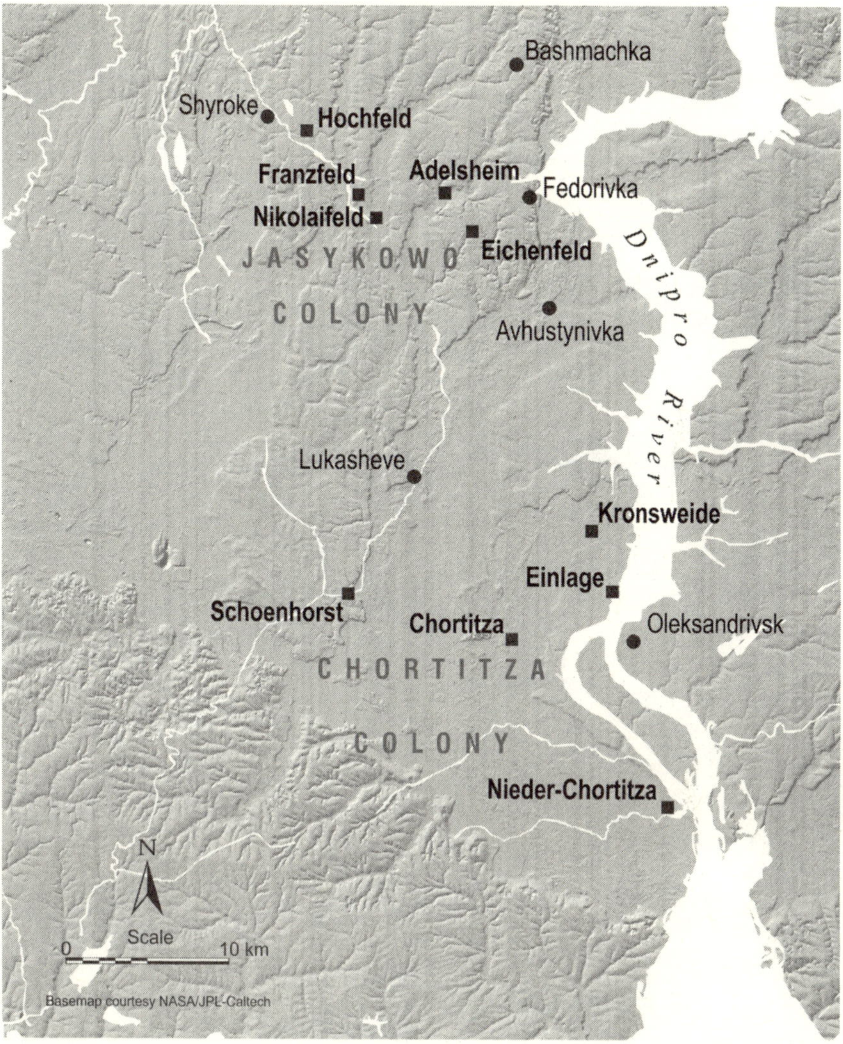


Map 3. Jasykowo and Chortitza colonies.

# INTRODUCTION

A legend circulates among the locals of Huliaipole that the anarchist Nestor Makhno, upon abandoning his struggle and fleeing Ukraine, ordered a cache of loot to be buried in a secret location. The intention was to safeguard funds for a renewed battle against the Soviet regime in some imagined future, but Makhno never returned to his homeland and, according to local lore, the treasure remains buried to this day.[1] Makhno's gold has not been confirmed as anything but a myth, but even if it did exist, what could be gained, besides the material riches, from its discovery? I believe the persistence of this story in the local collective mind relates to the belief that the materiality of historical artifacts can somehow make the past more substantial and present. If only metaphorically, discovering the gold would momentarily fulfill the promise of Makhno's return and all its attendant cultural meanings.

Historical writing similarly seeks to make concrete an ephemeral past, but, like Makhno's gold, it leaves us only with spectral traces trapped in documents, objects, landscapes, and receding voices. My research into Nestor Makhno and his movement's conflict with the Mennonites of southern Ukraine has led me to confront a multitude of competing histories, memories, myths, and legends all jostling to assert their own unique perspective. It is a topic fraught with folklore, ideological battles, and radically divergent cultural memories in which fact and fiction often seamlessly blend. Through the prism of history, multiple Makhnos are conjured, each one shouting over the other.

This book seeks to tell a difficult story from two sides. The historical memory of Makhno is especially contested between today's Mennonites and the global anarchist community. To the former,

Makhno is a sadistic character who perpetrated extreme violence against their parents and grandparents during the Russian Revolution and the ensuing civil war period in Ukraine. By contrast, many contemporary anarchists understand Makhno in heroic terms as the revolutionary leader of a movement that liberated workers and peasants from capitalist exploitation. Furthermore, Makhno is often celebrated in Ukraine as a regional hero. In his hometown, public statues, memorials, museum exhibits, and even a limited edition coin minted by Ukraine's central bank, all hail Makhno as a populist hero. Mennonite and pro-Makhnovist assessments of history could not be further apart.

This book is about the origins of these two radically diverging narratives. Through memoirs, histories, diaries, and archived documents, each group's narrative representations of the Mennonite-Makhnovist conflict are explored. Of particular concern to this study is how each group constructed the other as an enemy and how each side legitimized—and protested—its use of violence. Central to these narratives is Nestor Makhno and their authors' assessements of him as a hero or villain.

In certain ways, my personal relationship to the topic of Makhno embodies this narrative divide. As a young undergraduate I became fascinated by the philosophical writings of the Russian anarchist Peter Kropotkin. I was specifically attracted to Kropotkin's theory of mutual aid as a critical factor in human and animal evolution. Kropotkin himself visited Canada in 1897 and wrote a largely positive report about Mennonites living in Manitoba's so-called West Reserve.[2] Kropotkin's philosophy was also a major influence on Nestor Makhno. It is through this connection that I first encountered histories of the Makhnovist movement written by its participants Peter Arshinov and Volin. These histories emphasized the movement as a liberatory force championing direct democracy for peasants and workers and an egalitarian communal way of organizing society. However, when I returned home from university and told my friends and family about this fascinating movement I had read about, I learned of a completely different history.

My family history is linked to Ukraine in more ways than one. My grandmother was born in Ukraine's Volhynian region to a German Baptist family. They first arrived in Ukraine as colonists in the eighteenth century at the invitation of Catherine the Great. I remember as a child my great-grandfather telling me stories of how the Bolsheviks dug up his fields in search of money and hidden food. I also remember the stories of how my family fled the country by bribing a border guard only a few short years before Stalin's terror-famine struck Ukraine. On my paternal side, my father—of an Irish-Canadian background—converted to the Mennonite faith at a young age. He became a Mennonite Brethren pastor, and as a child I was raised in a largely Mennonite environment. I have fond memories of the people and activities at the West End church in Winnipeg I was raised in, and to this day the majority of my friends are from a Mennonite background. It was from these friends that I heard stories of the notorious bandit Nestor Makhno who murdered Mennonites during the civil war. These were harrowing accounts of extreme abuse and suffering, which had deeply impacted families that were, almost 100 years later, still experiencing inter-generational trauma from the violence witnessed.

Initially it was difficult to make sense of these two incompatible histories. The Makhnovist histories I had read made no references to these events. Indeed, they never mentioned Mennonites. At first I thought it could be a case of mistaken identity. Many forces were operating in Ukraine during the civil war and in this confused landscape the attacks of one group were sometimes attributed to another. However, as I burrowed deeper into the research I realized these attacks were undeniably perpetrated by Makhno and his army. I was forced to quite radically recalibrate my assessment of Makhno's movement, but I also wanted to understand the motivations behind these attacks. This book, which attempts to tell a balanced story, is the end result of that investigation. It is both the story of a movement that massacred innocents in the name of liberty and justice, and the story of a historically pacifist people driven to distress in the midst of violence, some of whom took up arms to protect life and property.[3] This book is written with a deep personal respect for both Mennonites and Ukrainians, for the Anabaptist faith and the Kropotkinite value of human mutual aid.

## HISTORICAL CONTEXT

Nestor Ivanovich Makhno was the youngest child of a poor peasant family from Huliaipole—a medium-sized town in Katerynoslav province (modern-day Zaporiz'ka Oblast' in southern Ukraine) roughly 100 kilometres east of Oleksandrivsk (Zaporizhia). In 1906, at seventeen years old, Makhno embraced philosophical anarchism and joined Huliaipole's anarchist-communist Union of Poor Peasants. Over the next three years this group would leave a trail of robbery, arson, and murder. In 1909, Makhno was arrested while attempting to bomb the local police station. Alongside his co-conspirators, young Nestor was sentenced to death by hanging for terrorist offences. By virtue of his age—and possibly his mother's intervention—Makhno's sentence was commuted to a life of hard labour (*katorga*) in Moscow's notorious Butyrka prison.[4] Following the 1917 February Revolution, Makhno's release was secured through a general amnesty for political prisoners issued by the new provisional government. Returning to his hometown, he and other anarchists organized the local peasantry to expropriate the land around Huliaipole.

Ideologically, Makhno was most strongly influenced by the anarcho-communism of the Russian thinker Prince Peter Kropotkin. Kropotkin described his philosophy as "the no-government system of socialism," which was unwavering in its rejection of both the state and capitalism.[5] In his writings, Kropotkin placed special emphasis on the realization of agrarian socialism through the self-motivated action of peasants. For example, Kropotkin writes that "only a peasant uprising can take the land away from the kulaks and landlords, and that the revolution will be all the more comprehensive, the more personal initiative and activity emerges from the peasantry and the less they wait for any alleged saviours."[6] Kropotkin also stressed the expropriation of all private property and the restructuring of society along communal lines. In the course of the coming social revolution both private property and the wage system were to be abolished. In their place, a society would emerge premised on mutual aid and the free distribution of goods according to the slogan "from each according to his means, to each according to his needs."[7] According to Kropotkin's vision property would not be nationalized under a centralized government but rather socialized into the hands of decentralized "voluntary associations." These associations would forge links with each other to create a federated "interwoven network" of societal administration.[8] In the context of nineteenth-century Imperial Russia, anarcho-communism very much followed in the footsteps of the nihilists and narodniks who placed their hopes in the revolutionary action of peasants. As Kropotkin asserted, "the liberation

Figure 1. Peter Kropotkin, c. 1890.

of the Russian peasants from the yoke of serfdom, which has oppressed them to this day, becomes the prime task of the Russian revolutionary."[9] This approach strongly contrasted with traditional Marxist views that the revolution would be led by urban workers. While both anarcho-communism and Marxism embraced class struggle and the necessity of violence to achieve their goals, the anarcho-communist social basis for revolution and its envisioned utopia frequently conflicted with those of Marxists.[10]

Makhno himself was an avid follower of Kropotkin from his time in the Union of Poor Peasants. Makhno recalls how in prison, "I got hold of Kropotkin's book *Mutual Aid*. I found it entirely absorbing and kept it with me constantly in order to discuss it with comrades."[11] Later when visiting Moscow in June 1918, Makhno managed to meet Kropotkin. The two spoke "at length about the Ukrainian peasantry," and Makhno was left feeling fully satisfied in his visit with "the venerable sage of Anarchism."[12] The two maintained contact and Makhno even supplied Kropotkin with food later in the civil war. In his memoirs Makhno expressed that he believed Kropotkin's philosophy "most closely approaches the peasant mentality."[13]

After the 1917 February Revolution and Makhno's return to Huliaipole, the movement's ideological leadership coalesced in the Huliaipole Anarcho-Communist Group, of which Makhno was a member. From its early stages the movement actively courted urban anarchists, and beginning in the middle of 1919 Makhno successfully attracted activists from Ukraine's anarchist Nabat Confederation to assist with propaganda and social reform.[14] The Revolutionary Military Soviet, an elected civilian-controlled body, was also established to coordinate political, economic, and cultural activity in the Makhnovist regions. In the midst of military hostilities and within an unstable territorial base, the Makhnovists attempted to implement a program of freely elected local councils (soviets) and an egalitarian redistribution of land to the peasants.

Throughout the movement's existence, four congresses were organized that elected peasants', workers', and soldiers' deputies. The largest of these convened between 28 October and 2 November 1919 in Oleksandrivsk, which gathered 300 delegates from across Makhnovist-controlled territory. As the Makhnovists were cynical of party politics, official election-style campaigns were forgone in favour of local assemblies in which representatives were directly chosen by those gathered. Workers and peasants who did not employ labour were allowed to participate in the elections, while business owners, estate owners, and wealthier farmers were disenfranchised. Despite the Makhnovists' extreme dislike of political parties, they nonetheless permitted individuals belonging to the various socialist parties to sit as congress delegates and on the Executive Committee of the Revolutionary Military Soviet.[15]

The movement also promoted the organization of large-scale communes on expropriated estates. For example, a formerly Mennonite-owned estate near Huliaipole was reorganized as the 300-member Rosa Luxemburg commune described in Makhno's memoirs.[16] The Makhnovist Draft Declaration also includes a clause encouraging the peasantry towards such "expanded cooperative organization and production ... [as] the most appropriate and natural step along the road to constructing the agricultural economy on new foundations."[17] The Makhnovists also formed a large-scale army, numbering as many as 100,000 troops, which the leadership considered to be guarding the labouring population and its right to self-organization without compulsion from outside forces. As a whole, the movement opposed the centralizing authority of the Bolsheviks and advocated a third revolution that would place power into the hands of the workers and peasants unmitigated by party bureaucrats.[18]

In St. Petersburg political change pushed forward at a frenetic pace. In November, Lenin and the Bolsheviks seized power in a second Revolution and on 3 March 1918 the new government signed the Treaty of Brest-Litovsk with the Central Powers of Germany and Austria-Hungary ending Russia's participation in the First World War. The treaty surrendered large swathes of Russian territory, including most of Ukraine. The Germans had also signed a protection treaty a month earlier with the Ukrainian nationalist Rada officially recognizing the Ukrainian People's Republic. The Rada subsequently invited Austro-German military units to assist in securing Ukraine's sovereignty. The Bolsheviks and their allies were forced to fully evacuate Ukraine. Makhno likewise abandoned Huliaipole, eventually making his way to Moscow. The German presence, however, was overwhelmingly perceived by the populace as an occupation, and after less than a month in power the Ukrainian nationalists were replaced by a German-backed puppet regime headed by the self-declared Hetman of Ukraine, Pavlo Skoropadskyi. Peasant insurgencies erupted across Ukraine in opposition to the occupation. A host of independent peasant armies led by local warlords named *otamans* and *bat'kos* created havoc for the occupying forces, killing some 19,000 Austro-German troops over a few weeks in the spring and summer of 1918.[19] Under these conditions, Makhno clandestinely returned to Huliaipole in July to organize a peasant insurgency in his region against the Austro-German occupation. From this rebellion emerged what would be called the Makhnovshchina (Makhno movement).[20] It was locally popular and notorious for harassing Austro-German units stationed in the region. It was also during this period that the Makhnovists first came into conflict with German and Mennonite *Selbstschutz* (self-defence) units.

At the same time, a civil war was deepening across Russia. Anti-Bolshevik forces led by former Tsarist generals alongside Kuban and Don Cossacks formed the White Army. The Whites, as they were known, were organized across Russia's vast territory and physically cut off from each other. The Whites fought on three main fronts, coordinated by General Anton Denikin in the south, Admiral Aleksander Kolchak in Siberia, and General Nikolai Iudenich in the northwest. Anxious to contain the spread of Communism, the Western Allies, led by the United States, Britain, and France, intervened on the side of the Whites, providing supplies, munitions, and troops. The Bolsheviks responded to the threat of counterrevolution by organizing their own Red Army under the command of Leon Trotsky. Peasants and workers were conscripted en masse in a bid to defeat the Whites and to secure control over the former territories of Imperial Russia. Between these two main armies emerged a range of other forces, such as Symon Petliura's nationalist Ukrainian People's Army based mainly in western and central Ukraine. Furthermore, a variety of independent peasant movements, collectively referred to as the Greens, complicated an already bewildering military situation. Distinct from the Makhnovists, the Greens were often ideologically vague and willing to shift their allegiances between the Whites and the Reds depending on the situation. By contrast, the Makhnovist leadership was consistently anarchist in its orientation and refused any alliance with the White Army.[21]

The end of the First World War in November 1918 led to the Austro-Germans' withdrawal from Ukraine, leaving a vast political vacuum. Given the Bolsheviks' weak presence in Ukrainian territory, a plethora of political movements and strongmen moved to assert control over Ukraine's various regions. The Makhnovshchina quickly consolidated its power around Huliaipole. In the ensuing civil war that engulfed the former Russian Empire, the Makhnovists battled any and all forces in a bid to establish an independent anarchist region in southern Ukraine.

At critical moments the Makhnovists played an important role in the Bolsheviks' military strategy along the southern front against General Denikin's White Army. Between 1918 and 1921 the Makhnovists and the Red Army entered into three periods of alliance, in which they coordinated their efforts against their common enemy. However, each truce was characterized by mutual suspicions that ended in open hostilities. A final alliance was agreed upon in October 1920, which resulted in the decisive defeat of the White Army in the Crimea. Almost immediately the Bolsheviks ended their truce with Makhno and initiated a campaign to eliminate the

Makhnovist army and its supporters. Makhno's struggle with the Reds lasted until August 1921 when he fled across the Romanian border before settling into exile in Paris. By September the movement within Ukraine was militarily defeated, although archival evidence suggests underground anarchist and Makhnovist groups potentially existed into the 1930s.[22]

The high tide of the movement came shortly after the White Army's thrust through southern Ukraine towards Moscow in fall 1919. In a desperate bid, Makhno directed his forces against the White Army's vulnerable rearguard, severely disrupting the White Army's operational capability. Makhno's campaign compelled Denikin to transfer a portion of his front line troops to deal with Makhno. Shortly thereafter the Red Army routed Denikin's forces, inspiring anarchist writer Max Nomad to dub Makhno "the bandit who saved Moscow."[23] In the shadow of Denikin's defeat, the Makhnovists greatly expanded their sphere of influence, occupying a substantial portion of southern Ukraine including the major cities of Oleksandrivsk and Katerynoslav (Dnipro). Amidst pitched battles with the White Army, the Makhnovists served as the main military-administrative power in the region until the Red Army's arrival in January 1920.

Throughout this period, the Makhnovists occupied a large number of Mennonite colonies. Due to the colonies' wealth—relative to the neighbouring Ukrainian peasant villages—the Makhnovists identified a large percentage of Mennonites as class enemies. Prior to the Austro-German occupation, Mennonite colonies and estates around Huliaipole were subjected to raids and their properties expropriated in the name of the Revolution. During the Austro-German occupation, a segment of the Mennonite community broke with hundreds of years of pacifism and established armed self-defence (*Selbstschutz*) units in an effort to protect their families and property. Lutheran and Catholic German colonists simultaneousely organized their own self-defence and sometimes integrated with Mennonite units. The Mennonite *Selbstschutz* was first organized by the Austro-Germans and was in theory independent and purely defensive. After the occupation, *Selbstschutz* units also coordinated their actions with the White Army, and during the spring of 1919 played an integral role in the White Army's front against Makhno and the Bolsheviks just north of the Molotschna colony. After the colonies were overrun in fall 1919, some former *Selbstschutz* members joined ethnic German battalions in the White

Army. Mennonites understood the Makhnovists to be a direct threat to their colonies' survival, but the decision to arm themselves deeply divided the community between *Selbstschutzler* and traditional pacifists.[24]

Under Makhnovist occupation, Mennonite families were subjected to constant harassment and abuse. The widespread rape of Mennonite women was particularly traumatic, and provoked many men to reject their pacifist roots. The horror of their experience peaked in November and December 1919 when Makhnovist troops perpetrated a series of massacres resulting in over 800 Mennonite deaths over a six-week period.[25] In Chapter 3, the context and motivations behind the massacre at Eichenfeld, in the Mennonite colony of Jasykowo, will be examined in detail.

## MAKHNOVIST AND MENNONITE NARRATIVES

The memoirs and histories produced by Makhnovists and Mennonites in the aftermath of these events present radically opposing narratives. To the former, Makhno and his movement illustrated a shining example of popular self-organization. Makhnovist authors present their movement's history through narratives of revolutionary heroism framed through the language of freedom and justice. Violence is likewise legitimized as a necessary element of the revolutionary process. In this way, the violence against Mennonites is subsumed by an overall narrative of the revolutionary peasants' struggle against southern Ukraine's landowning elite. In Makhnovist writing the Mennonites are never explicitly mentioned by name. Rather, they are included in the more general category of "German colonists" (*nemetskie kolonisty*), a term that also applied to German Lutheran and Catholic colonists. Furthermore, Makhnovist authors draw a tight correlation between "German colonists" and broad class categories like *pomeshchik* (landlord) and kulak (an affluent farmer). Although this construct of "German colonists" as wealthy rural elites is widely employed in the literature, working-class Germans and Mennonites were also recognized by the Makhnovists as potential allies, and some even joined Makhno. As I will explore in detail in Chapter 1, Makhnovist ideology considered class far more important than ethnicity. Ethnic difference is acknowledged in the Makhnovist paradigm, but class categories are used to differentiate enemies from allies. By paying careful attention to how identifiers like "German colonist," *pomeshchik*, and kulak are used, alongside place names mentioned in the texts, a detailed picture emerges of how Mennonites are constructed by Makhnovist authors. By contrast, while Mennonites are implicitly present in Makhnovist literature, during the course of my research I did not find a single mention of the 1919 massacres.[26] These events are only opaquely alluded to through generalized descriptions of large-scale violence.

Conversely, Mennonite memoirs and histories frequently reference both Makhno and his supporters by name. Mennonite literature presents the Makhnovshchina as a destructive force of extreme violence. With few exceptions, the social and economic motivations behind the movement are overshadowed in Mennonite accounts by the lived experience of terror and abuse. The Makhnovists are clearly identified as the perpetrators of the 1919 massacres and Makhno himself is most commonly described as a "bandit-terrorist." Mennonite narratives also highlight individual and collective persecution and martyrdom. Their interpretations of the Makhnovist experience range widely, but a common construction amongst pacifist Mennonites is of Makhno as a "scourge of God," as one survivor phrased it.[27] While the Makhnovshchina is framed as satanic, it is simultaneously a tool used by God to punish the community for its perceived collective sins. The Mennonite martyr thus bears double witness to the fallen nature of the Makhnovists and of their own community. As I will later discuss, in much of Mennonite literature the term Makhnovist frequently takes on added meanings overlain with spiritual implications.

Between Makhnovist and Mennonite narratives, it is impossible to explain Makhno, the person, from one totalizing perspective. There was a slipperiness to his personality that evaded definition, even for those who knew him closely. Makhno's close associate, the anarchist intellectual Volin (Vsevolod Eikhenbaum), struggled to write Makhno's biography.[28] The unfinished manuscript is revealingly subtitled "Contributions to the Study on the Enigma of Personality." Volin described his attempt to unravel the mystery of Makhno as follows:

> One may be in contact with a man for many years. But if his personal intimate life remains outside this contact you will not learn much about his true personality. During the six months in total I spent with

> the movement, I was in close contact with Makhno. I experienced with him episodes of "all kind" . . . I spoke and discussed much with him. . . . Often, I shared evening meals with him. The given conditions to determine the personality of Makhno, were therefore quite favourable. Yet I must emphasize that such knowledge always stopped short. His intimate, personal life remained absolutely unknown. Of it, I knew absolutely nothing. But it was above all just that which would have allowed me to penetrate the depths of his personality.[29]

It appears Makhno was no more penetrable to his close comrade than to today's researcher. In the historical literature Makhno is fragmented into an array of competing personalities and representations, variously described as a revolutionary anarchist, a peasant rebel, a Ukrainian Robin Hood, a mass murderer, a pogromist, and a devil.

Paul Ricoeur argues historical narratives perform a "configurational act" by "eliciting a pattern from a succession" of events. Plot is created by harnessing chronological events to service a story. The historical event in turn "receives its definition from its contribution to the plot."[30] Hayden White similarly describes this process as "emplotment," defining his term as "the encodation of the facts contained in the chronicle as components of specific kinds of plot structures."[31] Both Ricouer and White point to how narrativity, be it fictional or non-fictional, orders events in a story structure. The history of Makhnovist-Mennonite relations and their apparently irreconcilable narratives are what this book seeks to interrogate and unravel. I explore how Makhnovists and Mennonites have narrativized each other in their respective accounts and how specific characterizations of Makhno and his movement in Mennonite and Makhnovist literature serve broader collective narratives. An integral component of my argument is that the identity projects of each group have shaped their historical representations to such an extent, and often in such an exclusionary manner, that two radically divergent versions of history have evolved. Indeed, one could be forgiven for thinking that completely different events were being narrated. Particularly in the first two chapters of this book, I am concerned with how events were subjectively experienced, interpreted, and articulated by Makhnovist and Mennonite authors from the civil war period. I am equally interested in how each side contructed and defined the other. In this way, a narrative topography can be sketched, illustrating where Mennonite and Makhnovist memories divide and—sometimes surprisingly—overlap.

One historiographical tendency in particular motivated me to write on this topic. In certain radical leftist circles Makhnovist atrocities are denied or rationalized as justifiable responses to counterrevolutionary activity.[32] In exile, Makhno himself strongly denied the mistreatment of civilians by his movment, writing that "in relation to peaceful inhabitants, independent of what ethnic group they belonged to, entirely peaceable relations were maintained."[33] This is certainly not the experience found in Mennonite accounts of Makhnovist occupation. My work directly challenges such denialism, placing responsiblity squarely on the Makhnovists for the mistreatment and mass murder of Mennonites. While Makhno's personal involvement in the massacres is unproven, Mennonite sources make very clear that the movement at large perpetrated horrific crimes against innocent civilians.

My work also frames the motivations for these attacks within a broader socio-economic context. While presenting events of the civil war from the perspective of Makhnovist and Mennonite writers, I intersperse their narratives with socio-economic information to help situate the reader. This is part of a wider argument that, in addition to Mennonite collaboration with the Austro-Germans and the White Army, peasant land hunger was a critical component of the violence directed at German and Mennonite colonists. As I will show, the issue of land and labour relations between colonist and peasant is repeatedly referenced by memoirists on both sides of the conflict. The possession of land also reappears as a critical factor in the Eichenfeld massacre's pattern of murder, which specifically targeted landowners and their sons.[34]

I am especially interested in Mennonite economic success in the region and the wealth they accumulated over time, which allowed them to purchase large amounts of land, particularly from the 1860s onwards.[35] These purchases took the form of daughter colonies—to ease their own problem with landlessness—and private estates obtained from Russian nobles.[36] This increase in Mennonite land acquisition coincided with both the emancipation of serfs and a rural population explosion. The inadequacy of post-emancipation land allotments, coupled with widespread rural impoverishment, led many peasants to hire themselves out as farmhands on private Mennonite estates or as servants and workers in the colonies. This brought colonists and peasants into more direct contact distinctively marked by a master-servant relationship.[37] Peasants also found that lands they previously worked and now under Mennonite ownership were no longer available for lease.[38] According to Andreas Kappeler, by the late nineteenth century German and Mennonite economics, in relation to the local Ukrainian peasants, created "a fertile ground for the existence of social and inter-ethnic conflict."[39] Peasant unrest and rebellion related to land hunger intermittently shook the region, most notably in 1905. However, after the total collapse of centralized authority in 1917, the revolutionary peasants' resolve to forcibly expropriate the land led them into direct conflict with Mennonite estate owners and the colonies.

Throughout this book, the terms peasant and peasantry are used to indicate the largely ethnic Ukrainian rural population of southern Ukraine. Mennonites were also legally desiginated as "state peasants" by Imperial Russia, but for the sake of clarity I do not use the term peasant to refer to Germans and Mennonites in the region. The term colonist is widely used in sources from both sides, as well as by the Imperial Russian authorities, to describe the various ethnic groups invited by Catherine the Great in the eighteenth century to populate southern Ukraine, or New Russia, as it was then called. Bulgarians, Greeks, and Jews were likewise referred to as colonists living in colonies. In the context of late nineteenth- to early twentieth-century Ukraine and Russia the term should not be interpreted as derisive. Makhno in particular describes positive relations with Greek and Jewish "colonists." It must also be noted that the term never acquired the negative connotations it is associated with in modern North America and should not be read through this lens. Imperial Russia's colonization of southern Ukraine followed a unique process unto itself and should not be conflated with the North American experience, even if parallels, in certain regards, can be observed.[40]

It is also important to note that the region's peasants were not an undifferentiated mass. Some were farmers, others farmhands, and still others migrant workers, estate servants, wet-nurses, and seasonal factory workers, amongst a plethora of possible occupations. Peasants in southern Ukraine also came from differentiated pre-emancipation backgrounds, with some being former estate serfs, household serfs, and others state peasants. Culturally, peasants were from Ukrainian, Russian, Cossack, and mixed-heritage backgrounds, who lived in a regional multicultural tapestry unmatched elsewhere in Imperial Russia. Economically, peasants were divided into lower, middle, and upper strata, and by no means did they all support Makhno and his program. In fact, some even intervened to save their Mennonite employers and neighbours during the civil war.

Most Makhnovist and Mennonite writers speak of the peasantry in an abstract sense, without drawing the above distinctions. In the case of Mennonite literature, the peasants are universally referred to as "Russians" or "Little Russians." By contrast, Makhnovist authors and the movement's documents overwhelmingly identify peasants as "Ukrainian." In this book, unless otherwise indicated, the peasants being discussed are specifically those who sympathized with the Makhnovist program. This in itself is inevitably something of an abstraction, as no sure-fire statistical data on the movement's social composition exists. The closest we have is a Soviet census from 1920 that lists 265 Makhnovists who applied for amnesty from the Bolsheviks: 117 were landless, ninety-one owned less than four hectares, and fifty-seven owned more than four. The source also indicates the insurgents were mainly under the age of thirty.[41] In his memoirs, the Makhnovist Army Chief of Staff, Viktor Belash, offers a similar breakdown of the movement's membership with 40 percent being poor and middle peasants, 10 percent from the upper strata, and the remainder landless of varying occupations. He also confirms that 80 percent of the army was between twenty and thirty-five years old.[42]

Perhaps the best indicator of the Makhnovists' socio-economic concerns are their own resolutions. For example, in February 1919 the land resolution of the second congress of the Huliaipole district states: "In the interests of socialism and the struggle against the bourgeoisie all land must pass into the hands of the labouring peasantry. Based upon the principle that the land belongs to no one (*zemlia nich'ia*) and that it can only be used by those who work and cultivate it, the land should be transferred to the labouring peasantry without payment on an egalitarian basis."[43] These sentiments were echoed in the Makhnovists' October 1919 Draft Declaration, which rejected the nationalization of land under the Bolsheviks: "Lands seized from the great estate-owners should not be put at the disposal of the State but placed in the hands of those who actually work them: the peasant organizations, free communes, and other unions."[44] Both the Makhnovshchina's peasant nature and its overriding concern with the land question are dominant themes repeatedly emphasized in both Makhnovist and Mennonite literature.

It should be acknowledged that this book does not explore in depth how the Makhnovshchina has been represented and remembered by the southern Ukrainian peasantry at large. Makhno, Belash, and Kuzmenko were all of a peasant background but they cannot claim to speak for all of southern Ukraine's peasants. As such, they provide an important but unavoidably circumscribed view of events. Likewise, Makhnovist archival documents can help illuminate regional peasant attitudes but they are also from a decidedly partisan perspective. Written peasant accounts for this period and region are sparse, although the Ukrainian and Russian archives and oral traditions may proffer important finds. It is my sincere hope that future studies are able to deepen knowledge in this regard and give the region's peasants a stronger voice, and perhaps complexify their exact role in and interpretation of events discussed in this book.

Chapters 1 and 2 present Makhnovist and Mennonite narratives through eyewitness memoirs, histories, newspapers, and diaries. Chapter 1 provides a close reading of Makhno's memoirs alongside the historical writings of key Makhnovist intellectuals Volin and Peter Arshinov, the memoirs of Makhnovist Chief-of-Staff Viktor Belash, and the diary of Makhno's wife Halyna Kuzmenko. It is important to emphasize that the narratives presented in Chapter 1 are distinctly anarchist and written by the movement's ideological leadership. The works of Makhno, Volin, and Arshinov were published in exile, originally in French and German. Their target was primarily an international audience who sympathized with political anarchism. As such, these works represent how the exiled leadership wished to be perceived by the radical community at large. In this regard, these works are still important today in shaping contemporary radical leftist views on the Makhnovshchina. By contrast, Belash and Kuzmenko's memoirs provide something of a counterbalance, as they were never intended for publication. A detailed examination of these sources and their authors is presented before looking at events through the eyes of these Makhnovist writers.

Chapter 2 presents the Mennonite perspective predominantly from diaspora memoirs. Most important in this regard are the memoirs of

Gerhard Schroeder, Dietrich Neufeld, Gerhard Lohrenz, Jacob Toews, and David Rempel. Eyewitness letters collected by Mennonite historian Victor Peters have been used to supplement these sources. Additionally, extensive use is made of the Molotschna colony–based newspaper *Friedensstimme* as a source of first-hand accounts. Chapter 2 also contrasts pacifist and *Selbstschutz* narratives to gauge the extent to which their interpretations of events are complementary or divided.

Chapter 3 brings Makhnovist and Mennonite sources into direct dialogue through a case study of the 8 November 1919 Eichenfeld massacre. I argue it was a Makhnovist action while simultaneously exploring how both sides contributed to the creation of an environment marked by an escalating spiral of violent reprisals. To reconstruct the events around Eichenfeld, both Mennonite and Makhnovist sources are employed. A variety of memoirs are also explored to understand how the massacre was received and interpreted by the broader Mennonite community. Throughout this chapter's investigation I seek to understand and communicate the perspective of both perpetrator and victim in an effort to grasp the causes and motivations behind this tragic event. By examining Makhnovist and Mennonite accounts in this manner a multi-perspectival history unfolds, which I hope will encourage reflection and dialogue on the use and legitimation of violence in the civil war.

CHAPTER 1

# THROUGH MAKHNOVIST EYES

How Makhnovists understood class and ethnicity is a critical component of the Makhnovist-Mennonite conflict. In an account of his pre-revolutionary prison life, Makhno elaborated on his own sense of being Ukrainian:

> I couldn't really explain where I got my sympathies for Ukraine; of course, I had read a lot about its history, in particular the books of Kliuchevskii and Kareev. My mother often told me about the lives of the Zaporozhian Cossacks, about their free communes in the old days. I had once read Gogol's novel *Taras Bulba* and was thrilled with the customs and traditions of the people of those times. But it never occurred to me that the day would come when I would feel myself their heir, and they would become for me a source of inspiration for the rebirth of this free country. My convictions forced me to distance myself from separatist tendencies and did not allow me to give in to the temptation of contemplating an independent Ukrainian state, despite the sense of kinship I felt towards my Ukrainian prisoner comrades.[1]

In this passage Makhno admits a strong affinity with Ukrainian identity and Cossack mythology. He also acknowledges Ukraine as a distinct territory—as opposed to its official designation as southern or New Russia. The latter point is strongly emphasized in another memoir where Makhno describes personally confronting Lenin for using "southern Russia" to describe Ukraine.[2] Makhno also expressed disappointment that his memoirs could not be published in Ukraine or in Ukrainian.[3] Yet despite such cultural affinities, Makhno simultaneously signals his opposition to political nationalism and its project for an independent state. Indeed, as an anarchist Makhno rejected the idea of a centralized nation-state, instead advocating a federated network of locally elected worker and peasant councils. Throughout both Makhno's career and his movement's existence, nationalism was aggressively opposed in favour of an internationalist position, tolerant of ethnic expression, but centred on the unity of all working peoples. Later in exile, Makhno did display a growing interest in harnessing Ukraine's cultural awakening for a renewed struggle against Bolshevism.[4] This attitude is at times reflected in his memoirs, but is articulated in tandem with a passionate distaste for nationalism as an ideology. As historian Frank Sysyn succinctly observed, while Makhno "never became a nationalist, he did to a degree become a Ukrainian anarchist."[5]

Makhno considered political nationalism—as embodied in Ukraine's Central Rada during the civil war—as a traitorous manifestation of the urban middle-classes. In his memoirs, Makhno described the "spirit of the Ukrainian Liberation Movement" as "bourgeois and chauvinist through and through . . . which caused so much harm to the Revolution."[6] He derided them as "phony Ukrainians," for whom "language was the only thing that mattered, and not the total freedom of Ukraine and its population of working people."[7] He reserved special vitriol for the Rada's 1918 treaty with Imperial Germany, which allowed Austro-Hungarian and German troops to occupy Ukrainian territory in return for a recognition of Ukraine's theoretical independence. In his memoirs, Makhno describes a bitter battle with local nationalists for control over Huliaipole, in which he emphasizes their collaboration with the Austro-Germans and betrayal of the Revolution.[8] Throughout the civil war, Makhnovist-nationalist relations were likewise punctuated by open military conflict and a single, brief but tense truce.[9]

The ideological root of Makhno's disagreement with the nationalists lay in his rejection of using ethnicity to mobilize the masses and define enemies.

The Makhnovist movement repeatedly and aggressively denounced national antagonisms in its proclamations and resolutions. According to their world view, dividing enemies and allies along ethnic lines would break working class solidarity and undermine the Revolution. This attitude was forcefully expressed in February 1918 at the movement's second congress in Huliaipole. In addition to specifically condemning anti-Semitism, the congress unanimously resolved:

> Workers and peasants from all countries and nationalities face one great common task: to overthrow bourgeois oppression, class exploiters, and the yoke of capital and state power, and to introduce a new social system based on freedom, fraternity, and justice.
>
> The enslaved of all nationalities, whether they be Russians, Poles, Latvians, Armenians, Jews, or Germans, should unite in one close-knit family of workers and peasants, and then deliver a final and decisive blow to the class of capitalists, imperialists, and their minions to throw off the chains of economic slavery and spiritual enserfment.[10]

Volin cites a similarly worded proclamation issued by the Huliaipole Nabat Group of Anarchists on 15 May 1919, and signed by Makhno, reiterating that the enemy is not any one ethnic group but their capitalist representatives: "Peasants, workers and partisans, you know that the workers of all nationalities—Russians, Jews, Poles, Germans, Armenians, etc.—are equally imprisoned in the abyss of poverty. . . . We must proclaim everywhere that our enemies are the exploiters of all nationalities—the Russian manufacturer, the German iron magnate, the Jewish banker, the Polish aristocrat."[11] Furthermore, on 5 August 1919, Makhno issued a detailed order to all army commanders, again denouncing anti-Semitism and reminding his troops that the Revolution's enemy is "the rich bourgeois class, regardless of whether they are Russians, Jews, Ukrainians, etc." Furthermore, the order stipulates the death penalty for anyone who commits "violence against peaceful workers, no matter what nationality they belong to."[12]

The movement's official program entitled the Draft Declaration—adopted in late October 1919, just three weeks before the Eichenfeld massacre—addresses the national question in greater detail. Nationalism is once again described as a "profoundly bourgeois and negative" phenomenon leading to "absurd and bloody national conflicts." The Declaration also clarifies the movement's position on cultural expression:

> Clearly, each national group has a natural and indisputable entitlement to speak its language freely, live in accordance with its customs, retain its beliefs and rituals, draw up its school books and have its own managerial establishments and agencies: in short, to maintain and develop its national culture in every sphere. It is obvious that this clear and specific stance has absolutely nothing to do with narrow nationalism of the "separatist" variety which pits nation against nation and substitutes an artificial and harmful separation for the struggle to achieve a natural social union of toilers in one shared social communion.[13]

The Declaration advocates a kind of working-class multiculturalism, in which ethnic expression is considered compatible with the Revolution but national separatism is regarded as inherently counterrevolutionary. In terms of defining enemies, the movement rhetorically employs class as the primary determinant. According to Makhnovist ideology, violence against a Russian or German landowner is justified via their control over wealth and land but not their ethnic identity. In this way, the borders of legitimate and illegitimate violence are defined. This world view is imperative to consider when attempting to untangle Makhnovist motivations behind the attacks on Mennonites. While ideology was not the only factor involved, it did shape how violence was expressed and rationalized in important ways.

As previously mentioned, Mennonites are never explicitly referred to in Makhnovist literature. Rather they are subsumed in the general category of "German colonist." However, one pro-Makhnovist source does directly mention Mennonites. In March 1919, Stéphane Roger, a French Army deserter and left-wing journalist, embedded himself with the Makhnovists as they occupied the Mennonite Molotschna colony. Roger produced a glowing report of the movement for the French Socialist newspaper *La Vague*. Describing Makhnovist-Mennonite relations, he writes, "Always true to their own lying system of propaganda, the bourgeois and estate-owning Mennonites from the German colonies of Ukraine have for several months now carried on a deceitful campaign of slander with the goal of vilifying the reputation of Comrade Makhno. Only those without the slightest acquaintance with our Brigade Commissar Makhno could take seriously their perfidious insinuations."[14] It is likely the "propaganda" Roger refers to were articles from *Friedensstimme*—a Mennonite newspaper based in Halbstadt—which had been publishing eyewitness accounts of Makhno's fall 1918 raids on the Schönfeld colony. As a result of these attacks many Schönfelders fled south that winter to the Molotschna, which was still under the protection of the *Selbstschutz* and the White Army. By March 1919 the Molotschna colony itself was overrun by a joint Bolshevik-Makhnovist force.

Not addressing any specific Mennonite accusations, Roger then describes how Makhno gave an hour-long speech to a large, enthusiastic crowd in front of the town's main church, but Roger could not understand Russian and does not report on the speech's contents. However, a Mennonite memoirist, Jacob Toews, was also present and writes that Makhno "came himself to Halbstadt and held a public speech" in which he promised "peace and justice." Toews adds Makhno's troops "did not go by what their leader promised" and the villagers were subjected to "house searches, arrests and extortions, " while former *Selbschuztler* were "hunted down and arrested."[15]

Roger's account conforms with the Makhnovist interpretation of ethnicity and class as illustrated above. It is specifically the "bourgeois and estate-owning Mennonites" that he identifies as a threat. It must also be assumed that Makhno's speech was directed at Halbstadt's general populace, which included many landless and working-class Mennonites. Indeed, according to Chortitza resident and Mennonite historian David Rempel, some Mennonites actively joined revolutionary groups and even participated in expropriation campaigns.[16] Toews states the emphasis of Makhno's speech was on "peace and justice," reiterating the kind of rhetoric found in official Makhnovist proclamations. Roger furthermore reports how the speech ended with chants of "Long Live the Revolution! Down with the Bourgeoisie!" Roger's article serves as an example of how ethnic identity was qualified with class categories by the Makhnovists to construct an enemy.

Toews's comment that the Makhnovists "did not go by what their leader promised," is an equally important observation, indicating Makhnovist rhetoric did not always match reality. Especially in the area around Huliaipole, the tight link between wealth and Germans and Mennonites would have made it difficult to keep ethnicity and class strictly separated. There is unavoidably an ethnic dimension by virtue that the attacks, even if conceived in their perpetrators' minds in purely class terms, disproportionately targeted Germans and Mennonites as a result of how wealth was concentrated in the region. The colonies were treated with further suspicion due to collaboration with the German occupation and the organization of *Selbstschutz* units. At multiple levels an ethnic factor is implicit, even if it is not framed as such by Makhnovist literature.

Indeed, some Mennonites subjectively experienced the attacks as ethnic in nature. As one survivor asserted, "the Germans were murdered because they were Germans."[17] Rempel likewise felt the "Makhnovites had an intense hatred for these settlements, fuelled by vicious anti-colonist propaganda campaigns promulgated off and on from the time of Alexander III right up through the First World War."[18] However, these interpretations are complicated by other factors. The same survivor also describes a German colonist participating in a Makhnovist massacre, and Rempel acknowledges that during the colonies' Makhnovist occupation, "No matter how callous the brigands were towards everyone else, they considered teachers members of the working class and left them alone."[19] The question of whether the Makhnovist attacks on Mennonites can be conceived as ethnic pogroms will be returned to in Chapter 3. However, for the present purposes, it is important to note that Makhnovist literature itself never frames the attacks as ethnically motivated. Colonies and estate owners are described as German, but the assault on them is always narrativized as part of a rural class struggle. It should also be noted that while this study focuses on Makhnovist-Mennonite relations, Makhno's memoirs also frequently refer to attacks on Ukrainian and Russian kulaks and *pomeshchiks*. The latter terms should therefore not be interpreted as coded references referring exclusively to Germans and Mennonites.

Lastly, it is necessary to contextualize Makhnovist memoirs and histories as, in many ways, responses to the charge of banditry. A key concern for these writers was that the movement be seen by a Western readership as a liberatory, and not predatory, force. While Makhno is certainly not shy to describe violence, he appears especially concerned with proving its use was justified and that his movement adhered to a strict revolutionary code. In exile, Makhno was frequently confronted by charges of banditry and anti-Semitism. The archival trail is clear that Makhno aggressively opposed anti-Semitism. Jews also occupied important posts in the Makhnovist army, civilian body, and cultural-education section. Nonetheless, banditry and anti-Semitism were persistent problems at the rank-and-file level. The repeated orders from the leadership demanding troops stop wanton violence, robbery, and ethnic discrimination also strongly suggest a chronic problem. For example, the movement's third congress demanded the army "observe in their ranks complete comradely revolutionary discipline and cease all national harassment."[20] These problems were more explicitly recognized by Nabat anarchists in a March 1920 emergency meeting. Their resolution reads: "As there exists in this movement the basic desire of the people towards self-liberation, it is the duty of every anarchist to actively assist it in the struggle against the State. But the Makhnovist army is not an anarchist army. The absence of any significant number of ideological workers, on the one hand, and the continuous stress of a combat atmosphere, are reasons that among the revolutionary Makhnovist rebels undesirable behaviour is still observed, like drunkenness, anti-Semitism, etc."[21] Far from distancing themselves from the movement, the Nabat anarchists resolved to intensify their work within the army to order to produce an "advanced ideological anarchist vanguard" from among "the most conscious part of the rebels."[22] It is clear the ideological leadership consistently struggled to restrain behaviour they felt undermined the movement's social vision, including ethnic chauvinism. Nonetheless, given the region's dynamics it is not hard to believe anti-German sentiment would have also infected the army to some degree. However, unlike anti-Semitism, Germanophobia is never explicitly discussed in Makhnovist literature.

In the course of the civil war, the Makhnovist leadership consciously attempted to channel the peasantry's violence against class enemies and away from outbursts of overt ethnic persecution. However, while these efforts moulded how violence was articulated to an extent, the movement's ideology was never in full control and abuses of all types continued. This attempt to harness violence according to ideological prescripts is a recurrent theme throughout Makhnovist accounts. Makhno in particular emphasizes his role in this matter and largely depicts the movement as disciplined and rational under his leadership. The attacks on German and Mennonite estates and colonies are narrativized as heroic acts of resistance on the path to liberation. The other sources follow suit but do occasionally hint at the movement's darker aspects. These narrative deviations are vague for the most part, but do suggest some of the abuses exposed in detail by Mennonite narratives.

Autobiography is always a simultaneous exercise in personal disclosure and concealment, in confession and self-justification. Both Makhnovist and Mennonite writings must be taken seriously, but they should also be recognized as subjective accounts and susceptible to self-censorship. Murder and abuse, whether committed in the name of class or ethnicity, is clearly an unjustifiable and egregious human violation. However, by exploring the narrative constructions of the perpetrators a better understanding of their motivations can be grasped. The remainder of this chapter will provide background to the sources and their authors before examining Makhno's life and the civil war through Makhnovist eyes.

## ANARCHIST VOICES

The Makhnovshchina's history is an expansive and multi-faceted topic that reaches far beyond the focus of this book. The purpose here is not to provide a general history of the movement but to specifically interrogate how "German colonists" are narrativized by Makhnovist writers. The works of Peter Arshinov, Volin, and Makhno are particularly important in this regard. All written in exile, their books constitute something like a Makhnovist canon. They are the most referenced and accessible sources to the general public and they articulate the basic building blocks of a Makhnovist collective narrative. Arshinov and Volin's works in particular have been fundamental in shaping contemporary Western anarchists' interpretation of the movement. They provide indispensable insight into the Makhnovist paradigm, how enemies and allies are defined, and the movement's relationship to violence.

Peter Andreevich Marin (Peter Arshinov) was born in 1887 to a Russian working-class family in a small village near Penza, 500 kilometres southeast of Moscow. From the age of seventeen, he was involved in revolutionary activism. In 1905, Arshinov was working as a machinist in Turkestan where he joined the Bolsheviks and edited an underground newspaper named *Molot* (The Hammer). To evade the police's suspicions of his radical activity, Arshinov relocated to Katerynoslav, where he gained employment at a sheeting-rolling plant. It was here that Arshinov traded Bolshevism for anarchism and joined an underground anarchist group in which he organized attacks on the local authorities. On 7 March 1907 Arshinov killed an Oleksandrivsk railway boss in front of a large crowd of workers. He was arrested shortly thereafter and sentenced to death. According to Arshinov's memoirs he escaped twice from prison—the first time during an Easter mass—before being re-sentenced to twenty years in Moscow's Butyrka prison.[23]

Arshinov first met Makhno under these circumstances. In prison the pair quickly forged a strong connection and encouraged each other to read extensively and deepen their anarchist ideology. After the 1917 prisoner amnesty, Arshinov helped to organize Moscow's anarchists into the Federation of Anarchist Groups. In 1918, Arshinov was working as an editor of an anarchist paper in Katerynoslav before he reunited with Makhno in Huliaipole in April 1919. Arshinov became a key ideologue in the movement, influencing its ideological orientation while holding important posts within its cultural-educational department. He edited the insurgent newspaper *Put' k svobode* (Road to Freedom) and became involved in Ukraine's anarchist Nabat Confederation.[24] In summer 1920, he left the movement in an official capacity to begin writing its history.[25]

Arshinov fled the USSR for Berlin in 1922, before settling in Paris where Makhno and Volin also resided. He retained close ties with international anarchism, authoring the *Organizational Platform of the Libertarian Communists*.[26] The *Platform* sparked a vigorous debate and was harshly criticized by key international anarchist figures for embodying a type of Bolshevized anarchism.[27] The document also caused a rift between old comrades, with Makhno and Arshinov taking sides against Volin. In 1931 Arshinov broke with the anarchist position on the Soviet Union when he produced two pamphlets supportive of the regime. An enraged Makhno publicly castigated Arshinov as "vainglorious and powerseeking," while Volin reportedly warned Arshinov, "They will shoot you. Do not kid yourself, they will never forgive you."[28] Finally, in 1934, Arshinov renounced anarchism and returned to the Soviet Union. Three years later he was arrested by the Soviet authorities and executed for allegedly clandestinely promoting anarchism.[29]

Arshinov's book, *The History of the Makhnovist Movement*, was intended as the movement's official history. Arshinov began writing it "between battles," while still with the Makhnovists, although it was not completed until he was living in Berlin.[30] Arshinov writes that his work was based on a personal archive containing eyewitness accounts, newspapers, and official documents, parts of which were confiscated several times by the Soviet secret police. Arshinov states his manuscript was destroyed a total of four times.[31] Its successful publication finally came in 1923 in both French and Russian editions, and has since been translated into nine languages, including four English editions between 1974 and 2005. From its inception, the work was intended for an international audience. In his preface, Arshinov directly addresses "comrade-workers in other countries," warning them against competing accounts curated by Soviet authorities.[32] In this way, Arshinov sets up his history as an insider's report, giving authentic voice to the revolutionary masses' struggle for freedom.

Arshinov's history interprets events through a paradigm of uncompromising class conflict. It is propagandistic in its style and intention, and largely glosses over negative aspects of the movement.[33] The account is also characterized by the author's self-imposed detachment. Despite being an eyewitness, Arshinov never inserts himself into the narrative, refusing the reader insight into his personal experiences. Even the introduction, presenting a biography of Arshinov, was written not by himself but by Volin. This may have been an intentional device to promote the work as an unbiased account divorced from personal attachments. Arshinov's triumphalist writing style, combined with his narration in the objective third-person, constantly works to dissuade readers from any doubts. Moments of critical self-reflection are quickly overshadowed by hagiographic descriptions of the movement. Throughout Arshinov's narrative, German colonists are wholly subsumed within the category of class enemy. As kulaks, *pomeshchiks*, and Austro-German collaborators, they are regarded by Arshinov as a parasitical, reactionary element undeserving of mercy.

The second major Makhnovist source used in this study is Vsevolod Mikhailovich Eikhenbaum (Volin), born in 1882 to a family of

Figure 2. Vsevolod Eichenbaum (Volin). Paris, August 1927.

Russian-Jewish doctors in Voronezh province.[34] While studying law in St. Petersburg, Volin first became involved in revolutionary politics. In 1904 he withdrew from his program to focus exclusively on political agitation. During the 1905 Revolution, Volin played a crucial role as a founder of the first soviet in St. Petersburg. According to Volin, he rejected the offer of the soviet's presidency believing a worker, not an intellectual, should hold the position. During this period Volin joined the Socialist-Revolutionaries and donated the entirety of his inheritance to their organization. Leaving nothing of his family's wealth, this radical gesture consecrated a final break from his class origins. The following year, Volin was arrested and sentenced to exile in Siberia for participating in an insurrection at Kronstadt. Shortly thereafter he escaped to France where he became an anarchist.

A vocal dissident of the First World War, Volin caught the attention of the French authorities, who interned him. Once again Volin fled, leaving his wife and children behind, for America. Overseas, he continued his work with the Union of Russian Workers of the United States and Canada, where he staffed a weekly newspaper and gave lectures across North America. When the 1917 February Revolution broke out Volin returned to Russia. Operating out of St. Petersburg, Volin edited the weekly *Golos Truda* (The Voice of Labour), which soon became the most influential anarchist newspaper of the Russian Revolution. From the earliest days of the October Revolution, Volin was sharply critical of the Bolsheviks, prophesying they would assume authoritarian control of the country and subordinate the workers' and peasants' soviets to party control. In spring 1918, in the wake of the German occupation, Volin left St. Petersburg for Ukraine to agitate among its workers. In Kharkiv, he became a leader in the Nabat Confederation and developed an ideological position called "united anarchism," which sought to unify all streams of anarchism—anarcho-communist, syndicalist, and individualist—into a single organization.

In the summer of 1919 Volin travelled to Huliaipole where he met Makhno for the first time. Volin would spend the next six months as head of the Makhnovist cultural-educational section. He also served as the chairman of the Revolutionary Military Soviet—the civilian-elected body that oversaw the Makhnovist movement. In December 1919, on a mission separated from the army's main body, Volin contracted typhus, forcing him to take refuge in a village. Bedridden and violently ill, he was arrested by the Red Army in January 1920 and sentenced to death. After a sustained petition by his fellow Russian anarchists, Volin was spared the death sentence and transferred to Butyrka prison in Moscow. Seven months later, a treaty was signed between the Red Army and the Makhnovists and Volin's release was secured as part of a general amnesty for captured Makhnovists. He briefly rejoined Makhno, but when the treaty collapsed in November he was arrested once again. Volin languished in prison for another year until his release was once more secured by a delegation of visiting international workers who expressed concern over the incarceration of Russian anarchists. Lenin reluctantly agreed to their release and Volin fled to Berlin in January 1922.

In exile, Volin co-authored the first original work addressing anarchist persecution under Soviet rule.[35] During this period, he also translated Arshinov's history into German. Volin moved from Berlin to Paris, where he continued to write and became embroiled in the debates around the *Platform*. As previously mentioned, Volin broke with Makhno at this time and the pair did not reconcile until Makhno lay on his deathbed in 1934. During the growth of European fascism, Volin excoriated the

USSR, dubbing the party's rule as "red fascism" and comparing Stalin to Hitler.[36] Volin spent his final years in occupied France under crushing poverty and the chronic fear of arrest. It was in this environment that Volin completed *The Unknown Revolution* in 1940. Clandestinely working as an anarchist to his final days, Volin lived to see France's liberation. However, less than a month later, on 18 September 1945, he died of tuberculosis. Fellow Makhnovist Jacques Doubinsky salvaged Volin's *Unknown Revolution* manuscript and published it two years later in tribute to his deceased comrade.

Like Arshinov's history, Volin's work was intended for an international audience. Originally published in French, the book has seen various English incarnations since 1954. Volin's work was written at a time of failing liberal democracies and spreading dictatorships. It was also completed in the aftermath of the *Platform* debates, in which Volin feared the anarchist movement itself was at risk of becoming overly authoritarian. Throughout his book Volin seeks to highlight a third perspective, beyond liberalism and authoritarianism, by drawing attention to Russia's left-libertarian history, or what he termed "the unknown revolution."

A voluminous three-part work running over 600 pages, *The Unknown Revolution* explores the entirety of the Russian Revolution, from its roots in the nineteenth century to its bloody aftermath in the civil war. Volin offers a social-psychological interpretation of the Revolution in which the nineteenth century is presented as a period of growing revolutionary consciousness. According to Volin, the gradual loosening of Imperial Russia's paternalistic shackles over the masses culminated in their rejection of the empire and embrace of a self-organizing democracy represented by workers' and peasants' soviets. Volin accuses the Bolsheviks of manipulating and usurping this libertarian impulse for their own statist ends. To Volin, the Bolsheviks' ascension to power represented the masses' re-enslavement under a new state, differing in form but not structure from its imperial predecessor.

Part 3 of Volin's book chronicles the libertarian, or third revolution, against the Bolsheviks during the civil war. Dealing in turn with the Makhnovshchina and the 1921 Kronstadt insurrection, Volin relies heavily on other authors for his narrative. The section on the Makhnovshchina is in many parts a literal reproduction of Arshinov's book. However, Volin's work is unique for its brief, self-reflective moments and sometimes harsh criticisms of the movement. While a history in the formal sense, the book is also interspersed with memoir. Volin sees the Makhnovshchina as a fundamentally positive phenomenon, but he is particularly disturbed by the army's violence and Makhno's erratic behaviour. In exile, Volin would break sharply with Arshinov and Makhno while drawing closer to Makhno's wife, Halyna Kuzmenko.[37] Volin does not deal directly with the Mennonites, but his book does offer critical clues to the evolution and expression of Makhnovist violence.

Lastly, there are Makhno's memoirs, which can be divided into four separate works. The first piece, entitled "My Autobiography," provides a narrative of Makhno's youth and his time in prison up to his release after the 1917 February Revoluion. Critically, this memoir includes an account of his employment on a Mennonite farm. The work was first serialized in the Russian-American newspaper *Rassvet* in 1926. The same year a French translation provided by Volin appeared in the Parisian anarchist newspaper *Le Libertaire*. In 1927 a German version was serialized in Berlin's *Der freie Abeiter* newspaper. The memoir remained out of print until Alexandre Skirda republished heavily edited versions in Russian and French in 2006 and 2009.[38]

Makhno's remaining memoirs were published in three volumes, although Makhno lived to see only the first in print. All three volumes were drafted in Russian by Makhno. The first volume was translated into French and published in 1927, followed by a Russian version two years later. Volin posthumously edited Makhno's remaining manuscripts and published the final two volumes in Russian in 1936 and 1937. Volume One was republished in French in 1970. All three volumes were translated into French in 2009 by Alexandre Skirda, and most recently into English by Malcolm Archibald. Unfortunately, Makhno's narrative takes the reader only to the end of 1918, but it does provide us with rich material for understanding his relationship with Mennonites and German colonists.[39]

Some historians have argued Makhno was aware of the "colonist" perspective, which, if true, could have significant bearing on how Makhno constructed his personal narrative. In particular, an apocryphal story circulates that Makhno and his wife Halyna Kuzmenko were arrested in 1924 in Danzig, where it is claimed Makhno was indicted for crimes against German colonists.[40] Kuzmenko was quickly released, but Makhno remained imprisoned. In a peculiar historical twist, he was moved to Fort Neufähr, in Gross Plehnendorf—a former Mennonite settlement in the Vistula delta. While interned there Makhno fell ill with tuberculosis and was transferred to a hospital in Danzig. In a second twist of fate, a Mennonite nurse attended to him.[41] This hospital stay facilitated Makhno's escape, which was orchestrated by his fellow comrades who were trying to secure Makhno's passage to France. He then spent forty days in hiding, in desperate anticipation of a travel visa that failed to materialize.[42] Makhno eventually decided to risk making his way to Berlin by foot via Poland. In March 1925 he finally reached Germany, escaping what he called the "Danzig mousetrap."[43]

While the arrest did occur, its reason was likely unrelated to German colonists. Makhno himself described the reasons for his arrest in a letter to Volin dated 2 November 1924. The letter was written while he was still imprisoned at Fort Neufähr. He recounts that an official informed him, "Because you did not leave Danzig during the time limit set for you by the police, you have been interned and will now be sent to an internment camp."[44] After thirteen days in solitary confinement, Makhno explains he was transferred to Fort Neufähr, where he was waiting for his lawyer to secure a French visa. He describes the camp's conditions as inhumane and ends his letter, "I look forward to a visa, any visa, with impatience."[45] Another letter dated 16 September 1924 from Makhno's friend Alexander Berkman corroborates the latter account. Berkman clarifies Makhno was arrested twice in Danzig for visa-related violations.[46]

There is also evidence Makhno's arrest was linked to Soviet efforts to extradite him. Makhno later wrote that Soviet agents briefly kidnapped him prior to his arrest, in which he escaped by jumping out of a moving vehicle.[47] A German anarchist newspaper appealing for Makhno's release likewise claimed the Soviets had used their influence with Danzig's authorities to secure his arrest.[48] Berkman, who was in Germany attempting to secure Makhno's safe passage, also claims he discovered the Soviets had intervened to prevent Makhno's visa being issued.[49] In none of these sources are German colonists or a criminal indictment mentioned—an odd omission if one had occurred.

The original source for the German colonist claim is likely Makhno's wife, Halyna Kuzmenko. The Russian historian S.N. Semanov writes that in March 1968 he received a lengthy letter from Kuzmenko, who was then living in Kazakhstan. In it Kuzmenko writes: "In Danzig, we were arrested. The Germans expressed their dissatisfaction with the fact that in 1918 Makhno and his detachments expelled [*izgonial*] the German-'colonists' [*nemtsev-'kolonistov'*] from Ukraine. A few days later I was released and with my child we left for Paris via Berlin. About a year later my husband fled the Danzig fortress and also arrived in Paris."[50] A number of factors make Kuzmenko's statement difficult to interpret. Foremost, why is the word "colonists" in quotations and how is the term intended? It is true that German and Mennonite colonists around Huliaipole were raided in fall 1918 and many of them fled south to the Molotschna colony, but there was no attempt to expel them from Ukraine as a whole. Furthermore, the mass exodus of Mennonites from Ukraine did not begin until after 1921.

Kuzmenko's statement makes more sense if read in the context of the Austro-German occupation. Beginning in the summer of 1918, Makhno had organized an effective local peasant insurgency against the Austro-Germans and Hetmanate regime. In the fall, the Makhnovists forced the occupation out of Huliaipole on two occasions. In October an address was issued by Makhno stating: "The Huliaipole Military Revolutionary Staff again engaged on the path to overthrow the disgraceful, illegitimate Skoropadskyi Hetmanate regime, calls upon all citizens to rise up as one and contribute both in mind and body to this goal. The moment has come for the German-Hungarian-Austrian bands to depart."[51] These local successes were followed one month later by Germany's and Austria-Hungary's withdrawal from Ukraine as a whole. Arshinov similarly frames these events describing how Makhno retook Huliaipole, "chasing out the Austrians with the help of the local inhabitants." Arshinov further claims that the "insurrection also caused the disintegration of the Austro-German forces," which he argues contributed to the Austro-Germans' flight from Ukrainian territory.[52]

Kuzmenko gave a second, slightly different, account in 1973 of Makhno's arrest that corresponds more closely with the latter interpretation. She writes: "In spring 1924 we moved to Danzig. . . . One day Nestor was arrested in our apartment (I was not home). The Germans still hated

Figure 3. A young Halyna Kuzmenko, c. 1917.

[Makhno] from 1918, when he drove them out of Ukraine. They locked him up in a Berlin fortress."[53] In this passage, Kuzmenko is clearly referring to the German authorities and the 1918 occupation. In neither of her accounts, however, does Kuzmenko indicate Makhno was officially arrested for "expelling" Germans, nor does she mention any specific crimes against German colonists. Rather, it appears Kuzmenko believed the German authorities held a grudge against Makhno for his prior struggle against the Austro-German occupation. Kuzmenko's use of the term "colonists" in scare quotes is a curious turn of phrase. Although her exact meaning is debatable, it seems most likely she was referring to German occupation troops, in the sense that she interpreted them as an outside force attempting to colonize Ukraine in 1918. Regardless, Makhno's visa violations are a far less dramatic, but more plausible, explanation for his arrest.

Another important supplemental Makhnovist source is Kuzmenko's diary from 1920. Agafia (Halyna) Andriivna Kuzmenko was born 9 January 1897 in Kyiv. From a family of peasant origins, Kuzmenko's father worked at the local railway. He quit his job when she was ten years old and the family moved to Kherson province, where they took up farming.

Kuzmenko excelled at school, graduating from teachers' college in 1916. The following year she taught Ukrainian language and literature in Huliaipole before enrolling at Saint Volodymyr's University in Kyiv. A year later, she returned to Huliaipole to continue her teaching. There she gained a reputation as an intellectual and dedicated promoter of Ukrainian culture.[54]

In spring 1919 she met Makhno for the first time, and the couple soon began a romance.[55] It is unclear whether Kuzmenko and Makhno officially married, but this is apparently what the couple told her conservative parents and she became commonly known as "Makhno's wife." Kuzmenko's father was murdered by the White Army, an event she spoke of with "great bitterness and emotion." Her mother died in Ukraine's terror-famine of 1932–33.[56] During the war, Kuzmenko was frequently described as at Makhno's side, participating in battle and even operating a machine gun. She was known as a "tireless defender of women," reportedly going so far as to personally execute Makhnovists caught raping and plundering.[57]

On 28 August 1921 a pregnant Kuzmenko accompanied Makhno across the Romanian border into exile. The following year, in a Polish internment camp, she gave birth to their daughter, Elena. Eventually the family settled in Paris. During the rift between Makhno and Volin, Volin claims Kuzmenko was unfairly ostracized and accused by other Makhnovist exiles of negatively influencing Makhno.[58] After Makhno's death in 1934, she remained in Paris until 1943, when she and her daughter were conscripted by the Nazis for compulsory labour in Berlin. The two were arrested there in 1945 by Soviet authorities and repatriated to the Soviet Union, where both faced trial in Kyiv. Halyna was sentenced to eight years in a labour camp, and Elena was exiled to Kazakhstan. After Kuzmenko's release in 1954, she reunited with her daughter in Kazakhstan, where they resided for the rest of their lives. Kuzmenko passed away in 1978 followed by Elena in 1993.[59]

On 29 March 1920, according to R.P. Eideman—the Red Army commander of the Southern Front's rearguard—the diary of "Makhno's wife" was discovered. Eideman writes that she was killed in an assault on Huliaipole and the diary was found in a knapsack. The simple notebook, written in Ukrainian, contained entries spanning 18 February to 28 March 1920. Oddly, the diary was inscribed with the name Feodora Lukianovna Gaenko. Of course, Gaenko was not Makhno's wife, but Soviet authors continued to name her as such late into the 1920s. The diary, as reproduced

Figure 4. Makhno (right) and his daughter Elena (left) in Paris, c. 1928.

by Eideman, contains a less than savoury account of Makhno's character and activities. He is repeatedly depicted as a violent drunkard and one entry suggests Makhno sexually forced himself on the diary's owner.[60]

Given the diary's obfuscated origins and its controversial content, its authenticity has been questioned.[61] Both Makhno and Arshinov adamantly denied the diary's contents.[62] Part of the document's mystery was dispelled when Kuzmenko acknowledged she did in fact keep a diary during the period in question. Furthermore, she revealed to Semanov that "I borrowed a notebook from Fania Gaenko, she was a young woman, the mistress of Lev Zadov [the Makhnovist chief of military intelligence]. Her name was written on the first page of the notebook."[63] However, her account of the diary's confiscation differs radically from Eideman's. According to Kuzmenko, she and Gaenko were driving wagons when they were approached by Red cavalrymen and forced to trade horses. The diary was in one of these requisitioned wagons. She claims the Reds left them unharmed and they continued on their way.[64]

It appears Eideman was revising events for Bolshevik propaganda. It is difficult to believe Eideman was unaware of Kuzmenko's name given his direct involvement in the campaign against the Makhnovists. Furthermore, his account was published, mid-conflict, in early 1921. It stands to reason that the supposed death of Makhno's wife and the discovery of a diary portraying Makhno as a lecherous alcoholic would have served as a grand propaganda victory. By contrast, there is no obvious reason for Kuzmenko to lie about how the diary came into Red hands, and if she were concerned about its contents she could have simply denied its existence.

Regarding the diary's purpose, Kuzmenko explained that Makhno wanted a history of the movement written. When probed about the more controversial entries, she replied she could not remember exactly what was written, and wouldn't attest to their accuracy without seeing the original handwriting.[65] Kuzmenko specifically expressed concern over a passage that described a drunken Makhno dancing along a street while playing an accordion.[66] Kuzmenko's suspicions were well warranted as Eideman's reproduction of the diary differs from the original in critical respects. For example, in both the original and Eideman's version the 6 March entry begins: "Our host is a very agreeable person. Today he distilled some *samogon* [Russian moonshine] and treated us." According to Eideman the next sentence reads: "Nestor got tipsy [*podvypil*] and forcefully [*sil'no*] harassed/ molested me [*pristaval mne*]."[67] By contrast, the original Ukrainian diary reads: "Nestor got drunk [*pidvypyv*] and behaved very cheekily [*nakhabnym*] towards me."[68] The word used here can also mean "audacious," but it does not carry any implication of sexual molestation. By changing the word to one with a potentially nefarious meaning, Eideman transforms a rather harmless situation into a possible rape scenario.

Eideman's manipulations are illustrative of the caution one should take when approaching certain Soviet documents. Fortunately, Kuzmenko's original diary was preserved in the archives and a comparison is possible. Since Kuzmenko was not able to confirm its contents, it is theoretically possible parts of the original were manipulated or, as she suggested, entries added by Gaenko. Only a detailed handwriting analysis of the original could fully resolve any remaining skepticism. Regardless, it is highly likely it is authentic, otherwise Eideman would not have needed to create his own falsified version.

Viktor Belash's history-memoir *Roads of Nestor Makhno* is another important Makhnovist source. A native of Novospasivka and an anarcho-communist from age fifteen, Belash served as Makhno's chief of staff from 1919 onward. The White Army murdered his father, grandfather, and two brothers in response to his role in the Makhnovshchina. A renowned military strategist, Belash took command of Makhnovist operations after Makhno's flight to Romania.[69] On 23 September 1921, Belash was captured by the Bolsheviks and imprisoned in Kharkiv. Fated for execution, Belash saved his own life by agreeing to write a history of the movement. As previously mentioned, the Soviets hoped to extradite Makhno and hold a public trial in which testimony such as Belash's would be used against him. Belash was released in 1924 and operated as an informer for the secret police until his rearrest in 1937. In a final petition to the Soviet authorities for clemency, Belash wrote: "I want to exculpate my guilt before Soviet power, so I beg you to grant me the possibility of being useful either here or in Ukraine."[70] The Soviets refused his plea and Belash died in prison on 24 January 1938, prior to his slated execution.

Belash's memoir only came to light through the personal efforts of his son, who published the work in 1993. While a very detailed account and an extremely important resource, it must be interpreted in the context of its Soviet supervision. Belash sometimes attributes negative aspects of the movement to Makhno personally, perhaps in an attempt to whitewash his own role and appeal to his Soviet keepers. Indeed, in May 1922 the Soviet Union formally indicted Makhno with organizing a criminal gang, robbery, and the murder of civilians. The indictment specifically mentions Belash's "testimony" as foundational to the prosecution's case. Interestingly, despite offering a long list of villages where alleged Makhnovist atrocities occurred, the document does not mention any crimes against Mennonite or German settlements.[71] Nevertheless, Belash's work adds depth to the Makhnovist source base. While composing his book, Belash had access to the Soviet archives, which is reflected in his extensive footnotes and reproduction of Makhnovist documents. His account also provides an exhaustive chronology of events that exceeds Arshinov and Volin in detail and extends beyond Makhno's memoirs into the year 1919. Finally, for this book's purposes, Belash's account is vitally important for understanding the military context in which the Eichenfeld massacre occurred.

A final source used to a lesser extent in this study is Aleksei Chubenko's memoir. An anarcho-communist and former blacksmith, Chubenko was active with Makhno since 1917 and preceded Belash as Chief of Staff.

He often served as a diplomat for the movement and was briefly a sitting member of the Revolutionary Military Soviet in 1919. Chubenko was imprisoned by the Bolsheviks from January to September 1920. It was in this context that Chubenko wrote his memoirs.[72] The Bolsheviks released Chubenko as part of an amnestry for Makhnovists in the wake of a renewed alliance between Makhno and the Red Army. In April 1921, Chubenko officially broke with the Makhnovist movement. He wrote a "statement of repentance" for the Bolshevik authorities, in which he denounces his former comrades as "fake revolutionaries" and accuses them of banditry and indiscrimately shooting peasants and workers.[73] Chubenko writes, "From all this I concluded that you have to be a block head to believe in such a traitor as Makhno."[74] Given Chubenko's about-face and the possible pressures exerted on him by the Bolsheviks, the same caution must be exercised in approaching Chubenko's memoirs as Belash's. Nevertheless, Chubenko's memoir is unique in that outside of Makhno, it is the only eyewitness Makhnovist account of the movement's activities in summer and fall 1918. Like Belash, Chubenko sometimes portrays Makhno as erratic and excessively violent. For example, Chubenko describes how Makhno sadistically burned alive an Orthodox priest in a locomotive furnace.[75] However, despite Chubenko's later recantation, his memoirs on the whole depict the Makhnovists as a revolutionary movement heroically battling counterrevolutionary forces.

Significantly, Chubenko's memoir largely corroborates Makhno's memoirs. Indeed, whether produced in exile or in captivity, Makhnovist sources are chronologically quite consistent with each other. With minor differences in interpretation, the sources touch on the same major events. The memoirs also broadly conform with the archival record. Many of the proclamations reproduced or referred to in the memoirs match their archival equivalents almost word for word. Ukrainian historian B. Malinovskii likewise concluded that, barring slight adjustments for dates, the sequence of events described in Makhno's memoirs during the Austro-German occupation mirror archived governmental reports from the same period.[76] Of course, some experiences are unique to an author and cannot be corroborated. However, such unverified events are still important for how they are framed by the author and how they conform or deviate from broader narrative patterns.

As shown in the above survey, Makhnovist sources are fraught with pitfalls and should be approached with caution. As repositories of memories they are, like all sources, prone to narrative restructuring, whether it be for ideological or self-serving motivations. Additional care is necessary to take into account their intended audiences. In the case of the Makhnovist émigrés, their works should be understood in the context of international leftism and the attempts to promote anarchism as a legitimate alternative to both liberalism and authoritarianism. Their narratives also go to great efforts to refute accusations of banditry. Extreme violence is not excised from these accounts, but it is narrativized and rationalized through the language of freedom and justice. Those authors under Soviet watch similarly presented the movement in a noble light; however, it was also expected of them to help build a case against Makhno.

Taken as a whole, the Makhnovist corpus presents their ideological and social paradigm from a variety of perspectives and contexts allowing for a narrative investigation of how Makhnovists perceived German and Mennonite colonists. A narrative pattern emerges particularly in regard to Makhno, in which violence and murder are considered acceptable tools as long as they are guided by a set of revolutionary ethics rationalized by class struggle. Behind the triumphalist rhetoric of the sources, Makhno appears to struggle with ensuring these ethics are consistently applied. Makhno's presentation of himself as a just restraining force is offset by intimations of more unchecked behaviour both by himself and the broader movement. This tension is resolved within Makhnovist literature through constant references to themes of freedom and justice to legitimate the use of extreme violence.

---

According to local lore, during Makhno's infant baptism the village priest's cassock caught fire. In the minds of the local peasants, this indicated the child would become a famous bandit.[77] A second tale circulated in which Makhno had a son with a peasant girl. It was said that "at birth the baby already had teeth. This was an evil omen and people started saying that the Antichrist had been born. As it turned out, the 'Antichrist' soon died and the truth of the prophesy could not be gauged, but the tale began to be told."[78] Perhaps no more than fables, these stories direct the listener to themes of origins and infancy, suggesting that Makhno's violent career is inextricably related to childhood. There is also an emphasis on communal prophesy, suggesting his later personhood was socially prefigured by early life events.

Nestor Ivanovich Makhno was born the youngest child of an impoverished peasant family.[79] Makhno's identification with his family's social class is evident from his memoir's opening lines: "I am a peasant. I was born in Huliaipole in Katerynoslav *gubernia*. My parents were originally serfs, and later free peasants. According to my mother's stories, her life was miserable."[80] Most of Makhno's memories of his parents deal with unfair servitude. Even after their emancipation, he writes that his father was compelled by poverty to continue working for his former master before taking a job as a coachman for a Jewish factory owner in Huliaipole. Shortly thereafter—while Makhno was still an infant—his father died, leaving the family in financial straits.[81]

Makhno fondly remembers his mother as a headstrong woman who built the family's home with her own hands. He writes that she strongly resisted her serfdom and "while still a child she was twice beat with canes." The first time, she had refused degrading work, and the second time she was beaten for demanding higher pay.[82] Makhno evokes the image of a caring and dedicated mother who instilled in him a fierce sense of independence and justice.

Fatherless and occupying a half-finished home, Makhno describes how his family struggled to make ends meet on a four-hectare plot. Amidst these desperate conditions, Makhno recalls being briefly adopted out to a well-to-do peasant family. However, his brokenhearted mother could not bear to give Nestor up and she shortly reclaimed her son.[83] Reunited with his family, Makhno recounts being compelled to find summer employment on a Mennonite-owned estate. Arshinov's account of Makhno's childhood was the first to provide these details. Arshinov writes, "At 12 he left school and family to take a job. He worked as a farmhand on the estates of nobles and on farms of German kulaks. Already at this time, when he was 14 or 15, he felt a strong hatred toward the exploiters and dreamed of the way he would some day get even with them, both for himself and others, if he ever had the power to do so."[84] From Makhno's memoirs, he was even younger, around eight or nine, when he started working. Makhno writes extensively about this period and his experiences as a farmhand on local estates. He recounts his first job as follows:

> When summer arrived, I was hired as an ox drover by a landowner named Janzen. I was paid 25 kopecks per day or one and a half rubles per week. Every Sunday after receiving this sum, I joyfully went home, running most of the seven kilometers clutching the money in my fist. Once there, I gave the money immediately to my mother, just as my older brothers had done with their pay on earlier occasions. Now I was also earning money and just like them, passing it on to mother.... My young heart was filled with great joy.
>
> I remember once I forgot to water the oxen, and so when they were pulling a wagon filled with sheaves, they suddenly veered off the road towards a pond. Just then the overseer's assistant passed by (we called him "flyeater" because his mouth was often hanging open). He struck me twice with his whip. I was outraged and I almost ran home, but I was stopped by the thought of being paid on Saturday and the joy I could give my mother with it. And so I kept working the whole summer and earned a total of 20 rubles. This was my first self-earned money.[85]

Makhno's emphasis in this passage is on the love for his mother and his role in the family. His outrage, and potential rebellion, at being whipped is sublimated by his loyalty to his mother. In this manner, his language focuses less on the abuse endured and more on how his employment as a child labourer served to alleviate his family's poverty.

Another account, preserved through the family oral history of a peasant named Kornei Kolesnik, describes a sixteen year-old Makhno being publicly flogged. Kolesnik worked as a coachman for a wealthy German near the village of Podorozhne. According to the story, as told by Kolesnik's grandson, Kolesnik was driving the landowner to church when they saw Makhno harnessing three pigs to a sled:

> The German looked out the window of his carriage and couldn't believe his eyes. He ordered the overseer to flog Nestor.... More than twenty people witnessed the beating endured by Nestor. The

> overseer removed his trousers and whipped him so hard that blood spurted a meter away. As if that wasn't enough, the overseer struck him with the whip on the cheeks from ear to ear, and his face was covered with blood. People were really upset. Women were crying. Grandma [Kolesnik's wife] came running from her little room in a loft and punched the overseer in the face, while sobbing bitterly. Nestor was carried to Grandma's room (this was a room near the barn where harnesses were stored which the German owner had allotted to my grandparents). Grandma and other women began to bathe his wounds. Thus was born in Nestor his hatred for the rich. He spoke about this to my grandparents while convalescing at their place for more than two months.[86]

In this account, there is notable shift in Makhno's relationship to abuse. He is still the victim of it and does not personally resist but the community shares in his suffering. Violence is, however, employed on Makhno's behalf as a spontaneous form of resistance to the cruelties of the workplace. Moreover, the incident leaves Makhno with deep wounds, both physically and psychologically, transforming his former passivity into hatred for the wealthy.

Makhno does not mention the above incident in his memoirs but he does offer his own explanation for how he came to depise the rich. Makhno recounts that in the summer of 1899 he was working for a local landlord.[87] He does not specify the name or ethnicity of this employer. He was expecting to return to school that fall but his mother missed the enrollment date, forcing Makhno to continue working as a farmhand. Makhno describes his time on the estate as filled with injustices, explaining how he first came to question the system he had been born into:

> It was around this time I began to feel anger, bitterness, and even hatred towards the landowner and, especially, towards his children. Those young slackers often passed by me: sleek, well-dressed, and immaculately groomed and scented. While I was filthy, clad in rags, barefoot, and stinking of manure from cleaning the calves' barn. The injustice of this state of affairs was staring me in the face. My only consolation then was my childish reasoning that this was the natural

> order of things: they were the "masters" and I was a worker whom they paid so they wouldn't have to handle manure themselves.[88]

Makhno goes on to relate how he tried to ignore his cruel environment: "I often saw how the landlord's sons beat the workers . . . but I had turned myself into a workhorse and, like a true slave, I not only kept quiet, but pretended to see nothing."[89] However, Makhno's silent frustration soon reached a breaking point.

According to Makhno's account, in the summer of 1902, the landowner's sons levelled an exceptionally cruel beating on a farmhand. Makhno ran to inform the senior stablehand, Vania, who in turn assaulted the young masters. In response to the incident, the farm workers collectively marched on the landlord's home and threatened to quit the estate. The landlord pleaded with them to forgive his sons' stupidity and the workers agreed to let the incident pass. As for Makhno, he was particularly affected by Vania's words: "Nobody here should ever submit to such humiliation . . . and you, my little Nestor, if one of the landlords ever tries to hit you, grab the nearest pitchfork and strike him!"[90] Initially shocked by Vania's advice, Makhno came to "instinctively feel justice in it." For another year, Makhno laboured at the estate, replaying Vania's advice in his mind. Makhno writes, "More than once when I was pitching hay in the stable the thought came to me: if one of the landlords passed by and tried to hit me I would beat down that monster on the spot."[91] Some fifteen years later Makhno would adopt Vania's raw form of class conflict.

In Makhno's descriptions of workplace abuse there is no detectable trace of ethnic animosity. It is framed entirely by class categories and, in the latter account, set into the context of a labour strike. Makhno does not identify his first employer as Mennonite or German, and if the Janzen name had not been recorded there would be no indication of an ethnic dimension. It is very rare for such accounts to be recorded by peasants themselves, and Makhno's account offers a rare window into the psychological landscape of a peasant from the lowest stratum of society. For Makhno, the beatings and humiliation of hard labour represented in his text are narrated exclusively as symptoms of an unjust class system. The extent to which Makhno retroactively ascribed class categories to childhood experiences might be questioned. However, Makhno's formative years occurred in a highly politicized environment. Ample opportunities existed for disaffected and impoverished youth to become politically engaged.

Class divides in provincial Katerynoslav were often stratified along clear ethnic lines.[92] Alongside the Russian nobility, large wealthy Mennonite and German populations were particularly present in the Huliaipole *volost* (district) and surrounding areas. The Krasnopil *volost*, neighbouring Huliaipole, contained the Schönfeld colony, which was home to some of the richest Mennonites in Imperial Russia.[93] While the traditional pattern of a Mennonite colony consisted of tightly knit villages along a riverbank or streams, Schönfeld by contrast contained many estate settlements spread over a large area.[94] The Janzen estate where Makhno worked, or Silberfeld (Serebropol), was one such example, located seven kilometres southwest of Huliaipole.[95] Originally owned by a Russian noble named Serebriakov, 3,000 dessiatines (3,278 hectares) were sold to Heinrich Peter Janzen in 1839 at three rubles per dessiatine.[96] The estate was highly successful at sheep rearing, from which Janzen used the profits to acquire more land. Under Janzen's ownership, the property grew to 20,000 dessiatines (21,850 hectares). In 1897 the estate was subdivided into at least five separate properties, all owned by Mennonites. By the time of his death in 1899, Heinrich Janzen's operation owned 30,000 sheep and derived a yearly income of 100,000 rubles.[97]

Land ownership in southern Ukraine was the foundation of Mennonite wealth. The average full Mennonite farm in 1905 was sixty-five dessiatines (seventy-one hectares), while the average Ukrainian holding was just 6.3 dessiatines (6.9 hectares)—the bare minimum to meet subsistence requirements.[98] Makhno's family owned just over four dessiatines (4.4 hectares). By contrast, Schönfeld's estate owners commonly owned properties of hundreds, even thousands, of dessiatines.[99] Despite its relatively small population, Schönfeld owned roughly 10 percent of all Mennonite property in the empire by 1909.[100] To gain an idea of the economic disparity between landowning Mennonites and their employees, compare the average full farm colonist's annual income of 3,000 to 8,000 rubles to the 60 to 90 rubles a seasonal farmhand earned. Female servants earned 50 rubles per year and even skilled factory workers earned just two rubles per day. By contrast, the most successful estate owners could turn a profit of over 200,000 rubles per year.[101]

Figure 5. Silberfeld estate, c. 1910.

Figure 6. Wintergruen estate (formerly part of Silberfeld), 1900.

The emancipation of serfs in 1861, coupled with the rapid development of capitalism in the region and overpopulation in the villages, left a legacy of socio-economic inequality in southern Ukraine, where two-thirds of the peasant population were poor and one-in-six were landless. While peasants owned 57 percent of farms they occupied a mere 12 percent of the land.[102] Historian Colin Darch writes: "The provinces of Kherson, Tauride and Katerynoslav were a part of the Russian empire where the poor peasants' lot was extremely hard. The increasing poverty of the peasants contrasted sharply with the potential fertility of the black-soil regions and with the enrichment of the few *kulaks* and *pomeshchiki*."[103] Additionally, as the rural population rapidly increased in the region over the late nineteenth century, per capita land allotments in Katerynoslav province fell from 3.6 to 2.3 dessiatines (3.9 to 2.5 hectares).[104]

In an effort to offset the demands of a growing population, by the end of the nineteenth century Ukrainian peasants heavily relied on leasing land from private estates. Land-lease prices accordingly rose with demand. Prices were further exacerbated by a rash of Mennonite and German land purchases during this same period.[105] Such lands were largely purchased as private estates or as sub-colonies to ameleriorate landlessness amongst Mennonites. However, such land tended to be removed from the rental market or leased at even higher rates. Local peasants also targeted migrant peasant workers hired by estate owners and more well-to-do farmers. These workers were accused of taking local jobs and driving down wages.[106] In this context, as the historian Leonard Friesen notes, Ukrainian peasants came to see the Mennonites' "role to be that of usurpers constricting peasant livelihood."[107] With such mounting social and economic antagonisms, peasant violence against Mennonite landowners and property intensified.[108] However, according to historian Andreas Kappeler, Mennonites and Germans were rarely targeted on ethnic grounds during this period. Indeed, Kappeler states he was unable to find a single case of a "German colonist or landowner being killed by Ukrainian peasants."[109] Despite an increasingly vitriolic nationalist press that vilified German speakers as traitorous foreigners, the peasants' "protests were directed against all landowners" with the exception of Jews who were targeted in ethnic pogroms.[110] James Urry likewise concludes, "Unlike those on the Jews, the attacks involving Mennonites were based more on their perceived class than their ethnicity or faith."[111] In this context, the Russian nobility and wealthy Ukrainians equally found themselves victimized by a wrathful and impoverished peasant population.

Southern Ukraine's land crisis provoked large-scale disturbances, with eighty-eight peasant uprisings in 188 villages in the first decade after emancipation. Between 1881 and 1900 there were peasant revolts in a further forty-four villages.[112] In 1883, the Marshal of Nobility for Katerynoslav felt compelled to write the Minister of Interior: "The peasants firmly declared that they would take the land they considered theirs away from the landlords. They reasoned that even if the land was appropriated to the landlords

Figure 7. Huliaipole Peasant Union, 1909. Makhno is seated on the far left in the front row. Voldemar Antoni is seated next to him.

in the past, this was unjust because it was acquired by the blood of their parents and their peasant ancestors."[113] Peasant uprisings reached a climax in 1902, the same year Makhno describes the revolt at the estate he worked on. In neighbouring Kharkiv province peasants attacked numerous estates, forcing the military to intervene.[114]

In this explosive climate, Makhno writes that he took on numerous odd jobs, including employment at the Mennonite-owned Kroeger factory in Huliaipole.[115] After the outbreak of the 1905 Revolution, Makhno describes how he became involved in revolutionary politics and "for the first time in my life I began to read forbidden underground political literature." Initially Makhno spread social democratic leaflets before he joined a "small group of peasant anarcho-communists from Huliaipole," called the Union of Poor Peasants.[116] Prokop Semeniuta, whose brother Makhno knew from the Janzen farm, organized the group's activities.[117] However, it was the group's ideological leader Voldemar Antoni—nicknamed Jesus—that Makhno credits for "cleansing my mind once and for all of the slightest trace of the slave mentality and desire to submit to any authority whatsoever."[118]

Makhno recalls how the group expanded its activity in 1907 in response to the Stolypin land reforms, which allowed farmers to leave the traditional peasant commune (*obshchina*) and establish independent homesteads. Makhno describes how the government organized "propaganda tours" to encourage peasants to leave the village commune. According to Makhno, the Union of Poor Peasants responded with a campaign of "black terror" in which kulaks' and *pomeshchiks'* properties were targeted. Makhno describes the group "setting fire to the landlords' property and fields wherever possible."[119] While these actions would have certainly impacted the landowning Mennonites in the region, Makhno does not offer any specifics aside from noting that the "estates burned for a whole week and no one put the fires out."[120]

Makhno's activities with the Union of Poor Peasants must be placed in the context of an empire-wide rural rebellion and a wave of leftist terrorism that engulfed the country from 1904 to 1907. Historian Geoffrey Hosking described these years as a veritable "orgy of terror," in which 15 percent of the empire's estates were burned. From 1906 to 1907 alone over 9,000 government officials and civilians were victims of terror.[121] In Makhno's district, the Goosen family of the Wintergruen estate—neighbouring Silberfeld—fled to America during the height of the disturbances. Wintergruen survived intact and the family returned in 1907, but they felt compelled to hire "an armed Cossack or two for security."[122] The government repressions of the rural insurgency were organized by the Minister of Interior, P.A. Stolypin, who quickly gained a reputation for employing swift and often brutal methods. The army was dispatched to put down rebellions and field courts martial were established to mete out summary justice. The ropes by which rebels were hanged became colloquially known as "Stolypin neckties." Paraska Levadnyi, whose partner was a member of the Union of Poor Peasants, describes the repressions in Huliaipole: "The police made every effort to apprehend the anarcho-communists. They arrested their relatives, beat them bloody, and tried to find out where the revolutionaries were hiding."[123] Levadnyi also states that she was arrested and beaten in front of her two-year-old daughter until her blouse was soaked in blood and she passed out.

The Union of Poor Peasants' demise finally came about after a rivalry with the local police chief that ended in his assassination. Makhno was arrested and sentenced to death. Due to his young age, the conviction was commuted to a lifetime of hard labour (*katorga*) in Moscow's Butyrka prison.[124] Makhno survived seven years of imprisonment, according to his account often shackled hand-and-foot in an isolation cell, before a political amnesty led to his release in the wake of the 1917 February Revolution.[125]

Figure 8. A group of released Butyrka prison inmates after the February Revolution. Makhno is on the bottom far left.

Makhno returned to Huliaipole with a focused vision to upend the social system that had carved his path from the Janzen farm to Butyrka prison.

Makhno describes a hero's welcome upon his return to Huliaipole in March 1917. As the town's only returning political prisoner, he describes being received with reverence by the the locals, who referred to him as "the one who rose from the dead."[126] Makhno immediately devoted himself to pushing the Revolution forward. He recounts setting forth his social vision in a speech: "Here in Huliaipole and the surrounding region we should act decisively to dissolve government institutions and absolutely put an end to private property in land, factories, plants, and other types of enterprises. To accomplish this we must keep in close contact with the peasant masses.... We must convince the peasants we are fighting for them and are unswervingly devoted to those concepts, which we will present to them at village assemblies and other meetings."[127] Makhno's political program of profound socio-economic upheaval would have a major impact on the neighbouring landowning Mennonite and German populations.

Makhno describes establishing a peasant union in Huliaipole, with himself elected as chairman. In this union, Makhno and his supporters had formed an elected body capable of challenging the government's authority in the region. The provisional government's authority in Huliaipole was represented by a public committee—a temporary body intended for maintaining order before official elections could be conducted. Rural public committees were often controlled by liberals and moderate socialists, mirroring the composition of the provisional government. By contrast, peasant unions corresponded with workers' soviets, offering an alternative source of authority and a direct challenge to the provisional government.

In Huliaipole, Russian and Serbian army officers were stationed in the village to direct the town's Public Committee.[128] Makhno was successful in demanding the committee's re-election, which brought into it representatives from the Peasant Union. The goal from the outset was to dissolve the committee and neutralize its police force. Most importantly, Makhno became chairman of the body's land committee.

In spring 1917, Makhno writes that his main concern was preparing for the seizure and redistribution of land. His program was by no means uniquely radical. At a regional peasants' congress in Oleksandrivsk, attended by delegates from Huliaipole, Makhno states a resolution was passed proclaiming "the transfer of land into the hands of labouring society without compensation." Makhno recalls how a general fear existed amongst the peasantry that unless immediate action was taken "the Revolution will perish and we shall again be left without land."[129] This sentiment referred to the widespread feeling they had been robbed of their right to the land after emancipation.

Following the Oleksandrivsk congress, the Huliaipole Peasant Union issued a declaration stating, "The toiling peasants of the Huliaipole [*volost*] believe in their inalienable right to proclaim as communal property the lands of the *pomeshchiks*, the monasteries, and the State, and intend to carry this into effect in the near future."[130] In late June, Makhno describes assembling the region's landowners to inventory "a precise account of all the wealth in land at the disposal of the *pomeshchiks* and kulaks for their idle lifestyle."[131] On the basis of this inventory, the land was to be reorganized into free communes and equally divided amongst the peasantry. At a subsequent congress, it was resolved that landowners would be offered a choice between joining a commune or keeping a small individual plot.[132] Makhno's characterization of this period suggests that the initial goal was to level society by eliminating the wealthy rural classes through an egalitarian redistribution of land. While this policy certainly would have had a great impact upon the wealthy German and Mennonite estate owners,

Makhno does not indicate his policies extended to the colonies where the majority of middle- and lower-class Germans and Mennonites lived.

Although the provisional government regarded the Peasant Union's actions as illegal and even threatened to send troops, outside events proved fortuitous for Makhno. A crisis struck in September 1917 when General Lavr Kornilov, the Russian Army's commander-in-chief, threatened to march on St. Petersburg in a bid for power. Makhno writes that he was ordered by the central authorities to organize a defence force in Huliaipole to protect against potential counter-revolution. This pretext was used by Makhno to disarm the local middle- and upper-class landowners. Makhno writes that he told his supporters:

> Divide yourselves up into groups of 10 or 15, with 5 to a wagon, and don't lose any time—cover the whole Huliaipole raion and visit the *pomeshchiks'* estates, the *kulak khutors*, and the rich German colonies and confiscate from the bourgeoisie all the fire-arms you can find . . . but do not harm in any way, either by word or gesture, the bourgeoisie themselves. . . . With revolutionary honour and courage we must do this in the interests of the Revolution. For the leaders of the bourgeoisie, taking advange of the negligence of the revolutionaries, have organized their forces . . . I consider it appropriate to say to all the comrades setting out to disarm the bourgeoisie they must not get carried away and be involved in pillaging. Pillaging is not a revolutionary act, and so long as I am at the head of our movement any delinquent parties will find themselves before the Tribunal.[133]

This passages shows how Makhno perceived the "German colonies" as an inherent counter-revolutionary threat. The scope of Makhno's actions now extended to the colonies, suggesting he expected from them (or was already facing) resistance to his redistributive program. Makhno frames the action as a preemptive defensive measure and positions himself as a rational and just leader, stressing that he adhered to a strict set of revolutionary ethics. Makhno's passage also attempts to legitimize "disarming" the colonies through class. Makhno explicitly recognizes the tight link in the region between wealth and the "German colonies" by qualifying them as "rich." Throughout his memoirs, Makhno consistently prefaces the terms German colonies and colonists with the adjectives rich, wealthy, landowning, and kulak. Makhno's language indicates he was concerned with proving he was specifically targeting the wealthy landowning layer of society. According to Makhno, the colonies by virtue of their wealth fell into the latter category.

Arshinov's account of the same event presents Makhno as a personification of the peasants' revolutionary impulses. He writes, "During this time Makhno became, in this region, the soul of the peasant movement, which was taking over the lands and goods of the *pomeshchiks* and even, if necessary, executing them."[134] The "if necessary" is likewise used to stress Makhno's—and by extension the entire movement's—alleged discipline and restraint. Both Makhno's and Arshinov's accounts implicitly refute the charge of banditry by emphasizing the class-based nature of the action. However, unlike Makhno's account, Arshinov indicates violence and even murder did occur.

Soon after this action, Makhno writes that the peasants began seizing the land. By February and March 1918, a number of estates were designated as free communes, ranging in size from fifty to 200 people. Makhno emphasizes that he himself was a member of a commune, established on the former Klassen estate.[135] Additionally, livestock and farming implements were redistributed. Makhno states that "former owners were left with two pairs of horses, one or two cows, one plough, one seeding machine, one mower, one winnowing machine, etc."[136] Peasant families joining the communes left their villages to take up residence in the homes of the former estate owners. Management of the communes was "conducted by a general meeting of all its members."[137] According to Makhno, these communes were officially endorsed by the Huliaipole Anarcho-Communist Group but were considered purely voluntary. Makhno even claims "*pomeshchiks, kulaks,* as well as some German colonists, realized that one way or another they could not continue as owners of thousands of *dessiatines* of land. . . . Without hesitating any longer they sided with the Revolution and organized their lives on a new basis."[138]

Thus far Makhno's narrative characterizes himself as a bringer of freedom and justice to his people. Makhno's memoirs of his youth present a genealogy of injustice suffered first by his parents in their life of servitude and then by himself from the Janzen estate to his imprisonment. Juxtaposing these indignities is a narrative of resistance, first represented by Makhno's mother and his co-worker Vania, and then in his own career as a member of the Huliaipole anarchist group. Upon his release from prison and his return home, Makhno presents himself as a type of messianic figure in the eyes of the peasantry. He is "the one who rose from the dead." Within this context, Makhno sets forth to liberate his people, first from an outside authority symbolized by the Public Committee, and then from the enemy within symbolized by the local bourgeoisie and estate owners.

Within Makhno's narrative, Mennonites are subsumed under the general category of "German colonists" and also referred to as kulaks and *pomeshchiks*. From his account of life as a farmhand to his disarming of the bourgeoisie and to the land redistribution, Makhno is unconcerned with Mennonites as a distinct cultural group. For Makhno, landowners, like Janzen and the "rich German colonies," were merely pieces of a broader unjust class system that had been imposed upon the labouring peasantry. Seen from this perspective, the confiscation of Mennonite land is constructed by Makhno not as a cultural assault on Mennonites or Germans, but on a specific privileged landowning caste within the rural landscape. Makhno emphasizes that he opposed the pillaging of the colonies and even sought to smooth their readjustment to life in the new revolutionary landscape. Thus, while Makhno sought to destroy the foundations of socio-economic privilege in the countryside, he presents himself as eager to avoid violence, preferring to win the colonists to the side of the Revolution.

---

From March to November 1918 the Central Powers occupied the whole of Ukraine. By all accounts, the lower strata of the Ukrainian peasantry experienced the German and Austro-Hungarian occupation as deeply oppressive. By mid-1918 the occupation forces were dealing with multiple peasant uprisings across Ukraine.[139] Makhno describes in detail how the occupiers executed many of his close comrades and, in a targeted personal attack, burnt down his mother's home and executed his disabled brother Omelian.[140] After his brief flight to Russia, Makhno returned home in July 1918 to organize an insurgency in the Huliaipole region. This period saw the Makhnovshchina develop into a fighting army and the legend of "*Bat'ko* [father] Makhno" take shape. It was also a critical historical moment for Makhnovist-Mennonite relations.

During the occupation, many Mennonite and German colonists embraced the Austrian and German troops. Peasants in neighbouring villages watched as some historically pacifist Mennonites offered up their sons for military training under German supervision. On 21 March, the German command issued an order demanding the return of all previously expropriated land and property. Arshinov describes the early formation of the *Selbstschutz* units and their ties to the German occupation: "Local *pomeshchiks* in the major centres, the *kulaks*, and the German authorities, decided to eliminate Makhno and his detachment at any cost. The *pomeshchiks* created a special volunteer detachment consisting of their own sons and those of *kulaks* for the decisive struggle against Makhno."[141]

A key event described by Makhno in the evolution of the Makhnovshchina, and a pivotal turning point in Makhnovist-Mennonite relations, was the Battle of Dibrivka. In late October 1918, Austro-German authorities dispatched a large force cornering Makhno and thirty of his partisans near the village of Velyka Mykhailivka. Makhno describes how his force retreated into the nearby Dibrivka forest where they made contact with an insurgent detachment led by Fedir Shchus. A large enemy force composed of Austrian troops and German colonists surrounded Makhno and Shchus. The two leaders agreed to combine forces in an attempt to break out of their encirclement. Despite being grossly outnumbered, the rebel leaders were successful in their counterattack. The Austrians, not expecting a frontal assault, were caught off-guard. According to Makhno, they fled in panic, leaving their arms and horses to the insurgents. Arshinov describes how "a part of the *pomeshchik* detachment fled to the Volycha River, where they were drowned by peasants who had joined the battle."[142] Under these circumstances, Makhno was christened the leader of their insurrection and given the title of *Bat'ko*.[143]

Three days later, on 24 October, a large punitive detachment of Austrian troops and colonists—supported by German artillery—bombarded Velyka Mykhailivka and dislodged the Makhnovists from the village. According to the Makhnovist accounts, the Austrians and colonists then entered the village, setting aflame over 600 homes and executing a large number of peasants. The village burned for two days, during which Makhno claims the attackers raped and tortured many of its citizens. Makhno writes how he watched the village burning from a distance: "I sat up and reluctantly

Figure 9. Nestor Makhno (centre) and Feodir Shchus (right). Huliaipole, 1919.

gazed in the direction of Dibrivka [adjacent Velyka Mykhailivka]. One could no longer see any sign of flames. There was only a column of smoke which stained the blue sky with its terrible blackness and reminded us of the events of yesterday, events which I would never forget for the rest of my life."[144] In the aftermath of Velyka Mykhailivka's destruction, Makhno's focus was on achieving retribution. Initially, an eye-for-an-eye policy was adopted. In the surrounding villages, various executions were carried out and the homes of kulaks believed to have participated in the attack on the Ukrainian village were burned to the ground. Makhno writes that the insurgents adopted the slogan "Death! Death! Death for the death of each revolutionary, death for each violated peasant woman must befall every German and Austrian soldier and officer, every Hetmanite Guard or son of a *kulak*, who takes up arms against the Revolution or hires someone to do so."[145] This period initiated a campaign of terror directed against the Austro-Germans and their perceived collaborators. It is unclear whether any Mennonites participated in the attack on Velyka Mykhailivka, but both Mennonite and German estates and colonies were nonetheless targeted in the incident's aftermath.

Makhno describes meeting three armed "*kulak* colonists" from the German Lutheran colony of Mariental. While in disguise as a member of the provincial militia, Makhno recounts questioning the colonists: "You're traveling with weapons—you must be bandits. Where were you going?

'We're not bandits, we're bandit-killers,' was the answer I received."[146] The colonists explained that they were searching for Makhno and Shchus and proceeded to describe how they had burned Velyka Mykhailivka. Makhno writes that their graphic description provoked in him a psychological breakdown. He describes running off alone and watching the smoke rise from Velyka Mykhailivka. He writes, "I pulled a revolver out of my pocket, and quite unconsciously, cocked the gun and pointed the barrel at my forehead. But as soon as I felt its cold touch, I was filled with an overwhelming horror."[147] Makhno returned to his comrades and ordered the colonists' executions. He reflects, "I was no longer interested in whether the *kulaks* were to live or die. I saw them as low-life, vile scoundrels and I didn't even want to look at them."[148]

Capturing another set of armed colonists, Makhno writes that he learned the "most ferocious component of the enemy forces" involved in the attack on Velyka Mykhailivka was from the small German Catholic colony of Krasny Kut (Neu-Grüntal). Makhno proceeded to Neu-Grüntal where he describes encountering a number of armed colonists who were returning from Velyka Mykhailivka. Following a brief battle, the inhabitants of the village were assembled in a field and the colony of some sixty to seventy households was burned to the ground.[149] Makhno recalls one of his men telling the survivors: "You are free to go. . . . You are now in the same situation as those peasant men, women, and children whom your fathers, husbands, and sons jeered at, and whom they subjected to beatings, rapes and the burning of homes." Makhno then warned the colonists that "the road is open to you to join the toiling peasantry. . . . But speak frankly to those of the bourgeois class who are close to you and let them know why we burned your rich homes and killed your fathers, husbands, and sons. . . . The crimes of the bourgeosie will call forth retaliation by the Ukrainian toilers on a level such as the world has never seen before. No one will be spared unless they come to their senses and voluntarily renounce their position of lording it over the country."[150] The destruction of Neu-Grüntal was followed by more attacks on landowners in the region, including Mennonite estates, over the next few days.

While Makhno's speech to the colony's victims cannot be verified, it offers a key insight into his relationship with violence and how he legitimizes his movement's actions. Paradoxically, Makhno positions himself as his victims' liberator. He presents the attack on the colony as an act of socio-economic levelling that effectively frees its residents to join his revolution. Makhno's implicit argument is that his victims' class identity has been nullified through the destruction of their property and murder of their relatives. This sentiment is in line with Makhno's earlier claim he was able to win his class enemies over to the side of the Revolution by stripping them of their property and integrating them into the movement's communes. Makhno's language suggests he did not consider class as a fixed attribute and that former enemies could be redeemed through a conscious renunciation of wealth.

After such initial retributive actions as the destruction of Neu-Grüntal, Makhno writes that a number of ground rules were established for the occupation of estates and colonies. He recalls that he became concerned with the prospect of an uncontrolled bloodletting and positions himself as a voice of moderation over vengeance, noting, "I well understood that our goal was not exacting merciless vengeance of our enemies."[151] Makhno claims he sought to transform his supporters' anger into a focused revolutionary insurrection. To accomplish this task, Makhno says the following resolution was implemented:

> Starting in October 1918, to introduce into the operating procedure of our detachments the rule according to which each detachment which captures a proprietor-owned *khutor* [independent homestead], a German colony, or a *pomeshchik* estate must first of all call a meeting of all the owners of these properties and, after ascertaining the extent of their wealth, impose a financial levy and announce the confiscation of weaponry and ammunition. All this must be carried out under the direct supervision of the detachment commanders, who will exercise the strictest revolutionary discipline....
>
> If the owners are not willing to surrender weapons, the detachments must carry out careful searches.... If a search does not find any weapons, the owner is to be left alone, untouched. In the reverse case, if weapons are found, their owner is to be shot....
>
> All enemies of our movement and its Revolution who *actively take up arms against us* will be shot where they fought as soon as evidence concerning their actions has been gathered from the local population.

> The best method of applying revolutionary justice, which should always be practiced by all *Bat'ko* Makhno detachments, is to hold a preliminary inquiry conducted by village assemblies in those localities (villages and hamlets) where the accused were active and where they were apprehended by our detachment.
>
> Non-compliance with this procedure will result in revolutionary sanctions up to and including the public disowning of the offending detachments as having no connection with the general staff of the revolutionary-insurgent Ukrainian movement led by *Bat'ko* Makhno.[152]

Although this specific resolution has yet to be discovered in the archives, similar orders have been preserved. For example, a resolution from 1919 concerning the occupation of *khutors* and villages likewise places special emphasis on maintaining revolutionary discipline and warns against the Revolution "merging into robbery and violence." The order also prescribes the arrest of any insurgents engaging in such offences.[153] Another resolution signed by Makhno in December 1918 states that anyone committing unauthorized "robbery or violence" under the Makhnovist banner "will be ruthlessly shot."[154] Along these lines, the resolution produced by Makhno does broadly conform with the archival trail.

However, it is also at this point that there is a large increase in the number of robberies and murders throughout the Schönfeld region. Makhno himself describes the destruction of a second German colony (Eigenheim), which was home to a self-defence unit commanded by an estate owner named Lentz.[155] While "most of the colony was burned down," Makhno insists that only "those [farmers] who had shot at our partisans were annihilated on the spot."[156] This action was followed by what Makhno describes as a "tough, but necessary, march" in which his forces applied "fire and sword" to the region's *khutors* and colonies.[157] According to Makhno, the purpose of these raids was to confiscate "horses, *tachankas*, various kinds of weapons, and cash."[158] In this manner, the colonies were treated as supply depots for the Makhnovists in their war against the Austro-German occupation.

It is difficult to determine how strictly Makhno's resolution was followed. Officially, only those who refused to give up weapons, or had

Figure 10. Makhnovist unit near Huliaipole, March 1919.

Figure 11. Nestor Makhno in Romania, 1921.

participated in the "*kulak* detachments," were to be executed. However, Makhno's order left ample room for personal and community grudges to influence who lived and died. The imprint of these raids on the Schönfelder Mennonites was terrifying, causing the majority of them to flee to the Molotschna colony by winter.

The killings increased in frequency, but there were no massacres on the scale of 1919 during this period. Makhno emphasizes how the "executions could have taken on a mass character," but that the insurgency consciously avoided this. He writes, "These landowners could have been annihilated along with their mansions. In essence, this would have been an appropriate response for the losses sustained by the insurgents due to raids by *pomeshchiks*. But it wasn't necessary for the insurgency to take their lives, it was more important to demoralize them. . . . Death, even for those who had shown no respect for the lives of others was regarded as an extreme measure, applicable only for individual cases, not for masses of people."[159] Once again Makhno rationalizes the attacks from a revolutionary perspective and asserts that wanton violence was at odds with his movement's objectives. Arshinov's account similarly follows this pattern. He writes that "only soldiers known to have been guilty of acts of violence against the peasants were executed." In both narratives, Makhno is positioned as the movement's voice of reason and higher morality while simultaneously acting as "a harsh avenger of the oppressed people."[160]

However, with the responsibilities of leadership came an apparently violent inner struggle, most poignantly illustrated by Makhno's near suicide while he watched Velyka Mykhailivka burn. He even questions his title of *Bat'ko*: "I often asked myself: is it honourable to allow oneself to be exalted in this way by my fellow workers? What does it mean to be the object of the grateful admiration of people who trust you implicitly because they perceive you as someone sincerely devoted to their welfare?"[161] There is a tension in his memoirs expressed by fluctuations between self-doubt, rage, and revolutionary righteousness. The reader accompanies Makhno as he struggles to achieve balance between justice and unrestrained vengeance. The narrative tension between Makhno's simultaneous impulse towards vengeance and justice is never fully reconciled, leaving the reader with a distinct impression that the spectre of atrocity lay just beneath the events described. In the coming year, it would explode to the surface. Unfortunately, Makhno's memoirs abruptly end and the reader is forced to mine other sources from December 1918 onward.[162]

The year 1919 was by far the most tragic for Russian Mennonites. According to available statistics, 1919 saw 67 percent—827 victims—of Mennonite deaths. The vast majority of these murders occurred during a six-week period between 8 November and 18 December.[163] No fewer than four major massacres affecting the Molotschna, Jasykowo, Borosenko, and Sagradovka colonies would scar the Mennonite community. The Chortitza colony also experienced atrocities in the form of pillaging, executions, and mass rape. All of these crimes occurred under Makhnovist occupation.

The year 1919 saw the Makhnovshchina reach its fullest strength in numbers, but it concurrently saw the rapid disintegration of its army by the new year. With the end of the First World War, the remaining occupation forces in southern Ukraine withdrew to the German and Mennonite colonies, where they did not go on the offensive unless provoked. Makhno quickly filled the vacuum of power produced by this situation. In early 1919, Makhno's forces were in control over the region around Huliaipole, which provoked the flight of nearly all Schönfeld Mennonites to the relative safety of the Molotschna colony.[164] Arshinov refers in passing to this period as "the expulsion of the *pomeshchiks*."[165] Land and property were once again redistributed amongst the peasantry and the communes were reconstituted.

According to Arshinov, this period saw the establishment of a southern front against the new face of counter-revolution, General Denikin's White Army. The White Army was organized by former Tsarist officers—or as Arshinov described them, the "living debris of the overthrown monarchy"—who sought to overthrow Bolshevik rule and reinstitute traditional landed relations. Their ideology was distinctly pro-Russian and anti-Bolshevik, but it was vague in its long-term political goals. The White Army was given Allied support—particularly by the French in Odesa—and relied heavily on Allied armaments received along the southern ports of the Black and Azov seas. Over the course of the civil war, the White Army also gained a notorious reputation for the mistreatment of civilians and instigating Jewish pogroms.[166] Despite Makhno's distrust of the Bolsheviks, he would twice subordinate his troops to the Red Army in order to defeat the Whites.

The White Army became deeply entrenched in the Mennonite colonies. Close relations with the Mennonite *Selbstschutz* in the Molotschna colony were quickly established. Weapons, training, and operational advice were provided to the *Selbstschutz*. Soon, the "self-defence" was participating in joint offensive actions against Makhno.[167] As early as December 1918,

Makhno established a front at Polohy against a combined White Army-*Selbstschutz* force.[168] A seesaw battle ensued until Makhnovist and Red units overran the Molotschna colony in March 1919.

Of this period, but not specifically identifying the Mennonites, Arshinov writes:

> The liberation of the people in reality leads to the degeneration and return to savagery, not of the people, but of those who thanks to power and privilege, live from the labour of the people's arms and from the blood of the people's veins. The Russian revolution gives an example of how thousands of families from the privileged class—clean, well nourished and well groomed—fell to decadence and savagery. The revolution deprived them of their servants, and in a month or two they were covered with dirt, they were mangy. The liberation of the people leads to the savagery of those who live from its enslavement.[169]

It is an emotion-laden text communicating the extent to which the enemy had truly become "other." The "privileged class" is separate from "the people." There is a distinct sense that the wealthy are inhuman, vampirically feeding from the blood of the masses. Without a host to exploit, their true ugliness is revealed as "dirty, mangy" savages. Dirtiness is a typical trope employed by propagandists to dehumanize and distance themselves from the enemy and, in times of war, to rationalize murder.

The hatred expressed by Arshinov did have very real roots. The German occupation had taken its toll. It had returned the land to the *pomeshchiks,* confiscated the peasants' crops, and sent out punitive detachments which were sometimes accompanied by colonists. Peasants sympathetic to the Revolution watched as some colonists turned to the White Army to re-establish their property and arm the *Selbstschutz,* and they would again experience the loss of land and summary executions with each push of the White Army into Makhnovist territory. This downward spiral of vengeance only escalated the hatred between the opposing forces.

Belash recalls how the excesses of the occupation came to be visually linked with the colonies. While travelling by train, Belash recounts the following scene from the end of 1918: "I looked out the window at the road leading from the station to the nearest German colony. From the trees along the road dangled human bodies, around which a number of soldiers crowded. Those hung were captured Makhnovists."[170] Arriving in Makhnovist-controlled territory, Belash records a revealing interaction between three colonist travellers and the Makhnovist patrol: "A Makhnovist pushed three tall, thin Germans out of a train car. A group of Makhnovists came forward with a shout: 'Ah, here they are, my little birdies! . . . Kreutzer, where are your sons? In the punitive detachments? Do you remember how I served you? Remember how I joined the Red Guard? Do you remember how you and your sons led a punitive detachment to Temry and burned my home down?' asked a stocky middle-aged man. The German only shrugged his shoulders and cried."[171] Belash describes watching the colonists being impaled by Makhnovist bayonets. Deeper into Makhnovist territory, Belash was confronted by a mound of corpses guarded by a pack of dogs. He reflects, "Dogs brutalized, acquire the tendencies of wolves. And people? Are we any different than wolves?"[172] This question would haunt the movement throughout its history as it struggled to adhere to the principles of freedom, equality, and solidarity amidst the dehumanizing effects of warfare.

Another incident illustrative of the escalating violence during this period is mentioned in both Belash and Chubenko's memoirs. According to their accounts, Fedir Shchus was ordered to levy contributions on the German-Lutheran colony of Silbertal (Iablokovo). Every day, Shchus would return from the colony with pairs of boots but no money, sparking Makhno's suspicion. Finally, a grieving colonist confronted Makhno and requested she be allowed to bury her dead. Makhno's suspicions were confirmed and a serious confrontation erupted between Makhno and Shchus, in which Shchus was threatened with execution if he did not stop killing colonists.[173] According to Belash, the colonists assigned two of their own men to assassinate Makhno in revenge for Shchus's actions. The Makhnovist guard attempted to arrest the would-be assassins in Huliaipole and a shootout ensued, during which a Ukrainian boy was killed in the crossfire. Enraged, Shchus returned to Silbertal and massacred thirty more colonists. Apparently, a team of Makhnovists investigated the incident and, according to Belash, Shchus was disarmed and briefly arrested. However, after a heated argument Makhno released Shchus, who remained a prominent figure in the movement until his death in 1921.[174] Nonetheless, Chubenko recounts that relations between Shchus and Makhno were strained for a long time following this incident.[175]

This incident is notable for two reasons. First, it suggests Makhno did not have full control over his troops—even those close to him. Second, if the accounts are to be believed, it shows that while Makhno did not follow through with his threat of execution, he was disturbed by the indiscriminate murder of civilians. Belash recounts another incident from the end of October 1919 in which Makhno again intervenes with a commander ordering him to cease the unauthorized shooting of German colonists near Melitopol.[176] While these incidents cannot be confirmed outside of Belash and Chubenko, they do contribute to a narrative pattern that suggests Makhno was concerned with maintaining discipline within his army according to his own interpretation of revolutionary ethics. For example, Makhno and Belash also describe in detail their attempts to rout out anti-Semitic violence from the movement. Both recall the investigation of a pogrom at the Jewish colony of Gorky that left twenty-four dead. The perpetrators were apprehended and twenty-two "bandits" were summarily excecuted.[177] Commenting on the above incident, Belash reflects, "Innocent people were killed. Although the ideology of anarcho-communism preached internationalism, it is not easy to change centuries-old traditions."[178] The overall impression from these accounts is that violence often manifested itself in a highly localized manner often outside the direct oversight of Makhno.

Within the narratives of Arshinov and Belash a period is described in which the Makhnovists were locked in open conflict with the Mennonite and German *Selbstschutz* units. From these accounts it appears the situation easily devolved into unrestrained violence and the pursuit of retributive vengeance. This is most vividly communicated by Belash's accounts of the three colonist travellers and the massacre at Silbertal. Despite this proclivity to vengeful actions amongst the Makhnovists, we also encounter Makhno's apparent attempts to maintain a semblance of "justice"—even for those identified as class enemies. Nonetheless, the tension between vengeance and justice is present in both Arshinov and Belash's narratives. The murder of the colonists and the mounds of corpses disturb Belash, but he portrays himself as powerless to alter the situation.

Figure 12. Group of Makhnovists, c. 1920.

Likewise, Makhno is enraged by Shchus's actions, but he does not follow through with his threat of execution or, apparently, any kind of punishment. Nor does he follow his 1918 resolution and publicly distance the movement from Shchus. Perhaps it was Shchus's high standing within the movement that restrained Makhno. In this instance, vengeance was allowed to take precedence over justice. The inability to effectively institute strict disciplinary measures in the face of excessive violence would greatly contribute to the development of the Mennonite massacres in late 1919.

Volin provides additional insight into the army's moral decline and slide into terror in 1919:

> Any army, of whatever kind, is an evil, and even in a free and popular army, composed of volunteers and dedicated to the defence of a noble cause, is by its very nature a danger. Once it becomes permanent, it inevitably detaches itself from the people and the world of labour. Its members lose the inclination and the ability to lead a healthy working life. With an imperceptible and therefore all the more dangerous gradualness, it becomes a collection of idlers, who acquire anti-social, authoritarian and even dictatorial leanings, who acquire also a taste for violence as a thing in itself, for the brute force even in cases where recourse to such means is contrary to the very cause it purports to defend.[179]

While Volin's historical account follows Arshinov's very closely, he breaks form with regard to the army's behaviour and Makhno's role in 1919. A different vision emerges of an army elite, drunk with power and obsessed with violence.

Following a disastrous breakthrough by the White Army into the Makhnovist sector, and a bitter falling-out between Makhno and the Bolsheviks, the Makhnovist army was forced to retreat into central Ukraine over the summer of 1919. A special White Army unit was ordered to pursue Makhno and eliminate his forces. By September, Makhno's forces had been squeezed into a small patch of territory controlled by Ukrainian nationalists. In the city of Uman, Makhno was compelled to negotiate a short-lived non-aggression pact with the Nationalists. Meanwhile, General Denikin issued his famous "Moscow Directive," with the goal to capture the city. Major centres such as Katerynoslav and Kharkiv quickly fell to Denikin and by October the White Army was 240 miles south of Moscow. Denikin's offensive marked the high point of the White Army movement and the last time it would critically threaten the Bolshevik regime.

At Uman, Makhno was encircled by the White Army and faced a desperate situation. In an action reminiscent of his breakout at Dibrivka, Arshinov writes that Makhno ordered his troops to make a frontal assault on the White Army near the village of Perehonivka in an effort to smash through the encirclement. Makhno's plan was a success and the consequences for Denikin were disastrous. In an all-or-nothing bid, Denikin left his rearguard extremely vulnerable. Believing Makhno was a spent force, White Army reserve forces were thinly spread across central and southern Ukraine.

Capitalizing upon his victory at Perehonivka, Makhno made a dash for Huliaipole. Arshinov narrativizes this event in highly mythologized language: "The following legend about Pugachev is told among the peasants of Great Russia. After his uprising he fell into the hands of the authorities. He told the noblemen sitting around him: 'In this uprising I only gave you a foretaste. But wait: soon after me will come the real broom—it will sweep all of you away.' Makhno showed himself to be this historic broom of the people in all his revolutionary insurrectionary activity."[180] The army fanned out in the direction of Katerynoslav, Huliaipole, and Nikopol. The Makhnovists rapidly occupied Oleksandrivsk, Huliaipole,

Figure 13. Makhnovist Army Staff. Huliaipole, 1919.

Berdiansk, Melitopol, and Mariupol. On 20 October, at the height of their advance, they briefly captured Katerynoslav and bombarded Taganrog, where Denikin was stationed. At Volnovakha, the White Army's major supply lines were severed and Denikin was cut off from Allied support along the Azov seaports. Within this context, the Makhnovists came to occupy the Mennonite colonies of the Molotschna, Chortitza, Jasykowo, and Sagradowka.

The policing of civilian life within the Makhnovist zone became a major concern. The Makhnovists' capture of an expansive territory led to the establishment of a *kontrrazvedka* (counter-intelligence). The *kontrrazvedka* was divided into military and civilian sections and quickly gained a notorious reputation for being uncontrollable. According to Belash, by autumn 1919 the *kontrrazvedka* had developed a network that reached down to every squadron. Furthermore, the service employed locals to provide information on White Army collaborators. Given this description, the *kontrrazvedka* would have been keenly interested in hunting down Mennonite *Selbstschutzler*. Belash writes that the *kontrrazvedka* shot all individuals with any connection to the White Army, including officers, police, prison guards, spies, and provocateurs.[181] Makhno likewise writes that the *kontrrazvedka* was "authorized to search any home in the martial law zone" and detain any suspected individuals.[182]

Volin looked upon the influence of the counter-intelligence with horror. Theoretically, it was subordinate to the Revolutionary Military Soviet—the civilian body that served as the executive of the movement of which Volin was chairman—but, practically, it functioned outside of civilian control.[183] In November 1919, a special commission, which included worker and peasant delegates, was established to investigate the reckless activities of the service.[184] Volin also claims that Makhno's behaviour was increasingly authoritarian during this period, which he attributes to the development of a "warrior sentiment" and "military clique" around Makhno. Most seriously, Volin accuses Makhno of reckless drunkenness, excessive violence, and rape.[185]

In exile, Volin's relations with Makhno became severely strained, although he did not print his accusations until quite some time after Makhno's death. In his unfinished works, Volin explains that he had withheld certain information for fear of retribution from Makhnovists in exile. He also accuses high-ranking commanders of driving a wedge between Makhno and Halyna for fear of her influence, and preventing Halyna from speaking out about Makhno's "darker side."[186]

Volin's account offers us a contested memory of Makhno from within the movement itself. Many anarchists have questioned the truthfulness of Volin's accusations, as he does not provide specific details. Makhno's close friend in exile, Ida Mett, regarded Volin as an "unscrupulous character." Concerning the rape accusations, she pointed out that Makhno's wife, Halyna, was a defender of women and had personally executed rapists.[187] Halyna herself continued to give positive assessments of her husband and the movement throughout her life.[188] Leah Feldman, a Makhnovist nurse, likewise rejected Volin's charges. She commented in an interview, "Who in Russia is he supposed to have raped? His wife was always riding on a horse beside him and would have soon put a stop to that."[189]

Conversely, other Makhnovist intellectuals came to disdain the movement's violence. In exile, Mark Mratchnyi—who was briefly involved with the cultural-education section—refused to be printed in the same journal as Makhno. He also accused Arshinov of covering up Makhno's dirty past and downplaying the extent to which anti-Semitism had infected the army.[190] Aron Baron also vocally protested the army's excessive violence in 1919 at a Nabat Confederation meeting.[191] The problem with all of these sources, however, is that they provide few details that can be further investigated. Even such critics as Volin and Mratchnyi remain self-restrained, maintaining a code of silence over the murkier aspects of the movement.

One source, however, that does not submit to such self-censorship is Kuzmenko's diary. She complains of Makhno's drinking bouts and erratic behaviour. In one instance, a drunk Makhno is described as cursing and yelling in front of children and then nearly falling off his horse into the mud. Over the following days in Huliaipole, Kuzmenko describes a still drunk Makhno ordering his cavalry to publicly whip a number of former partisans. Kuzmenko complains of a "raid on innocent people" who were "beat for no reason." The resulting effect was to terrorize the villagers of Huliaipole who became afraid "to protest the violence of the drunken Makhnovists."[192]

The most egregious example of violence recorded in the diary is a massacre perpetrated against the German-Lutheran colony Mariental. According to the entry for 16 March 1920, the village's *Selbstschutz* killed a Makhnovist scout. Kuzmenko writes that the colony "paid dearly for this rash murder." The Makhnovists burned down the village and "almost all residents were killed, except for the very old and very young, they say women were killed." A surviving German attempted to flee to the neighbouring Greek village of Komar, but was turned over to Makhno and executed on the spot.[193] Kuzmenko's decription of the massacre is reminiscent of the attack on Neu-Grüntal in 1918 but more indiscriminate in nature and devoid of ideological justifications. Kuzmenko's following paragraph causually describes the sunny weather, stopping for lunch, and talking a walk along the river bank where they encountered a corpse.[194]

The Makhno encountered in Kuzmenko's diary is an unruly character suffering from bouts of heavy drinking and fits of rage. It is perhaps a Makhno driven to his end by an unending civil war and thoroughly desensitized to extreme levels of violence. The matter-of-factness with which dozens of executions are listed in the diary, and the callousness with which life is so easily eliminated, chillingly illustrates Volin's observation that "the continued existence of an army within the movement, of whatever kind it may be, always and inevitably ends by being affected by certain serious faults, by a special kind of evil mentality."[195] Whatever the truth of Volin's specific allegations, Kuzmenko's diary provides evidence that excessive violence and civilian mistreatment were problems within the army that extended to Makhno personally.

It is also from this later period that we encounter Belash's last mention of "German colonists." Belash recounts the changed situation in 1920: "The German colonists—our former irreconcilables enemies—now resigned themselves. In all the colonies, where we stayed, they were doing reconnaissance, stood in the outposts, warning us of any movement of the Red Army. They carefully, apparently out of sympathy, or perhaps because of fear, hid the place of our stay from the Reds: we were out of danger."[196] The impression given is that the Makhnovists had worn down the colonists' will to resist, and "perhaps out of fear," had terrorized at least a portion of the civilian population into submission and even collaboration. The longevity of the war had taken its toll, with violence giving way to terror.

CHAPTER 2

# THROUGH MENNONITE EYES

At the Winnipeg Mennonite Heritage Centre there hangs a clock known less for its ability to tell time than to tell of a time passed. The clock's hands reach out at awkward angles and its faceplate bears the distinct impression of a boot. The artifact's description reads:

> Marauding anarchists, led by the infamous Nestor Makhno, destroyed many Kroeger clocks. When they plundered Mennonite villages the clock became a favorite target because they mistook its burnished metal for gold. They'd seize a clock, gallop out of the village and later cast it aside after ripping out the weights and chains.
>
> One clock is known as the Nestor Makhno clock. The brutal bandit was known to take over a village and make himself at home in the most prosperous house. From there he would lecture village leaders on how life would now proceed under the revolution. On one occasion a Kroeger clock bonged while Makhno was in mid-speech. The interruption startled him and in fury he tore the clock from the wall and trampled on it.
>
> When he left, the family collected the pieces. Years later Arthur Kroeger was called upon to create a duplicate faceplate. The damaged original was donated to the Mennonite Heritage Centre in Winnipeg, where it still bears the dents of Nestor Makhno's boots.[1]

As a memorial artifact Makhno's clock communicates the essence of the collective Mennonite experience of Nestor Makhno and his movement. During the Revolution the boot of Makhno trampled the finely tuned world of the colonies. The meeting of Makhno and the Mennonites marked in time a deeply destructive moment, one that would ultimately end in the decimation of the colonies and the overseas exodus of the Mennonites.

The Mennonite narrative of Makhno is steeped in the collective memories of a people that suffered enormously in the face of war and revolution. The vast majority of Mennonite accounts about the Makhnovists are dominated by recollections of murder and robbery. Understandably, this deep narrative script colours the representation of Makhno and his movement in Mennonite histories. An example of this is contained in Victor Peters's biography, *Nestor Makhno: The Life of an Anarchist* (1969). The passage in question is from H.B. Wiens's memoirs, in which he describes the situation on the Makhnovist-*Selbstschutz* front line on 21 January 1919. Peters quotes Wiens at length: "Rumor had it that the home guard [*Selbstschutz*] of the neighboring *volosts* would come to free the Krasnopol (Schönfeld) *volost*. In the engagement, which took place about thirty *versts* away, the home guard was beaten. The following nights hundreds of carriages and wagons, carrying partisans, plunder and women, returned and were once more quartered in the villages of our *volost*."[2]

By contrast, the original German document sent by Wiens to Peters reads:

> The *Selbstschutz* was advancing (*Der Selbstschutz näherte sich*) and there was talk amongst the Russians (*im Gerede gings bei den Russen*) that the *Selbstschutz* would kill them all (*der Selbstschutz brachte sie um*). So hundreds of wagons loaded with women and children and things (*Wagen mit Frauen und Kindern, auch mit Sachen*) departed for Alexandrovsk. The *Selbstschutz* were defeated thirty *versts* away, and returned to the colony [Molotschna]. For the entire next day, the Russians returned to their village. We were not yet free of the bandits, which was what we had really believed.[3]

Peters's English translation substantially alters the context. In Peters's version, there is a rumour that the *Selbstschutz* are coming to "free" the

Schönfeld district. By contrast, Wiens writes that the "Russians" feared the *Selbstschutz* would kill them all. Furthermore, in the original, Wiens writes that "women and children" fled to Oleksandrivsk in wagons as a result of this rumour, but they returned when the *Selbstschutz* was defeated. Peters rearranges the scenario. The returning wagons are now filled with "partisans, plunder, and women" and the children are excised entirely. The effect of this loose translation is to transform the *Selbstschutz* from a menacing threat into a liberating force.

It appears that cultural expectations about who constituted heroes and villains led Peters to reconstruct the event in translation. Collective Mennonite memory does not conceive of the *Selbstschutz* as a destructive threat. While sometimes condemned for abandoning pacifism, it is widely interpreted as a defensive response to a desperate situation.[4] The Makhnovists, by contrast, are overwhelmingly associated with plunder, murder, and rape. Indeed, Wiens's memoir on the whole negatively assesses the Makhnovists as disorganized and violent thugs. However, Wiens's account of the fleeing peasants constitutes a deviation in the plot that is strikingly at odds with the expectations of Mennonite cultural narratives.

One difficulty in handling Mennonite memoirs from this period is that their authors normally experienced only the Makhnovists' destructive side. House searches, expropriations, murder, and rape dominate Mennonite accounts. They were keenly aware of the ubiquitous presence of the *kontrrazvedka* but rarely mention the movement's cultural-educational section or the Makhnovist political program. For example, Chortitza resident Gerhard Schroeder recalls the election of the October 1919 congress in Oleksandrivsk, but he appears to be unaware the Makhnovists had organized the election, attributing it exclusively to the efforts of the "workers from Alexandrovsk and Chortitza." Schroeder insists: "The [Makhnovists] had no interest in establishing any form of formal government on the ruins of the old; their main concern was to maintain a state of anarchy as long as possible."[5] However, a close reading of Mennonite sources reveals a greater range of experience and interpretation than might be expected. A number of Mennonite sources even reveal a degree of neutral, or at least non-violent, interactions with Makhno and his supporters.

The Mennonites were privy to the darkest side of the Makhnovshchina and have recorded it in painstaking detail. For this reason, Mennonite sources are critical to understanding the Makhnovshchina. It is perhaps surprising that, outside of Mennonite scholarship, these sources have rarely been examined. Many anarchist and non-Mennonite scholars are quite sympathetic to the Makhnovist perspective.[6] Historian Alexandre Skirda, for example, writes that he is pleased with the efforts to "rehabilitate in academic circles Makhno and the Ukrainian insurgent movement." According to Skirda, the most important objective is to "make the experience of the Ukrainian libertarian communists known to a wider public and to extract from it lessons of use to the contemporary revolutionary project."[7] The problem is that such ideologically driven histories, inside or outside of academia, often ignore the mass of Mennonite sources that do not conform to personal politics. That said, Mennonite sources, similar to the Makhnovist sources, are perspectival and should also be approached with care. Any fair assessment of the Makhnovshchina must therefore acknowledge both its constructive aspirations and destructive aspects. Only then can a more comprehensive multi-perspective history of the movement be achieved.

## MENNONITE VOICES

A variety of Mennonite sources are used in this chapter, but a number are more worthy of detailed mention. The Victor Peters collection held at the Harvard Ukrainian Research Institute is important for the letters of correspondence with Mennonites who directly witnessed Makhno and his movement. The letters were solicited in the 1960s as part of Peters's biography on Nestor Makhno. Anna Goerz and H.B. Wiens's memoirs are particularly insightful. Gerhard Lohrenz's published memoirs and Peter J. Dyck's diary are also indispensable sources regarding the pre–civil war period. Dyck's diary was self-published by the author's son in 1981. Dyck was a resident of the Molotschna and recounted in detail events from the beginning of the First World War to the end of the civil war. Gerhard Lohrenz was raised in the Sagradowka colony and fought in both the *Selbstschutz* and White Army. Lohrenz later immigrated to Canada where he wrote a number of works on the history of Russian Mennonites. His study of the Sagradowka massacre, *Fire Over Sagradovka,* is especially important for its collection of deeply personal eyewitness accounts from Mennonite women.

Dietrich Neufeld's diary and memoir stand out amongst the primary sources. The diary spans September 1919 to March 1920, offering a reflective real-time account of Makhnovist occupation. Originally composed in French, the diary was first self-published in German in 1921 under the pseudonym Dederich Navall. In 1922, Neufeld published two memoirs which, in English translation, were combined with the diary to produce the book *A Russian Dance of Death* in 1977. Originally from Sagradowka, Neufeld resided in Chortitza during autumn 1919. As a teacher and intellectual, his writings are penetrative and even philosophical. They delve into the heart of the conflict, often challenging traditional Mennonite self-perceptions. Neufeld was a pacifist, and his writings reflect this stance in his harsh criticism of the *Selbstschutz* and Mennonite pre-revolutionary colony life.

Another pacifist memoir that deals explicitly with the Makhnovshchina is Gerhard Schroeder's *Miracles of Grace and Judgment*. Schroeder was also a teacher who resided in Schönfeld. He self-published his memoir in English in 1984. The book details the Mennonite experience in the Schönfeld district. Schroeder recounts a number of personal encounters with Makhno, making this an invaluable source. I have also used the history of the Janzen family, for whom Makhno worked as a youth. Their story was published in 2010 in the *Saskatchewan Mennonite Historian* by the grandchildren of Abram Janzen, an owner of the Silberfeld estate. The family's history contains an account of Makhno's experience at Silberfeld and a further encounter during the civil war.[8]

Finally, the Molotschna newspaper *Friedensstimme* provides a host of useful articles on both the Makhnovists and the Mennonite *Selbstschutz*. *Friedensstimme* was founded in Halbstadt in 1903 under the editorship of Abraham Kroeker. Originally written for a Mennonite Brethren audience, it became the only colony newspaper during the civil war, which greatly expanded the scope of its readership. Kroeker personally occupied an intermediate position between self-defence and pacifism. He was strongly critical of Mennonite enthusiasm for the Austro-German occupation and the punitive expeditions to retrieve property. He also frequently admonished the broader Mennonite community for what he perceived as its lack of faith and attachment to material goods. At the same time Kroeker believed it was legitimate to employ self-defence to protect one's family and community. He firmly believed it was wrong to condemn those men who had taken up arms and that self-defence was not necessarily anti-biblical.[9] During the First World War, *Friedensstimme* was suspended and was frequently under military censure throughout the civil war. Its pages offer a wealth of information, including reports of Makhno's activities, debates over pacifism, and reflections on the Makhnovist massacres.[10]

## NEW RUSSIA

There is a fundamental paradox at the heart of Russian Mennonite history that must be addressed in order to contextualize the colonies' tragic civil war experience. Cultural anthropologist James Urry has argued that in various historical settings Mennonites have adopted "paradoxical rhetorical strategies" where we simultaneously find "*separatist* arguments derived from their faith's tragic orientation" and "*assimilative* arguments derived from the comic orientation of their yearning to be good citizens."[11] In the Russian context, through the process of escaping an oppressive Prussian state and founding their community in "New Russia," Mennonites became an essential ingredient in Russia's colonization of this newly opened frontier.

The role played by the colonies in the socio-economic makeup of southern Ukraine strongly supports Urry's conclusion that "Mennonites have never been far from politics and not all have been unwilling participants in the power plays of the 'world.'"[12] In the Prussian Mennonite search for a new home, their interests became entangled with the objectives of an aggressively expansionist Russian empire, which inevitably meant the subjugation of certain groups and the elevation of others. In this context, despite an identity rooted in pacifism, Mennonites found themselves part of a broader imperial agenda that necessarily involved violence on the part of the government in order to reshape the socio-economic landscape of New Russia. Yet, the imperial system was unable to colonize the colonizers. In the eyes of late nineteenth-century Russian nationalists and the government during the First World War, Mennonite pacifism and cultural foreignness was perceived as a threat to the empire. Therefore, for reasons of survival the Mennonite political leadership frequently adopted a deferent attitude towards the tsar, but simultaneously defended the privileges they had received as foreign colonists who had settled New Russia.

Prior to the arrival of Mennonites in New Russia, the region's Zaporizhian Cossacks were resettled, co-opted and enserfed by the expanding Russian empire. Under Catherine the Great, the Zaporizhian Sich—the Cossacks' main military-settlement—was surrounded by imperial troops and destroyed on 14 August 1775. In the aftermath of this victory Catherine issued a decree stating, "The Zaporozhian Sich has already been destroyed, together with the eradication for all time, of the very name of the Zaporosky Cossacks, for no less reason than the outrage of Our Imperial Majesty at the behavior and audacity of these Cossacks in disobedience of Our Supreme commands."[13] In 1783, Catherine issued a decree abolishing all local political institutions and privileges, followed by the introduction of serfdom to the region the same year.[14] Former Cossacks and peasants sometimes found themselves registered as serfs and forced to pay dues (*obrok*), in the form of labour, to newly settled Russian landowners.[15] Massive land tracts were gifted to Russian nobles, who in turn imported their own estate serfs from central Russia to work the land. In this manner, the region's population of serfs rose from 1.32 percent in 1764 to 27.9 percent in 1781.[16]

In further efforts to populate New Russia, state peasants were resettled by the government from Russian territories. Religious dissenters, like the Doukhobors and Old Believers, were also granted freedom of religion to attract settlers to the region. A large number of fugitive serfs from Poland and the northern Russian provinces were tolerated as well.[17] Nonetheless, the nature of Russian serfdom greatly restricted the empire's ability to rapidly grow New Russia's population, and Catherine found it beneficial to entice European settlers with wide-ranging privileges far beyond what Russian peasant subjects had received.[18] Foreign settlers—including Germans, Bulgarians, Greeks, Serbians, and Mennonites—made their new home in what became the southern Russian provinces of Katerynoslav and Tauride. Each ethnic group established separate settlements, or colonies, where they preserved their traditional cultural patterns.[19] The impact of imperial colonization on the region's cultural and economic development was vitally important. Historian Terry Martin remarks that "the conquest and settlement of New Russia represented a complete break in the region's history; indeed, some argued state action created the region."[20] A diverse collection of peoples were funnelled into this frontier region, whose experiences of New Russia ranged from freedom and opportunity to enserfment and impoverishment.

Mennonite historians emphasize the social insularity of the colonies in this early period. The original Mennonite colonists, who settled on the lower reaches of the Dnipro River's right bank, were especially noted for their belief in establishing a nonconformist community of believers that stood apart from the state and the worldly ways of non-believers. Mennonite historians Cornelius Krahn and Leonard Sawatzky describe the "old colony" pattern of living as follows:

> In the total pattern of Mennonite history they could be compared in some respects with the Kleine Gemeinde of the Molotschna, the Hutterites, or the Amish, although more conservative.... Their utmost concern centred around the preservation of their way of life. From their point of view the total cultural pattern including language, clothing, education, furniture, self-government, mutual aid, village pattern, and all forms of customs were integral parts of their church concept. They preserved the most extreme form of separation from the world and the practice of church discipline by means of the ban and avoidance. Contact with the outside world was kept at a minimum.[21]

In the spirit of Psalm 35:20, they sought a life as the "quiet in the land," separate from but at peace with their neighbours. In time, the colonies achieved a great degree of prosperity and came to be described as a virtual "state within a state" or, as termed by Mennonite historian and Chortitza colony resident David G. Rempel, a "Mennonite Commonwealth."[22] Gerhard Lohrenz described the Mennonite village at the turn of the nineteenth century as "from afar looking like an oasis in the steppes."[23] In their relative seclusion, Mennonites established themselves as an affluent *Völklein* ("little nation") within the larger context of Imperial Russia.

A key element of Russian Mennonite history is the colonial privileges acquired from the Russian tsar. In 1800, Tsar Paul granted the Mennonites extensive privileges in a document called the *Privilegium*. The *Privilegium* included the guarantee of religious freedom, exemption from military service, ten- to fifteen-year tax exemptions, the assurance of Mennonite non-redistributional inheritance and property practices, and sixty-five dessiatines (seventy-one hectares) of land per family.[24] This was the largest land allotment awarded to incoming colonists. By contrast, Lutheran and Catholic German colonists received sixty dessiatines (65.6 hectares), Swedes fifteen dessiatines, and Greeks eight dessiatines (8.7 hectares).[25] Bulgarian colonists proved an exception, who settled on terms comparable to Mennonites and Germans.[26] In New Russia's frontier landscape, the *Privilegium* with its attendant promises comes close to a kind of founding constitution for the Russian Mennonites and embodied the Mennonites' special relationship with the Russian Crown. It is symbolic that the Mennonites carefully preserved the original copy in its own room in the Chortitza colony almost as a holy relic.[27]

A common refrain in both Mennonite and Slavic sources is that Mennonite colonists were particularly desired due to their reputation for efficiency and industriousness. The Russian government did indeed recognize Mennonites as highly effective agriculturalists and intended for them to serve as model farmers in the region. The preamble to the *Privilegium* reads in part that their "excellent industry and morality may, according to the testimony of the authorities, be held up as a model to the foreigners settled there and thereby deserves special consideration."[28] The *Privilegium* came to represent an earthly confirmation of divine favour. Urry comments, "If, in the hope of salvation, Mennonites believed they possessed a special covenant with God, the Lord's anointed tsar had provided an earthly covenant in the form of the *privilegium*. Under the protection of God and the tsar, Mennonites and their descendants were free to seek heavenly salvation in peace and security."[29] Cultural insularity, combined with narratives of divine selection, would profoundly affect the development of Mennonite social relations within the broader Russian landscape. In the hierarchy of New Russia's colonist communities, the Mennonites were considered first amongst equals.

The Mennonites lived up to their benefactor's expectations, setting a shining example of agricultural efficiency in the region. Mennonites proved to be excellent innovators, being amongst the first farmers in the region to replace sheep rearing with wheat cultivation in the 1840s.[30] They also led the way in the production and adoption of new agricultural technologies.

These innovations sometimes benefited the neighbouring Ukrainian peasants, who embraced the most successful methods and technologies spearheaded by Mennonite farmers.[31] Furthermore, under the leadership of Johann Cornies, Mennonites were mobilized by the government to assist with the sedentarization of the region's nomadic Nogai Tatars. Mennonites were also recruited to deliver agricultural apprenticeships for Ukrainian and Jewish farmers in the region.[32]

The economic wealth of the colonies rapidly grew throughout the nineteenth century. Lohrenz comments, "Most of our people in Russia were prosperous, quite a few were rich, and some very rich."[33] By 1914 there were 104,000 Russian Mennonites inhabiting four major settlements and fifteen sub-colonies amongst a multitude of smaller hamlets and estates. Beyond agriculture, Mennonites were successful as millers, merchants, craftsmen, and industrialists. By 1911 Mennonites owned over 50 percent of the milling industry and were responsible for producing 10 percent of the region's agricultural implements.[34]

At the economic level, Mennonite separation from the outside world declined. As the colonies grew in wealth and size, contact with outside groups became inevitable and even beneficial. However, internal pressure to remain religiously and culturally distinct, by maintaining radically different social patterns from their Ukrainian neighbours, worked against broader integration. Extensive contact with the neighbouring peasantry did, however, come in the form of hired help on the colonies and estates. The sight of hired help on the colonies from local Ukrainians and migrant Russians increased rapidly after the serfs' emancipation, so that by 1904 "practically every farm employed 2–4 seasonal workers and some a worker for the entire year."[35] This was in addition to maids, wet-nurses, and other servants. The servant economy employed lower-class Mennonites as well, many of whom worked on the large estates.[36] This arrangement was not restricted to wealthy estate owners but penetrated the very heart of Mennonite socio-economics.

Mennonite relations with Ukrainian peasants expanded further with the establishment of so-called "daughter" or sub-colonies in the second half of the nineteenth century. These new colonies were a direct response to a landlessness crisis amongst Mennonites. Mennonite land tenure was hereditary and generally indivisible. As Leonard Friesen has convincingly

Figure 14. Peasant field workers on the Wintergruen estate, 1900.

argued, this indivisibility of landholdings provided a stable basis to build economically profitable farms through capital investment and techonological innovation.[37] In sharp contrast, peasant land tenure was communal and divisible in nature. While peasant practices ensured a minimum safety net for village members, they also led to diminishing allotments as the rural population expanded. Furthermore, the divisibility of peasant land encouraged a risk-averse attitude towards investment and innovation.[38] At the same time, Mennonite land tenure inevitably produced its own landlessness crisis within the colonies. On the one hand, the scarcity of land encouraged many Mennonites to become skilled tradesmen and successful business owners. On the other hand, social tensions within the colonies reached a boiling point by the mid-nineteenth century as the landless became a majority. Some Mennonites even advocated adopting a redistributional model. Only after state intervention was a solution arrived at in which the colonies' reserve lands were allocated to the landless and the traditional sixty-five-dessiatine (seventy-one-hectare) farms were allowed to be divided in half. Additionally, colonies were granted permission to collectively purchase new lands to establish so-called "daughter" colonies.[39]

These new colonies were often located on land formerly worked by Ukrainian serfs. For example, the Jasykowo colony was purchased from Russian nobles in 1869. A year later an agreement was signed between the colony and neighbouring Ukrainian villagers establishing lease prices for land and access to pasture now under Mennonite administration.[40] In the case of the Sagradowka colony, Dietrich Neufeld observed how the local peasants were forced to pass through the colony to reach their distant strips of land. According to Neufeld, this arrangement greatly irritated the local peasants.[41]

Like Makhno, many Ukrainians worked as farmhands or servants on Mennonite and German estates and colonies. The working arrangement was often described by Mennonites as amicable. Gerhard Lohrenz writes of his relationship with the family farmhands, "My relationship with our workers was always the very best. I spoke their language perfectly, knew them, understood them and liked them. I think they always considered me their friend."[42] Indeed, there are numerous examples in the pages of *Friedensstimme* in which servants intervened to save the lives of their Mennonite employers during the civil war.[43] Jacob Toews writes fondly of the bonds he forged with his farmhand Grischka, who had worked with the family since he was eight years old. Grischka developed a drinking problem, but Toews remained loyal to his old friend and helped him to quit alcohol. Toews recalls how in time, Grischka "got to be a perfect example for other workers. He became very faithful to us, counted himself as part of our family. Our assets were his assets."[44] Toews also describes how when he was drafted as an army medic in the First World War he became affectionately known as *dobriy kulak* (the good kulak). Given such relationships, it is understandable that for many Mennonites the extreme violence that accompanied the Revolution came as a shock.

Nonetheless, physical abuse, as described by Makhno, was not an uncommon occurance. While Toews stresses his positive relationship with his peasant employees, his narrative reveals another side:

> The Russians had one great passion, and that was drinking and gambling. Seldom a Sunday would pass by that someone would not get drunk and you'd have to try and settle it in a fair way. Sometimes I'd lose my patience and give them a good box on the ears. If once in a while I'd hit an innocent one he didn't seem to mind much. All said I could do with my Russian personnel very much as I pleased. They loved me in spite of it all. Probably because they knew I meant them

> well. They wouldn't bear you a grudge because of one beating. This was their way of life.[45]

Toews seems unaware of the resentment his own behaviour could cause, asserting that "we Mennonites treated our labourers humanely" and accuses Russian and Swiss landlords of having "no consideration for them [the workers] as human beings."[46] Regardless of who was committing the abuse, this potential source of resentment left the rural workforce vulnerable to radical agitation. For example, a *Friedensstimme* article published during the German occupation reproduces excerpts from a Moscow anarchist journal in which the servant economy is openly challenged and the workers encouraged to "throw open your master's gates to the tide of revolution."[47] Toews also recounts in his memoirs how political agitators would spread revolutionary propaganda amongst the peasant workforce. However, he writes that prior to the Revolution, "We were used to the labourers talking about dividing up the land; had heard this since childhood days, and used to laugh about it."[48]

Distinct ethnic labels also accompanied the servant economy. Mennonites consistently referred to Ukrainians as "Russians" or "Little Russians" and Ukraine as "south Russia." While these labels were not intended to be pejorative or patronizing, they reveal a lack of awareness amongst Mennonite writers about the changing self-identification of ethnically conscious peasants in the late nineteenth and early twentieth centuries. In this manner, the use of "Russian" to describe Ukrainian peasants is similar to how Makhnovist writers collapse Mennonite distinctiveness under the category of "German colonist." The use of these terms by Mennonites and Makhnovists betrays a certain lack of intimacy with each other, in which the complexities of identity in the New Russian context are subsumed by generalizations.

Implicit negative stereotypes about peasants are also common in Mennonite writings. For example, Gerhard Lohrenz describes the living arrangements between Mennonites and their workers:

> If the labourers were Mennonites they slept in our home and ate at our table, but if they were Russian the girls slept in our home and the boys slept in a room with a bed in one corner of the barn. The Russian labourers ate apart, but the same food was given to them as we had....

> To a Canadian this eating apart and sleeping in the barn may seem discriminatory. It was not meant that way, and the Russians did not take it that way either. They would have felt uneasy eating with us, since their table manners were different. They liked to use their fingers as much as the fork. . . . As far as sleeping in the barn is concerned, the Russian peasant was used to it from home.[49]

As Lohrenz indicates, these prejudices were not characterized by hatred or even dislike but rather assumed cultural differences. For example, Schönfelder H.B. Wiens remarks in his memoir that "since stealing is the custom of most Russians, this could not be prevented in Machno."[50]

Accounts from Mennonite employers generally do not challenge how cultural prejudices negatively coloured their perception and treatment of peasant employees. However, other memoirists like Dietrich Neufeld argue that Mennonite socio-economics were embedded in a broader imperial system that had engendered a great degree of bitterness and hostility amongst land-hungry and impoverished peasants. Neufeld writes: "Long before the War the Russian peasant was already casting envious glances at the much more prosperous colonist, who only too often was his employer and master. As a hired hand he was not as badly treated by the Mennonites as by the Russian landed proprietors, but the relationship was still that of capitalist master and inferior servant and not that of equals or brothers. The situation was even more common in the rest of Russia. The downtrodden masses of Russia were finally no longer willing to bear this afflication. They yearned for rebellion."[51]

The region's systemic inequalities deepened peasant resentments. In the peasant revolts that would shake the final decades of Imperial Russia, estate owners were especially targeted. As previously discussed, from the 1860s onwards wealthy Mennonites and Germans increasingly purchased the Russian gentry's estates. This new class of estate owners became integrated into a system of labour relations, which had barely emerged from serfdom. Many peasant farmhands, such as Makhno's father, were themselves former serfs who continued to work the lands of their former masters. To the land-hungry farmhand or rentee the Mennonite estate owner was simply a new face in a familiar system of economic expoitation.

In the closing decades of the nineteenth century, Mennonites and Germans found their traditional privileges increasingly under threat as a surge of ethnic Russian nationalism swept the empire. In the era of Alexander II's Great Reforms, a profound social restructuring occurred from the emancipation of serfs in 1861 to the introduction of compulsory military service in 1874. Facing a dual wave of revolutionary activism and non-Russian revolts within the empire, the government increasingly utilized nationalism as a diversionary tactic to stabilize internal support.[52] The government adopted a policy of forced integration and the foreign colonists' special legal status was abolished in 1871. The latter provoked an existential crisis within the Mennonite community, who considered it a direct attack on the *Privilegium*. Some feared the erosion of their special rights would lead to the assimilation of Mennonites and, in the long term, a loss of faith. Mennonites felt especially threatened by the possibility of military conscription given their religious injunction against taking up arms. Delegates were dispatched to St. Petersburg in a failed effort to renegotiate their exemption. A compromise was eventually reached for alternative service in forestry and medical units, but not before a wave of emigration had begun. Between 1874 and 1880, 18,000 of the most conscientious of objectors resettled in North America.[53]

The era preceding the First World War marked the height of the Mennonite commonwealth and is traditionally depicted as a lost golden age. However, perhaps in part due to the increasing discrimination against Germans and Mennonites, it was also an era of intense devotion to the tsar. The words of the influential Mennonite minister and historian Peter M. Friesen from 1911 illustrate this sentiment:

> As long as we are in Russia, we fear, in the final analysis, only God and the tsar, and likewise we only trust in God and the tsar. We also believe that as subjects, citizens and Christians we will not only be able to live in Russia with an untroubled conscience, but that we will also be able to stand as a patriotic, culturally useful, small member in the large family of Russia (into which we have been adopted by Divine Providence), and will learn to do this more and more as a total body. If individuals among us [Mennonites] at times should act contrary to

> the general interest and to the law, then we as a fellowship of believers confess "Let every person be subject to the governing authorities."[54]

Such declarations of fealty to the tsar were in no small part authentic, but they were equally intended to dispel nationalist charges of dual loyalties and position Mennonites as faithful Russian subjects. As Urry phrases it, "peoplehood became politicized" in narratives that emphasized Mennonite Russianness and their contribution to the Empire's development.[55]

With the outbreak of the First World War, anti-German sentiments intensified dramatically. The government viewed Germans, including Mennonites, as potential fifth columnists despite their displays of patriotism or support for the war effort. Since the 1880s, the nationalist press had fanned the flames of anti-German hatred, imploring Russians to cast out the kaiser's agents. In many of these articles Mennonites were specifically targeted as an internal threat.[56] The government, sensing a potential scapegoat, declared all Germans to be "of enemy descent" and passed a series of land liquidation laws in 1915 that aimed to expropriate their properties and forcibly resettle ethnic Germans to the outer reaches of the empire.[57]

Dietrich Neufeld recalls how the war "gave cunning nationalists a golden opportunity to deflect the dissatisfaction of the lower classes from themselves to the ethnic aliens in the country."[58] Anti-German riots were reported throughout the empire, including a major one in Moscow in 1915 that saw eight deaths and 70 million rubles worth of damage.[59] Molotschna resident Peter J. Dyck recalls how the use of German in public was banned and that all colonies were renamed in Russian.[60] Fines were issued for violating the ban and in one case a Mennonite man was arrested and exiled to Siberia for speaking German with his neighbour.[61] However, since the ban applied only to High German, Mennonites—unlike most other German-speaking colonists—were able to adapt by using Low German publicly. As the war deepened, all German state employees were dismissed. In the case of Peter Dyck and his colleagues at the Molotschna Credit Union, a mere twelve days' notice was given before their discharge.[62] Many Mennonites felt it was only a matter of time before the land liquidation laws took effect and they would be forced to relocate.

According to Lohrenz, anti-Germanism at the local level of the colonies did not affect relations with their neighbours as much as might be expected. Nonetheless, he recalls "the situation poisoned relations somewhat." Lohrenz recounts an encounter between his younger brother and a Ukrainian peasant teenager who called out, "Ah here comes one of those damned Germans. We should put all of you Germans with your head on the block. We should exterminate you."[63] What the anti-German propaganda accomplished was to encourage an atmosphere of mutual distrust on the eve of revolution. According to Neufeld, anti-German propaganda convinced the peasant that the colonist was "nothing but a traitor and scoundrel."[64] Such growing distrust is illustrated by Toews, who recalls how a tin pipe, laid across a wheelbarrow on his property, started a rumour that German cannons were aimed at the neighbouring Ukrainian village.[65]

The liquidation laws greatly enflamed pre-existing tensions, encouraging the peasantry to see the expropriation of German lands as a legitimate and accomplished fact. Anti-Germanism both masked and gave vent to deeper socio-economic resentments. Toews writes: "more and people voiced their opinions that this was the way to treat all Germans—confiscate all their properties, especially their land, in order to stop the imbalance of the German wealth in Russia." He argues that the Russian nobility especially advocated for this policy because "they hoped that by focusing public attention on the lands of the Germans, their own properties might be spared."[66]

At this time a type of political accommodation called *Hollanderei* began in the Mennonite colonies. The *Hollanderei* argument asserted Mennonites were not ethnically German but Dutch and their Low German tongue was a Dutch dialect. The argument was historically true to an extent, as many Mennonites traced their lineage to the Netherlands. However, others traced their roots to parts of Germany and Switzerland.[67] Furthermore, the Bible was studied in High German and Mennonite schools taught their pupils to read and write in High German. *Hollanderei* was a politically expedient decision on the part of the Mennonite leadership and arguably avoided their colonies' imminent liquidation.[68] Others, like Peter Dyck, felt the argument to be inauthentic:

> Today at the *Schulzenbott* [governing village body], a sample petition was read. Each individual is to hand in his own petition to His Majesty, the Emperor, in regard to the land requisition and expropriation of their homes. In this we are to state that we are actually not German,

> but Dutch, and that the Boers of Africa are our *Rodneje Bratja* [true brothers]. There is a fair amount of self-praise in the petition. We really seem to lack faith in God, as Pastor Kuegelgen is to have said in Petrograd. The other Germans [non-Mennonites], who also wish to remain German, and are not suddenly turning into Dutchmen, are, I believe, not working nearly as hard as the Mennonites.[69]

Jasykowo resident Julius Loewen, likewise, asserted that Mennonites during this period "felt strong ties with [German] culture, language, and literature . . . they were and remain German in spite of their civic duties to the tsar."[70] In certain ways, Dyck and Loewen's perspectives foreshadow the difference of opinion that would later emerge between pacifists and *Selbstschutzler*. Dyck believed the civil leadership was compromising Mennonite identity to avoid persecution, which, according to him, was indicative of the community's spiritual malaise and lack of faith. Dyck may also have seen the *Hollanderei* position as abandoning their Lutheran brothers, some of whom faced the law's full effect. The charge of insufficient faith and the abandonment of Mennonite identity would be renewed when some Mennonites chose a path of armed struggle over pacifism.

## *SELBSTSCHUTZ* AND *WEHRLOSIGKEIT*

The question of Mennonite ethnicity would resurface in the wake of the Austro-German occupation in March 1918. Mennonite accounts describe the arrival of German troops with widespread anticipation and enthusiasm. An eyewitness describes the occupation's arrival in the Molotschna: "[They were] greeted by cheering crowds of Mennonites jubilant over their rescue by soldiers from the ancient 'homeland.' Pretty blonde Mennonite girls carried bunches of flowers and their mothers offered *zwieback* and thick slices of ham to the astonished but delighted young liberators. They then all joined in the singing of 'Deutschland, Deutschland, über alles.'"[71] Adolf Reimer reflects on the Mennonite embrace of the Austro-German occupation: "What must our Russian neighbours have thought of our enthusiasm for the Germans, of our festive reception, or of the fact that we now shared their weapons? The Germans would not always be there, but our Russian neighbours would. We did not behave tactfully."[72] The thoughts of the pro-revolutionary peasants were later poignantly articulated by the commander of a joint Red-Makhnovist unit in 1920: "You damned apostates from the faith of your fathers, for 400 years you could not take any weapons into your hands, but now [you do] on behalf of your damned Kaiser Wilhelm."[73] In many ways the political decisions of the colonies during the civil war had unintentionally confirmed the suspicions aroused by anti-German propaganda.

The response of some Mennonites who took up arms during the occupation was a critical moment in their relations with their peasant neighbours. While the embrace of the Austro-German troops was almost universal, the degree of collaboration varied. Viewpoints fractured between those who wished to uphold traditional pacifism and those who sought armed self-defence. Both came to view Makhno as a direct threat to the colonies, but they interpreted events in very different ways.

Traditionally, Mennonite rationalizations for self-defence have been framed within the context of Makhno. The first reports of Makhno's activities reached the Molotschna colony with the arrival of fleeing Schönfelders in the fall of 1918. The November and December issues of *Friedensstimme* devoted a large amount of space to accounts of Makhnovist murder and robbery.[74] Two reports directly refer to the battle at Velyka Mykhailivka as a catalyst for the raids.[75] The torture of a young Mennonite to extract a confession that he fought the Makhnovists at Velyka Mykhailivka is also described.[76] The image of Makhno and his band as a force of senseless terror and destruction from these reports was solidly established in the colonies. The response from one segment of the Mennonite population was to call for the physical protection of the colonies.

In hand with reports of murder and torture were the reports of rape. The rape of Mennonite women in particular is stated as a motivating factor for joining the *Selbstschutz*.[77] For example, a Mennonite farmer described how his son had joined the *Selbstschutz* under the firm conviction that he must "protect his mother and other village women from Makhno and his bandits."[78] Indeed, Makhnovist raids became synonymous with rape. Lohrenz collected the harrowing experiences of Mennonite rape victims. He reports that in numerous cases husbands were tied up and forced to watch their wives and daughters raped by Makhnovists.[79] One case in particular communicates the horror faced by Mennonite women:

> Four bandits entered the home of the Boschman family. Husband and wife with their three small children were in one room. The bandits cut Boschman down with their swords. While he lay gasping and bleeding on the floor they gang raped his wife in front of the children. When they were through with her, her husband was dead. She took her children and left the house. She walked through the garden into the open steppe walking towards another village. When they had gone some distance, two riders came after them. They raped the woman there in the open field with her children standing around them. About a year later the house this woman was living in was broken into at night by half a dozen bandits. They ransacked the house, shot the proprietor and gang raped the widow. I have known this woman. She was the daughter of a highly respected family, sensitive and intelligent. The inner conflict and turmoil such a person goes through is hard to describe.[80]

Another survivor expressed the collective rage of her people: "I have one wish and one wish only, namely that all those murderers and bandits in there would have one common throat and that I be permitted to put my hands on that throat for a little while!"[81] The importance of recording these events is in helping us to fully understand the psychological pressures that led a people who had upheld pacifism as an integral part of their identity to embrace armed resistance as a solution. These memories of atrocity show how the attacks extended beyond wealth and property.

As a weapon of war, rape strikes at the foundation of societal bonds. Tuba Inal writes that wartime rape should be understood within the overall context of military strategies and the societal meanings attached to rape. According to Inal, social representations of what it means to be feminine make woman into "military targets in a war of masculine pride" in which a woman's physical pain is transformed into social pain.[82] In this manner, rape symbolically "domesticates not only the women survivors who were its immediate victims but also the men socially connected to them."[83] In the case of a tightly knit socially conservative community like the Mennonites, the infliction of social pain through rape had the power to radically disrupt a people's sense of self and motivate the male population to take up arms.

Figure 15. Mennonite homestead displaying flags of Imperial Germany. Ohrloff, Molotschna colony, 1918.

The murder and rape experienced during the fall raids deeply traumatized the Schönfelder community. For many *Selbstschutzler* these experiences were a prime motivator in their war on Makhno. The Germans and the White Army were certainly aware of this and took full advantage of the Makhnovist threat to recruit young Mennonites. At a village assembly in Alexandertal, a White Army officer described the Makhnovists as pestilence in need of extermination: "You farmers destroy the weeds among your grain, without pangs of conscience. Who is Makhno? A weed that is worse than weeds, and he must be destroyed. Furthermore, if a rabbit destroys a young tree in your garden, you shoot without further consideration. Who is Makhno? An animal, worse than an animal who must be shot down."[84] Recruitment into the *Selbstschutz* was so successful that by the spring of 1919 3,000 Mennonite and German colonists in the Molotschna colony alone helped to form a joint front with the White Army against Makhno's forces.

A common narrative found in Mennonite memoirs and histories is that Makhnovist atrocities directly inspired the *Selbstschutz*'s organization. While the attacks certainly accelerated recruitment, according to Mennonite sources, *Selbstschutz* formations existed before October 1918, preceding the first reports of widespread murder. *Friedensstimme* first mentions a Mennonite *Selbstschutz* in 18 May 1918.[85] Molotschna resident A. Reimer dates the *Selbstschutz*'s origins even earlier, recalling that "young men belonging to a secret *Selbstschutz* already organized before the German occupation and almost immediately obtained arms from the German command."[86] Toews likewise mentions a Lutheran unit in Eigenfeld in April 1918, described as "a troop of twenty armed men, a sort of *Selbstschutz* . . . organized under the auspices of a courageous pastor's daughter."[87] Furthermore, the decision of the Lichtenau Conference—composed of religious and secular leadership—to tolerate Mennonite self-defence occurred in July 1918.[88] This situation was paralleled in the colonies beyond the Molotschna, where there was no Makhnovist presence in 1918. In the Chortitza, Sagradowka, and Jasykowo colonies, self-defence units made their first appearance in summer 1918 amidst the German occupation.[89] The chronology and geographic dispersion of the *Selbstschutz* suggests armed self-defence was less a direct response to Makhno and more a consequence of the German occupation's influence and the general fear of banditry.

The recovery of lost property and goods also played an important role in the growth of the *Selbstschutz*. Reports of Mennonite colonists accompanying German punitive detachments into Ukrainian villages predate the organization of the self-defence units. In a unique letter to the editor from *Friedensstimme* a Mennonite author describes one such punitive expedition in detail:

> They wanted to take revenge for all the insults suffered from the Russian peasantry. Indeed, not only did they meditate upon but practiced revenge. Small groups were formed which broke into the homes of the Russian peasants and miserably thrashed them with the *nagaika*. House searches were also conducted by our side, and the surrounding Russian villages were pretty much robbed. Initially, some Germans were also brought along, so it might appear that everything was done in the name of the Germans. But it should be noted that this author knows of no theft by German soldiers, and firmly believes that they committed no rude acts unless provoked by trickery. The blame rests on us![90]

Another *Friedensstimme* report from 2 July 1918 details property requisitions carried out with the aid of Austrian troops in Huliaipole. The action was resisted by several Huliaipolians who were executed by the

Figure 16. Mennonite *Selbstschutz* unit from the villages of Blumenort, Tiege, and Ohrloff. Molotschna colony, 1918.

Austrians.[91] From this same time period, Makhno also describes his mother's house being burned down and his physically disabled brother being publicly executed in Huliaipole by the occupation.[92]

The eagerness to retrieve property extended into the colonies themselves. Poor and landless Mennonites and Germans that had participated—voluntarily or otherwise—in expropriation campaigns were in turn targeted by their former victims. By June 1918 tensions within the colonies were such that the occupation's district commander felt compelled to issue the following warning:

> During the period of the Bolsheviks, Anarchists, etc. some inhabitants of the Mennonite and other German villages, mostly poor people, were forced . . . to work with the Bolsheviks. They were often forced, under threat of arms, to collect all sorts of contributions from the well-to-do. . . . Now the former owners, most of them well off, demand the return of their goods—in part through all kinds of threats, evictions, etc. . . . Such behaviour . . . is designed to arouse a sentiment among the poorer classes, which eliminates all peaceable and profitable work together. It is a great mistake for a few well-off people to think that the German troops came into the land only to protect the rich. . . . I hope this warning will suffice and that in the future more tolerance will prevail, especially among one's ancestral brothers. I would hate to see

> myself forced to take severe action against anyone who threatens calm and peace by his quarrelsome, aggressive behavior.[93]

The sudden fluctuations between positions of power and total vulnerability made it difficult to resist seeking retribution when it presented itself. Toews, who acted as a German informant, remembers how peasants "came running to me from everywhere, begging that I put in a good word for them . . . and it did give me satisfaction, when these people, who had been for liquidating our lands and had despised and mistreated us, now had to come and humble themselves before us when they had something to do with the German commandos."[94] However, Toews was also disturbed by the Austro-German methods wherein "anyone who was suspected, was shot."[95] Toews instinctively understood this policy would come to haunt his people. Thus, while openly sympathizing with the occupation, he simultaneously strove to temper its actions. He writes, "I made up my mind not to practice revenge. . . . And here I have saved many a life."[96] How should Toews's confession be interpreted? The honest attempts of a conflicted colonist or the rationalizations of a guilty conscience? The reader is placed in a similar position as in Makhno's memoirs. This is not to morally conflate Toews's and Makhno's actions but to acknowledge that both authors' texts struggle with a tension between seeking vengeance and achieving justice, each from within their own moral universes.

This same dichotomy between justice and vengeance, and arguably the erosion of Mennonite pacifism, in certain regards predates the Revolution. In the wake of the 1905 Revolution, it became common for Mennonites to employ armed Cossacks to defend against peasant attacks on their property. Cossack guards were given the authority to beat and even kill for such minor offences as pasturing on estate lands. Sometimes, Mennonites meted out justice themselves. Urry and Loewen write that "landowners, usually with the acquiescence of the local authorities and police, hunted down horse thieves, tracking suspects to villages."[97] In some cases houses, and even whole villages, were burned in retribution. Set in this context, the slide into armed self-defence was not entirely an aberration of the civil war but, in some ways, an extension of pre-existing practices in a more chaotic and hostile environment.

Makhno's fall raids and the influx of Schönfeld refugees to the Molotschna in winter 1918 certainly encouraged the growth of the *Selbstschutz*. However, as shown, the *Selbstschutz*'s origins cannot be exclusively attributed to Makhno. Mennonite armed self-defence must be contextualized by the Austro-German occupation and a broader peasant insurgency that extended beyond Makhno's territory. Furthermore, the abandonment of pacifism has earlier roots in the reactions of some Mennonite landowners to the 1905 Revolution, as well as the use of violence on estates to enforce workplace discipline. A narrow focus on Makhno obscures these latter factors. In Mennonite accounts, Makhno often functions as an archetypal bandit symbolic of broader Mennonite suffering. A telling example is an account where Makhno is fully depersonalized and referred to, like a plague, as *the* Makhno.[98] In this way, Makhno achieves the status of *the* bogeyman or *the* Devil; an abstract embodiment of pure fear and evil. As Mennonite author Anne Konrad writes, "Makhno was a man every Russian Mennonite child in Canada knew was close to the devil."[99] Indeed, Makhno's movement undeniably caused enormous suffering for Mennonite communities. At the same time, such abstracted representations of Makhno risk simplifying the conflict's complex roots.

In contrast to *Selbstschutzler* narratives, pacifist accounts emphasize the importance of preserving Mennonite identity through Anabaptist doctrines. Pacifist narratives frequently stress a theology of martyrdom which presents "an integrated Anabaptist vision of victory for the church and the kingdom of Christ through suffering and martyrdom, in which the Anabaptist martyrs are seen as following in the footsteps of the suffering saints of the Old and New Testaments and most of all in those of Christ Himself."[100] Ethelbert Stauffer, the author of a seminal text on Anabaptist martyrdom, fittingly describes it as the "apocalypse of martyrdom."[101] In this theology of history, suffering for one's faith is elevated to the prime vehicle for the progression of God's plan and a "causal and teleological necessity ... of the cosmic battle between God and Anti-God."[102] In a literal blood sacrifice, pacifist martyrdom propels history towards a new "kingdom" reality. According to this belief, the Anabaptist is a soldier of Christ who considers death as a kind of "baptism by blood."[103] Stauffer views the blood of martyrs "as a seed which will bring forth fruit in its time, to wit not only at the end of all times but in history proper."[104] The Mennonite theology of martyrdom takes a radical stance against the secular world, in which "history is the contest between the people of God and the powers of this world, a contest which presses to a final decision through the suffering of the martyrs."[105] Stauffer describes Anabaptist disciples as "like sheep among wolves."[106] This conception of martyrdom informed the paradigm of many pacifist memorists. As Stauffer wrote, martyrdom constituted the "hidden sanctuary or crypt of Anabaptist Christianity."[107]

In the context of the civil war, martyrdom was tightly related to maintaining *Wehrlosigkeit*—literally "defencelessness"—or non-participation in war. It was believed that if this spiritual core could be maintained, even in the face of persecution and death, God would reward the Mennonite people for their faithfulness. Conversely, abandoning this spiritual identity would incur God's anger. In some cases, Mennonite writers sometimes referred to the civil war as a kind of purification of their people, implying that God was attempting to set his people on a renewed path of faithfulness by allowing the atrocities to take place. A report from *Friedensstimme*'s 14 September 1919 issue reads, "Like in the Book of Job, God gave us up into the hands of Satan. It seemed as if Hell itself was let loose."[108] Likewise, in the 14 December 1919 issue an author implores his co-religionists to "private and corporate confession," asking, "What is marked on God's debit sheet against our people?"[109] Within this fatalistic narrative God plays an intervening role, meting out rewards and punishments based upon obedience. The failure to obey endangers not only the individual soul but the community as a whole.

The pacifist narrative was often harshly critical of Mennonite *Gutsbesitzer*, or estate owners, for their perceived greed and materialism. Some pacifists also saw a state of spiritual degeneracy within the colonies predating the Revolution but finding its logical conclusion in the acceptance of German militarism in 1918. While the Germans were initially embraced as saviours—even by pacifists—the decisive juncture occurred when the youth were enticed by the Germans to form self-defence units. *Friedensstimme* editor Abraham Kroeker was deeply critical of Mennonite efforts to recover stolen property. In April 1918 Kroeker wrote, "Why did we suffer? Not because of 'higher things' as did our martyred ancestors, but because of our wealth. We have suffered for the sake of Mammon, which we have so eagerly emulated. We were too materialistic, too selfish. Therefore

God sent the first liquidation and when it did not achieve its purpose, he had to cut the knife deeper. Thus, as a man sins so he is punished."[110] Pacifist Adolf Reimer similarly wrote, "The basic attitude toward the Lord was not right. People were not sufficiently surrendered to Him and so their attitude toward their possessions was not correct."[111] This basic argument became a constant refrain in the pages of *Friedensstimme* for the remainder of the civil war.[112] In the wake of the German withdrawal and the first Makhnovist raids, one writer bemoaned, "Never before has the avarice and greed in our society been greater than now . . . our people have suffered greatly in the recent year but seem to have learned so little."[113] In another article from 4 August 1919 the author asks why the Mennonites are hated so violently by the peasants. He concludes that his co-religionists "did not act correctly before God," were attached to "earthly goods," mistreated their servants, and lusted after land and riches.[114]

In the aftermath of the Makhnovist massacres, a pacifist writer presented one of the most extreme criticisms in a *Friedensstimme* article from 21 December 1919. Noting that the *Gutsbesitzer* (estate owners) suffered most during the Makhnovist occupation, the author points out that there appears to be little sympathy amongst Mennonites for the wealthy, believing they got what they deserved. The author then asks whether this attitude is justified and proceeds to argue in the affirmative. Derisively referring to the estate owners as *Steppenkönige* (kings of the steppe), the author chides them for their lack of education and failure to provide spiritual and cultural leadership. The author's final assessment is scathing, accusing the landowners of arrogance, alcoholism, inter-marriage that "stunted their abilities," "flirting" with servant girls, and the abuse of hired help.[115] The author's vitriol aside, this article illustrates the deep and bitter divisions within the Mennonite community in the wake of the Makhnovist occupations.

Pacifist memoirs are likewise critical of the *Selbstschutz*. Dietrich Neufeld reflects on the matter: "For the Mennonites the blunder of abandoning pacifism for militarism was particularly incriminating. Have we not always, with justified pride, pointed to our 400-year tradition, which signified a strict pacifism? And at the very moment when, as a result of a bloody war without parallel, militarism in all its worst aspects, and pacifism had begun to spread with unprecedented popular appeal—even in

Germany—then we abandoned our noble position. A Mennonite who surrenders the fundamental idea of peace and affirms war has judged himself. He is henceforth no longer a Mennonite."[116] Neufeld cuts to the heart of the pacifist critique: by taking up the sword Mennonite identity had been forfeited, in turn making the physical survival of the colonies a moot point. For Mennonites like Neufeld, armed self-defence was an untenable stance that would lead to the physical and spiritual destruction of his people. Adolf Reimer starkly defined the Mennonite pacifist's task as follows: "What does it mean to be completely nonresistant? It does not mean that one is completely defenceless. It does not mean giving oneself over to fatalism or the caprice of evil without self-will. No, it is the highest commitment possible. It means to have God and to be militant in Him. It means to be so yielded to Him that one does not inwardly rebel against God's leading . . . that one submits even if He sends Makhno and allows him to rage. One accepts this as from God's hand. . . . There is no fear, no reaching for self-help. He knows that God's protection is more real than the *Selbstschutz*."[117]

Mennonite analyses of the civil war remained highly metaphysical, filtered through an Anabaptist religiosity and Mennonite cultural patterns. Materialism and greed might be condemned on theological or moral grounds, but the basic sacredness of private property and capital accumulation generally remained unchallenged.[118] Speaking of the Mennonite Brethren in particular, Lohrenz writes that prior to the civil war, "Smoking, for instance, was considered a grievous sin, but considerably less was said about underpaying the labourers or exploiting people one way or another."[119] Kroeker virulently attacked the suggestion that socialism could be compatible with Christianity. In response to a letter from a "revolutionary Mennonite" who referred to Jesus as "the greatest socialist," Kroeker identified the eight-hour workday as an ally of Satan.[120] Nor did Kroeker challenge triumphalist frontier narratives. In a 1914 issue of *Friedensstimme* Kroeker wrote, "We were called to Russia to cultivate the steppes and we have done that. This has accrued to our benefit, but also to our neighbours, the Russians and other groups."[121] While the latter was true in certain respects, narratives of this kind tended to overlook the systemic socio-economic inequalities that were historically tied to the region's development.

Makhno was also as much a devil to the pacifist as to the *Selbstschutzler*, but narrativized in a way that required a non-violent response. Neufeld describes Makhno in his journal as a fearsome entity, an "inhuman monster . . . whose path is literally drenched in blood."[122] Elsewhere his followers are described as "devils in human form" who exhibited "the bestiality of men who had become raging animals."[123] The monologue of a Makhnovist, given to us by Chortitza resident Gerhard Schroeder, is particularly illustrative:

> Do not try to change me with advice to read the Bible and believe in God or with anything of that kind of advice. We Makhnovtsy as partisans and as anarchists have only one program, only one desire and aim—to enjoy living off someone else's property, to rob and kill as we please. We will not change, and will be a menace to others as long as we live. Nothing will change us, not the Bible nor God, neither Hell nor Heaven. We will live this way as long as possible and when that is not possible we will commit suicide, and only when soft Mother Earth has covered us, will we be harmless.[124]

Whether or not Schroeder's account is recollected verbatim is less important than how it positions the pacifist in relation to the Makhnovist. A spiritual battleground is painted for the reader in which the Mennonite is confronted by an entity that embodies a materialistic philosophy of unrestrained self-indulgence. For the pacifist, it was a test that had to be met with the patience of a martyr.

## MEETING MAKHNO

Given Makhno's importance to Mennonite narratives, it is perhaps unexpected that first-hand encounters with him are relatively rare. Even more surprising is that the encounters recorded are often neutral or even positive in character. The earliest account comes from the Janzen family, whom Makhno worked for as a youth. Their account of the young Makhno was "brought down through oral tradition" and put into written form by the great-granddaughters of Abram Jakob Janzen—one of the Silberfeld estate's proprietors.[125] How Abram came to Silberfeld, and his exact relation to the estate's original owner, is unclear. However, some details have been reconstructed by consulting property and genealogical records, alongside information provided by the Janzen family.[126]

It appears Abram Janzen was sent to Silberfeld after his mother's death in December 1891. Abram's father had previously passed away when he was an infant. In 1897, a 925-dessiatine (1,010-hectare) subdivision of Silberfeld was listed as belonging to Abram and his brother Heinrich Jakob Janzen.[127] That summer, thirteen-year-old Abram met the nine-year-old Makhno who was employed on the estate. In 1909 Abram married Maria Friesen and they established themselves on Abram's subdivision of the estate. In 1915, Maria gave birth to their son, named Heinrich. The couple's life together was cut short when Abram died of an asthma attack in August 1917. One year later an advertisement by Maria Janzen appears in *Friedensstimme* for the sale of two bulls.[128] The final mention of the Janzens comes from Makhno's memoirs, in which he writes, "Towards the middle of February [1918] three sailors from the Black Sea Fleet arrived in Huliaipole. Two were peasants from Huliaipole, the third was a stranger to us. He was visiting his father who had been a coachman for the *pomeshchik* Abraham Janzen."[129]

According to the Janzen family's oral history, Makhno and Abram grew up together at Silberfeld, where they "were friends and spent many evenings playing together."[130] Years later during the fall 1918 raids on Schönfeld, Makhno returned to Silberfeld where he encountered a widowed Maria and her children. According to the Janzen family, "When Makhno realized that this was the widow and children of his old friend, Abram Janzen, he ordered his men to drop all the precious belongings they had already put in their bags and to leave this house without taking anything or harming anyone."[131] It is possible a young Abram and Nestor—perhaps having bonded over their shared experience of growing up fatherless—had forged an authentic childhood friendship. Regardless, Maria Janzen found herself the unexpected beneficiary of this relationship, which likely saved her from robbery or worse.

The next encounter comes from Anna Goerz, the daughter of the Ebenfeld estate's owner Jakob Neufeld. In the 1860s or '70s, Ebenfeld was purchased by Heinrich Kaethler, possibly from the same Russian noble that had owned the neighbouring estate of Silberfeld. Jakob Neufeld came to the estate as a teacher and soon fell in love with Kaethler's daughter Maria. The

Figure 17. Abram and Maria Janzen.

Figure 18. Worker with horse in front of the Silberfeld estate.

couple married and the estate was later transferred to Neufeld. Makhno had also worked for Neufeld as a youth and they apparently had a positive relationship. Early in the Revolution, prior to the German occupation,

Makhno stayed overnight at Ebenfeld. Anna Goerz recalled that "since their relationship had been good, Makhno showed no hostility . . . he made every effort to establish a friendly basis and when he was offered a key for his room for greater safety, Makhno refused to take it, saying that he felt safe among friends."[132] Goerz describes how Makhno proceeded to the Klassen estate the next morning, where a redistribution was conducted. Here, Klassen was invited to take an equal portion of the goods.[133] While it must have struck Klassen as supremely unjust to be apportioned a share of his own property, the account supports Makhno's claim that he initially adopted a strategy of integrating former landowners into the movement's social experiments.

An interaction recorded by Gerhard Schroeder between himself and Schönfeld's school board president further corroborates Makhno's fondness for Neufeld:

> But you know, Makhno has promised [Neufeld] not to touch his property or him personally. The question is whether anyone can trust the words of a man like this one. When the period of anarchy broke out, [Neufeld] tried to resist the plundering raids with the help of several German soldiers, and succeeded for awhile in repelling the bandits. However, one day Makhno sent a messenger to this Mennonite landowner. The message read, "[Neufeld], I have not forgotten how in 1906 I found a place of refuge on your estate. There I succeeded in eluding the cruel dogs of the Tsarist police. It was only through your help and cooperation that in 1906 I succeeded in eluding the police and thus was saved from being shot by them. I have not forgotten the old practice of *khleb-sol'* [hospitality]. . . . Do not shoot anymore, and we promise not to touch either you or your property."[134]

Combined with Goerz's account, it appears Makhno left Neufeld's estate intact, while moving on to redistribute the neighbouring Klassen estate. The school president is distrustful of Makhno, but the story communicates how personal relationship shaped Makhno's treatment of landowners.

Schroeder also provides an account of Makhno's first appearance near Schönfeld. Rumours of Makhno's approach led the colony's men to arm themselves and prepare for a battle. However, "as luck would have it, Makhno did not advance to our village, but sent word the next day that he would leave us unharmed if we surrendered all our weapons at a specified place. This was done."[135] Schroeder confirms Makhno left the colony in peace after the surrender of all arms. This account suggests that Makhno, at least in certain cases, was following a policy similar to the fall 1918 order he references in his memoirs. What dictated the order's enforcement is difficult to determine. The reports from *Friedenstimme* clearly indicate atrocities were committed. Whether it was Makhno's personal presence or his relationship with a specific landowner, the above accounts nevertheless suggest a range of interaction was possible between Makhno and Mennonites.

Personal favouritism is also a recurring theme in Mennonite encounters with other Makhnovists. Dietrich Neufeld wrote in his journal with astonishment how a group of Makhnovists billeted in his home wanted him to write a poem as a personal tribute to Makhno. As Neufeld was a teacher, the Makhnovists considered him part of the working class and assumed Makhno was also his hero.[136] Schroeder likewise developed a strange personal relationship with an ill-tempered Makhnovist commander named *Bat'ko* Pravda. Simeon Pravda was a former beggar known as "the wooden one," by virtue of his artificial legs. He allegedly lost his legs in a mining accident prior to the Revolution. Pravda was apparently carried around in a wheelbarrow from which he barked orders at his subordinates.

Between the winter of 1918 and spring 1919, Pravda and his men terrorized the area around Schönfeld. According to Mennonite accounts, Pravda murdered his own brother in a drunken dispute.[137] He was immediately arrested by Makhno for this incident, but was released shortly thereafter and, apparently, congratulated for maintaining discipline. Pravda's importance within the movement is sometimes exaggerated in Mennonite accounts. Neufeld described him as the "chief of the intelligence department" and "Makhno's right-hand man."[138] However, in Makhno's memoirs Pravda achieves a single passing mention of no consequence.[139] Belash, on the other hand, described Pravda as an irrational drunkard and potential liability for the movement.[140]

Although Pravda was an unstable and violent character he was nonetheless capable of forming friendly relations with those who gained his respect. Both Schroeder and Wiens managed to cultivate a relationship with Pravda in which he at times deferred to their advice. On one such occasion, Wiens dissuaded Pravda from executing his foster son.[141] The younger Makhnovists also took a liking to Wiens and his wife, affectionately referring to them as "Papascha and Mamascha."[142] Pravda would sometimes demand Wiens's presence at private functions. Wiens writes:

> At 11:30 pm on New Year's Eve I was woken up, and told I should immediately come to the headquarters. Pravda insisted I should await New Years with him and the other neighbors. When I came to the road his bodyguards were already there for me. One called to another from 50 steps away that H. Wiens is coming. When I came to Pravda's door I was greeted warmly. Then we had to sit around the table and drink *samogon*, but I said the doctor had forbid me to drink. At midnight we were ordered to go outside, where many gunshots were fired simultaneously.[143]

Pravda enjoyed Schroeder's and Wiens's company so much he invited them to share tea with Makhno in summer 1919.[144] Makhno was boarded at Schroeder's residence, about which he writes: "I cannot say that we relished the affair but I must say that on this occasion we found Makhno to be a very friendly man, and we had a rather nice visit with him."[145]

A final encounter with Makhno from September 1919 is recorded by Schroeder. Schroeder had relocated to the Chortitza colony, where a Makhnovist forced Schroeder to exchange his horse for a camel. Schroeder then noticed Makhno passing by and called out to him, "Comrade Makhno, you know me. You have been to our place in Schönfeld. I am a teacher. Just now I returned from plowing a field for my relatives. Your men have just taken my horses and wagon. You know that I am a teacher, a labouring man, not a capitalist. Could I have my horses back?" Makhno intervened on Schroeder's behalf, but Schroeder's horse was retaken once Makhno moved on.[146]

Mennonite accounts agree on the importance of personal relations to Makhno and his desire to pursue what he considered just. Makhno commonly behaves in a way that seems aimed at projecting himself as a reasonable arbiter. These accounts stand in direct contrast with more generalized Mennonite descriptions of Makhno as an embodiment of evil. Yet, he simultaneously appears to be leading an army of ill-disciplined and criminal characters. For example, in fall 1919 Maria Peters's aunt billeted Makhno in the village of Petersdorf, Chortitza. Peters recalls that "There were no murders whenever Makhno was present."[147] However, after Makhno left his troops terrorized the villagers and murdered Peters's husband and father-in-law.[148] In Makhnovist and Mennonite sources paradoxical images emerge of a movement and its leader characterized by both a pursuit of justice and a descent into wanton violence.

Mennonite and Makhnovist narratives frequently construct a highly abstracted Makhno that avoids addressing this contradiction. In the words of Mennonite historian Harvey Dyck, "This part-targeted, part-random horror lives on in the Mennonite imagination as a kind of ultimate Manichean abomination."[149] By constrast, Makhnovist accounts sometimes present Makhno as the literal incarnation of peasant aspirations for freedom and justice. Arshinov writes that a story circulated amongst the peasants that Makhno was the fulfillment of a prophecy told by the famous eighteenth-century Cossack rebel Emelian Pugachev: "[Pugachev] told the noblemen sitting around him: 'In this uprising I only gave you a foretaste. But wait: soon after me will come the real broom—it will sweep all of you away.' Makhno showed himself to be this historic broom of the people"[150] In both cases Makhno becomes a metonym for historical forces far greater than his person. Future historians would do well to make the distinction between Makhno the metonym and Makhno the man, if such a task is possible. Makhno was undeniably violent in the extreme. However, a close reading of the primary literature suggests a character far more multi-dimensional, and even contradictory, than the dominant images of Makhno found in either Mennonite or Makhnovist narratives. These same narrative tensions between justice and vengeance continue as central themes in the literature describing the 1919 Eichenfeld massacre.

CHAPTER 3

# THE EICHENFELD MASSACRE

On the night of Saturday, 8 November 1919, a squadron of Makhnovist cavalry surrounded the Mennonite village of Eichenfeld in the Jasykowo colony. The village was blocked off at both ends and a massacre ensued. By the time the riders left, seventy-five Mennonites lay dead, numerous women had been raped, houses were burned to the ground, and cartloads of personal belongings were stolen. On Tuesday, the survivors that had fled for safety returned to Eichenfeld to bury their loved ones in twelve unmarked mass graves. The terror continued over the following week, with the death toll rising to 136 in the surrounding area.[1]

Eichenfeld—alongside other massacres in fall 1919—is an important event in the historiography of Russian Mennonites, marking the high point of their collective persecution during the civil war. Mennonite histories often attribute the Eichenfeld massacre directly to Makhno. It is widely assumed that Makhno, as commander-in-chief of the insurgent army, must have ordered the village's liquidation. For example, Dyck, Staples, and Toews argue that the Makhnovists' "disciplined, purposeful actions and clear-cut criteria in singling out their victims bespoke careful planning, and in Makhno's territory, Makhno was the chief planner. Makhno exercised close military discipline over his forces, and it is almost unimaginable that the Makhnovites carried out the massacre without his approval."[2] By contrast, the whole of Makhnovist literature is silent about Eichenfeld and the other Mennonite massacres. While not specifically addressing Mennonite accusations, anarchist researcher Alexandre Skirda has gone as far as to argue that the Makhnovists are innocent of all charges of banditry. He writes, "It is consequently noticeable that none of the charges of banditry aired by this one or that, stands up to a serious examination of the facts. In spite of all that, how are they to be explained? Perhaps in terms of the age-old fear that the rural bourgeoisie and squire-archy felt of the dark, nameless peasant mass, these 'yokels' whose wrathful vengeance they rightfully feared."[3]

This chapter challenges both narratives in certain regards. On the one hand, numerous eyewitness reports show beyond doubt that the massacre occurred under Makhnovist occupation and was perpetrated by segments of the army. On the other hand, there is strong evidence the massacre was motivated more by local tensions between Ukrainian villagers and Mennonites than by Makhno's personal enmity. An analysis of primary sources shows that a Makhnovist cavalry unit supported by local Ukrainian peasants perpetrated the massacre amidst a massive troop transfer between Oleksandrivsk and Katerynoslav. Local peasants had become embittered against the colony in the face of Mennonite collaboration with the Austro-Germans and the White Army. Jasykowo had established a particularly stubborn *Selbstschutz* that engaged a number of different forces over the course of 1919. In June 1919, while under Red occupation, the *Selbstschutz* murdered four members of the local militia. This incident in particular would later be used as a pretext for targeting Eichenfeld. The state of the Makhnovist army in the weeks leading up to the massacre and Makhno's increasingly violent rhetoric were also relevant to the evolution of these events. When examined together, these factors provide a detailed chronology of the context and events that resulted in the Eichenfeld massacre.

As mentioned, references to the Mennonite massacres are absent from Makhnovist sources. Nonetheless, a careful reading of Makhnovist literature does shed light on certain aspects around Eichenfeld. Volin and Arshinov provide a sense of the Makhnovist army's composition and behaviour in fall 1919. Volin in particular paints a picture of an increasingly militarized and violent movement. Belash provides an even richer source for the reconstruction of events. His work traces both Makhno's and the army's movements in November 1919. The archived orders and internal communications of the Makhnovist army that detail the breakdown of troop discipline during this period are also important. Finally, there are the memoirs of White Army officer A.V. Bipetskii and Red soldier E.P. Orlov, who both visited Eichenfeld in the massacre's aftermath.

A unique source is a collection of interviews with twenty-four Ukrainian residents in seven villages in the district where Eichenfeld was formerly located. They were conducted in 2001 by a three-person team led by Svetlana Bobyleva from the Ukrainian-German Institute at Dnipro National University. The express purpose of the project was to preserve any remaining memory of the massacre. Excerpts were subsequently published in the book *Nestor Makhno and the Eichenfeld Massacre* (2004). The interviews confirm Mennonite eyewitness accounts on a number of important details. However, most of the accounts are from individuals not yet born in 1919, and the oldest with first-hand memories was eight years old when the massacre occurred. Historian John Staples cautions that "none had been old enough in 1919 to recall events in detail. Their stories are secondhand passed down from parents, older siblings, and relatives." Staples also points out that "accounts vary wildly on details."[4] Working with elderly subjects who were children at the time of events presents a greater possibility for mistaken or false memories. Indeed, certain memories deviate substantially from, and even contradict, eyewitness Mennonite accounts.

A further problem involves assessing to what degree Soviet propaganda may have influenced the collective memory of Makhno in the region. Ukrainians were exposed exclusively to anti-Makhnovist narratives for the entire Soviet period. Makhno was presented as the mentally deranged leader of a "kulak" uprising responsible for anti-Semitic pogroms and every other manner of atrocity.[5] It is difficult to imagine that these negative stereotypes did not impact the interviewees' narrative construction of Makhno in some fashion. Nonetheless, the data collected by Bobyleva and her team is an impressive achievement, offering an important case study in regional memory which can be used to compare against Mennonite accounts.

Aleksandr Beznosov's research is a critically important source which makes use of Bobyleva's interviews, in addition to archival documents from the Nikolaipol District Soviet in the Dnipro State Archives.

Beznosov wrote a study about the Mennonites in the Nikolaipol *volost* (Jasykowo's district), which was first published in 2002 in the Ukrainian-German Institute's academic journal. In 2019 the Nordost-Institut at the University of Hamburg published a German translation. Beznosov's archival research clarifies many important details and largely corroborates Mennonite accounts.

In contrast to the dearth of Makhnovist sources, Mennonite literature abounds with eyewitness accounts and commentary on Eichenfeld. Marianne Janzen's document collection, gathered in preparation for her paper, "The Story of Eichenfeld," is most helpful in this regard. The collection contains numerous first-hand accounts of the massacre and information on Jasykowo's *Selbstschutz*. Janzen is the niece of Eichenfeld's *Selbstschutz* leader, Heinrich Heinrich Heinrichs. Her family relations afforded her unique access to critical sources such as Heinrichs's memoirs. She also corresponded with Heinrichs's brother Cornelius who outlines important events of 1919 in detail.

As a whole, Mennonite accounts present a coherent and detailed picture of events, but they also deviate from each other in some critical respects. For example, the exact nature of the Eichenfeld *Selbstschutz* and its leadership is sometimes contested. The exact chronology of events in 1919 is also confused at times, with different authors giving different dates for the same incidents. Finally, the exact identity of the massacre's perpetrators and their motivations is an issue of contention. All accounts indicate the presence of Makhnovist cavalry on the night of the massacre, but some accounts assert the neighbouring Ukrainian peasantry was as much, if not more, to blame for the tragedy.

Lastly, there is Nikita Saloff-Astakhoff's memoir. Astakhoff was a Ukrainian Stundist (Evangelical Protestant) convert present in the Jasykowo colony as part of a religious tent mission. Astakhoff was in the neighbouring village of Adelsheim during the massacre but a number of his co-religionists were murdered in Eichenfeld. The source is deeply reflective and unique as it is the only surviving Ukrainian-written eyewitness account. Astakhoff also records a number of conversations with Makhnovists that provide insight into the mind of the perpetrators. Furthermore, he reveals that just prior to the massacre Makhno personally granted permission to the tent missionaries to evangelize in the district.

Commentary from Mennonites outside Jasykowo is a step removed from eyewitness accounts. Dietrich Neufeld, Gerhard Schroeder, Anton Sawatsky, and the Heinrichs's cousin David G. Rempel are particularly helpful in this regard. All four resided in the Chortitza colony at the time of the massacre. Their accounts provide a broader context and insight into how the tragedy was received and interpreted by the Mennonite community at the time.

A common source of confusion regarding the chronology of the massacres is the presence of two competing dating systems during the civil war. Pre-revolutionary Russia employed the Julian (Old Style) calendar, which fell roughly two weeks behind the Gregorian (New Style) calendar used in Western Europe. Only on 1 February 1918 was the Gregorian calendar officially adopted by the Soviet regime. However, the new system was not immediately or uniformly adopted. In fact, its adoption tended to divide along political lines with radicals embracing the new calendar and opponents of the Revolution retaining the Old Style. Significantly, in 1919 the majority of Mennonite sources still used the Old Style while the Makhnovists used the New Style. Furthermore, contemporary Mennonite histories often use Old Style dates without clarification.[6] For example, the Eichenfeld massacre is usually dated 26 October, but it occurred on 8 November according to our current calendar. For consistency, this chapter uses New Style dates.

Difficulties emerge when attempting to cross-reference Mennonite and Makhnovist sources, since it must first be determined who is using what calendar. The failure to do so can lead to a confused chronology of events. A case in point is historian Natalia Venger's proposed reconstruction of the events leading up to the massacre. Venger assumes the massacre occurred on 26 October (New Style) and that Belash was using Old Style dates in his memoir. On the contrary, Belash was using New Style dates, and 26 October is the Old Style date for the massacre. Belash wrote his account after the civil war, and in Soviet custody, when the Old Style calendar was no longer in use.

As a result of the confusion between Old and New style dates, Venger concludes from Belash's account that on the eve of the massacre Makhno was in Huliaipole organizing an attack on the White Army's supply depot at Volnovakha. As part of this operation, the Makhnovist commander

Taranovskii was assigned to blow up a stockpile of armaments near Volnovakha. According to Belash, Taranovskii set out for the station where, "arriving at some colonies, he started drinking heavily, stole some *tachankas* and returned."[7] Venger, in turn, suggests that "since the period of absence of Taranovskii's detachment corresponds with the date of the punitive expedition to the village of Dubovka [Eichenfeld], it is possible to conjecture that he was the initiator of those bloody events."[8]

This interpretation is problematic for a number of reasons. Eichenfeld was located on the Dnipro Rivers's right bank in the Jasykowo colony, quite far from Huliaipole and in the opposite direction of Volnovakha. There would have been no reason for Taranovskii to make a two-day trip across the Dnipro to Eichenfeld to carry out a massacre on a community of no strategic importance. Moreover, Belash writes that Taranovskii returned to Huliaipole after his foray into the colonies. Taranovskii could not have travelled such a distance, organized a massacre, and returned in a single day. Finally, Belash says nothing about Taranovskii killing colonists. To the contrary, Belash mentions, on the same page, the case in which Makhno intervened to stop the murder of German colonists in Melitopol.

Nonetheless, it is important to confirm conclusively what calendar Belash was using. To do so, an objective event must be identified in two separate sources and their dates compared. From Belash, I chose the arrival of the Makhnovists in Chortitza and their crossing of the Einlage (Kitchkas) Bridge in Oleksandrivsk, in which two Mennonite guards were forced to jump into the Dnipro. This event is described by both Belash and Dietrich Neufeld. The relevant passages are as follows:

> Belash [October 5, New Style]: Our cavalry brigade, led by Makhno, swooped into Khortytsa and destroyed a white squadron. At 4am they took the Kichkas bridge and drowned the watchguard in the Dnieper. At 5am they entered Aleksandrovsk. At 10am on the 5th, part of our infantry entered the city, occupied its outskirts and continued to the next village.[9]

> Neufeld [September 21, Old Style]: They're here! Who they are and under what political banner they are fighting nobody knows. We see nothing but brutal madness, looting and killing. . . . How long will they stay? From our house we can see an endless train moving from

Figure 19. Mennonite homestead in Franzfeld, Jasykowo colony.

> here to Einlage-Kichkas, the nearby village at the Dnieper bridgehead. Presumably, they are crossing over to Alexandrovsk.[10]

In a footnote to Neufeld's entry it states that on 21 September two Mennonite guards on watch at Einlage "were given the macabre choice between execution on the spot or jumping off the bridge."[11] Neufeld later confirms that the troops crossing Einlage were in fact Makhnovists. The discrepancy in days between the two sources corresponds to the difference between the Old and New Style calendars. As such, to derive relevant information about the Eichenfeld massacre from Belash, his description of events around 8 November must be analyzed.

---

Jasykowo was established as a sub-colony of Chortitza in 1869. It was located roughly thirty kilometres north of Chortitza and fifty kilometres south of Katerynoslav. In 1868, the Chortitza colony purchased 8,733 dessiatines (8,012 hectares) from a Russian noble named "Yazykov," in an effort to address their community's landlessness crisis.[12] By 1911, the colony owned 9,722 dessiatines (10,621 hectares) divided into thirty-two-dessiatine (thirty-five-hectare) farms. An additional 2,252 dessiatines (2,460 hectares) were privately owned by Mennonite estate owners.[13] The official census for 1873 lists 957 residents in six villages.[14] By 1910, the colony's population had diversified to an extent, adding 461 Orthdox, 210 Lutheran, and sixty-one Catholic residents, all of whom were landless.[15] Each village was legally designated with a German and Russian name in addition to a number.[16] The colony's administrative centre was Nikolaifeld/Nikolaipol, which was also the name of the *volost* in which the colony was situated. Eichenfeld's Russian name was Dubovka. It is estimated that Eichenfeld had a population of 306 in 1919 prior to the massacre. The nearest Ukrainian village was Fedorivka, four kilometres northeast. Eichenfeld had nine businesses, including a number of mills and handicraft businesses, as well as a brick factory. The land where Eichenfeld previously stood belongs today to the village of Novopetrivka.[17]

In 1915, Chortitza resident David Rempel accompanied his father to visit the Nikolaipol *volost*. There, the pair visited various relatives, including Rempel's uncle, Heinrich Heinrichs, whose son of the same name would become an important *Selbstschutz* leader a few years later. Rempel described Heinrichs as a "scion" descended from "two of the most select families of the *Gutsbesitzer* [estate-owning] class."[18] Rempel recalls, "I became fast friends with two cousins, Heinrich and Kornelius. I was awestruck by that family's prosperity. . . . My father pointed out the affluence evidenced by their landscaped gardens, impressive structures, and well-tended fields; he also drew my attention to the stark contrast between these estates and the few Ukrainian peasant villages interspersed among them in this veritable Mennonite paradise. . . . Father also voiced his concern that so few of his Mennonite contemporaries seemed to be aware that their good fortune could instantly crumble to nothing if the tsarist government collapsed."[19]

In 1917 Rempel's father's prediction came true. As Soviet power asserted itself in the Nikolaipol district, a number of Mennonite properties were raided. Archival documents show that, in addition to Ukrainian peasants, at least six Jasykowo colony residents also participated in these early actions. In April 1918 Austrian troops reached Nikolaipol and occupied the district. The occupation immediately began repressions, executing fourteen people, including four Germans and two Mennonite Bolsheviks. Soon, German and Mennonite landowners were participating in punitive raids on Ukrainian villages alongside the Austro-German occupation.[20] A report from this period reads: "There appeared a detachment of the

Figure 20. The Heinrichs Family in Eichenfeld. A young Heinrich H. Heinrichs (centre, back row) and Cornelius H. Heinrichs (left, back row).

German-Austrian army joined by German colonists from the Nikolaipol *volost* and the German landowners of the Novopokrovskoi *volost,* who were armed with machine guns and rifles. They would enter each village and collect all citizens without exception who were shot and beaten mercilessly."[21] In one instance, two landowners named Friesen and Neustaedter personally shot seven Ukrainians accused of robbery.[22]

By the summer of 1918 *Selbstschutz* units were organized and armed by the Austrian officers stationed in Nikolaipol. The Mennonites' embrace of the Austro-Germans appears to be a direct response to the robbery endured after the Bolsheviks seized power. Many young Mennonites in particular reacted by questioning the wisdom of their forefathers' pacifism. However, the *Selbstschutz* was resisted by certain pacifist community leaders who warned the use of violence would draw the colony into open warfare with the neighbouring peasantry.[23]

In fall 1918, a draft of all men aged eighteen to thirty was introduced. In total, 250 men served in the *Selbstschutz,* organized by Peter van Kampen, Jakob Niebuhr, and Jakob Dyck.[24] All members were Mennonites with the exception of three Cossacks.[25] In Eichenfeld, a group of eighteen men was led by Heinrich Heinrich Heinrichs. However, according to Heinrichs' brother Cornelius, the group did not necessarily consider itself within the structure of the official *Selbstschutz.* He writes, "Eichenfeld never had a

*Selbstschutz*. They never drove out, never practiced, and were never organized. Heinrich Heinrichs was always the leader whenever an emergency arose."[26] A report in *Friedensstimme* likewise describes the Jasykowo's *Selbstschutz* as "poorly organized and lacking in uniform leadership, military training and discipline."[27] It is possible the Eichenfeld group considered itself more of an impromptu force, or it may not have recognized van Kampen's authority as legitimate.

Jasykowo resident Julius Loewen remembers the draft, stating that cavalry units of ten to twelve men were organized in each village, with the remaining men serving as infantry. They were subordinate to a German commandant until the withdrawal of the occupation.[28] Heinrich Heinrichs likewise writes in his memoirs, "In 1918 the *Selbstschutz* was organized by us, and I, too, had to join. . . . [The Germans] gave us orders to form a *Selbstschutz* so that our village would experience less robbery from the little bands that had formed."[29] The origins of Jasykowo's *Selbstschutz* in the German occupation would have firmly placed them in the counter-revolutionary camp in the eyes of the revolutionary peasantry.

According to some pacifist Mennonites, the Jasykowo *Selbstschutz* became questionably aggressive in their protection of the community, enflaming already tense relations with their Ukrainian neighbours. Anton Sawatsky writes: "Hungry Russian neighbors also visited the village of Eichenfeld and hoped to obtain food from these nonresistant Mennonites. For the past three and one-half years [these Mennonites] were not obliged to take up arms or crouch in the trenches, suffer thirst and cold or get sick and die. [Thanks to alternative service] almost all [Mennonite young men] returned home. Yet what happened? These starving Russians who came at night were shot or lay wounded until the morning when Mennonites came and killed them. Peter van Kampen had a strong *Selbstschutz* and they never took prisoners."[30] Sawatsky, as a dedicated pacifist, had reasons for portraying the *Selbstschutz* in as negative a light as possible. Whatever the level of violence actually employed by the *Selbstschutz,* Sawatsky's observation points to the rapidly deteriorating relations between Ukrainian and Mennonite neighbours. Following the Austro-German withdrawal from Ukraine, a 19 November 1918 report published in *Friedensstimme* suggests local tensions were reaching a critical point. The author notes that

Figure 21. Jasykowo *Selbstschutz* leader Peter van Kampen (centre), 1913.

Figure 22. Eichenfeld *Selbstschutz* leader Heinrich Heinrich Heinrichs.

in Nikolaipol "there is division as to whether [the colony] should telephone Chortitza and Alexandrovsk for help. In that area a terror prevails."[31]

From an early stage, the Jasykowo *Selbstschutz* distinguished itself by successfully repelling attacks on the colony. *Selbstschutz* member David Penner recalls, "Our *Selbstschutz* managed to defend us as long as the bands were not too large. The bands were held at bay on several occasions."[32] The

*Selbstschutz* faced its first major challenge in December 1918 after the withdrawal of the Austro-German occupation. Jasykowo resident Julius Loewen describes a band of "several hundreds," led by a peasant named "Glatshenko," that attacked the colony from the north. T.F. Gladchenko was a commander in the nationalist Ukrainian People's Army, who later declared himself an anarchist and joined Makhno in 1919.[33] The Nationalists had captured Katerynoslav on 27 November 1918 and declared their intent to expropriate the land from wealthy landowners. Likely with the intention of establishing nationalist power over the district, Gladchenko, accompanied by an artillery unit, attacked Jasykowo.[34] According to Loewen, the *Selbstschutz* successfully repelled Gladchenko with only a single casualty.[35] Between December 1918 and January 1919, the Nationalists would make several more unsucessful attempts to take Jasykowo. In another incident recalled by *Selbstschutz* member Jakob Dyck, Jasykowo was confronted by a large group of "bandits" who demanded they surrender their weapons. At the arranged exchange spot, the Mennonites turned their guns on the invaders and forced them to retreat after four hours of battle. Dyck writes that the captured intruders "were tried and taken to Katerynoslav," however, "whether or not they arrived there is debatable."[36]

During this period a battle for Katerynoslav erupted between the Nationalists, Bolsheviks, and Makhnovists. An alliance was struck between Makhno and the Red Army, in which a joint force under his command seized Katerynoslav on 27 December. However, Makhno's triumph was short-lived, as the Nationalists counterattacked and recaptured Katerynoslav. A month later, the Red Army regained the initiative, capturing Katerynoslav on 27 January, once again with Makhno's assistance. In the aftermath of this victory, Makhno signed a treaty with the Bolsheviks, in which his forces were incorporated into the Red Army as the 3rd Trans-Dnieper Brigade.

In early February, the Jasykowo *Selbstschutz* received information about a large unknown force marching towards the Nikolaipol district. En route, it had raided the German colony of Jamburg and a series of Ukrainian villages. Cornelius Heinrichs recalls that "there were many people coming towards the colony. Three shots were fired signaling 'all is not well.'"[37] According to an archived Soviet report, contact was established and the unknown force identified itself as a Bolshevik unit, led by a commander named Ivanchenko. Jasykowo's leadership declared itself as loyal to the Soviet government and requested Ivanchenko not pass through their colony. Ivanchenko refused and ordered the Mennonites to turn over their arms.[38]

The Mennonites refused to lay down their arms and were attacked by Ivanchenko. An intense battle ensued resulting in three dead and thirty-five wounded Mennonites. The Soviet report states that the neighbouring Ukrainian villages also sustained casualties. Ivanchenko received reinforcements from Katerynoslav and the outmatched *Selbstschutz* laid down its arms.[39] Jakob Dyck's and Cornelius Heinrichs's accounts largely corroborate this report.[40] Heinrichs recalls fifteen Eichenfelders, including himself, his brother, and father, engaged the Red Army. He also confirms three Mennonites died in the battle.[41] Dyck writes that at four in the morning the colony was surrounded by 200 Reds, who began their attack two hours later. The *Selbstschutz* held their ground and successfully repelled the invaders.[42] Heinrichs explains that the *Selbstschutz* from Petersdorf attacked the Reds from behind, who "could not see over the hill, so they thought they must be surrounded and ran away leaving behind their machine guns and artillery. They were pursued by the men from Petersdorf and killed on sight (took no prisoners)."[43]

According to Heinrichs, it was only after the battle that "we found out the government [Bolsheviks] had sent this group."[44] An archival report states that the colony voted to recognize Soviet power and a large fine was imposed on the colony as punishment for the incident. Heinrichs remembers that a delegation, headed by G. Andres, travelled to Katerynoslav where "they told them they were sorry and that they thought they were bandits."[45] A Bolshevik official, in turn, visited the colony and issued a statement on 14 February acknowledging the Mennonites' recognition of Soviet power, concluding the incident was a result of a misunderstanding due to the unfortunate actions of Ivanchenko. Beznosov writes that Ivanchenko was likely a Makhnovist who joined the Red Army after the 1919 alliance. He was also listed as a Makhnovist commander in 1921.[46] Following this incident, Dyck writes that "our young men gave up their weapons freely to the Reds."[47] However, Cornelius Heinrichs states, "We wanted to make good but no arms were surrendered. The government came and examined but nothing was ever done."[48] It is possible the majority of

Jasykowo's *Selbstschutz* surrendered their weapons, while the Eichenfelder group around Heinrich Heinrichs concealed theirs.

Despite the negotiations between the Bolsheviks and the colonists, requisitions continued unabated. Food, horses, and transport were continually demanded by the Red Army. In some cases, rich landowners were held hostage to extract "contributions" from the colony. In one instance, Eichenfelder Susanna Klippenstein writes: "Some riders came and threatened to set our village on fire. They had it surrounded so that no one could get out. A plane flew over us. A lot of people were standing on the street. I don't know what they demanded, or why they didn't set fire to the village, but everyone was thankful that we were saved once more."[49] Tensions were coming to a head as the colonists felt themselves increasingly oppressed under Bolshevik rule. Bolshevik party workers were sent from Katerynoslav and members of the local Soviet militia exercised unrestrained power over the colony by summer 1919.

In this environment, both Cornelius Heinrichs and Jakob Dyck describe how a fellow *Selbstschutzler* named Daniel Hiebert turned traitor. It was believed Hiebert had passed the names of *Selbstschutzler* to the Soviet militia in return for a position as militia sergeant. Threatened with exposure, the Eichenfelder group decided to eliminate members of the local militia. Heinrichs writes, "The group decided to clean up these men. Heinrich was the leader—they decided they would kill everybody, take no prisoners and not one person would utter a word."[50]

Thirteen-year-old Jake Dyck was assisting his father with morning chores when they saw three armed men appear on a steep bank before disappearing upstream. Jake's father warned him, "You have seen nothing. Nothing. Do you hear?" Later that day at school Jake witnessed the Hiebert children being told their father had been shot by the *Selbstschutz*. Years later Jake's younger brother, John, reflected, "The three armed men glimpsed by Jake earlier were even then on their grim errand of revenge. Or justice? Leading Reds, Russians as well as Jews, lost their lives that day too at the hands of the *Selbstschutzler*."[51]

On 13 June 1919 the militia headquarters in Nikolaifeld was attacked. A one-hour shootout between the militia and Heinrichs's group ensued. The militiamen were forced to surrender, but after laying down their arms four were executed including the militia chief Snissnarenko, Daniel

Hiebert, and two party workers from Katerynoslav.[52] A fifth individual escaped by hiding in an oven and later reported the murders to the Soviet authorities in Katerynoslav. The Cheka [Soviet secret police] was subsequently sent to Jasykowo to investigate the incident. It was at this time Heinrich Heinrichs fled Eichenfeld.[53] According to David Penner, in the aftermath of the incident the district soviet "arrested two to three men in each village and took them to Ekaterinoslav where they suffered a great deal."[54] Loewen writes that these prisoners were kept by the Bolsheviks in a ship anchored in the Dnipro but were saved when the White Army seized the city on 26 June.[55]

Numerous Mennonite sources argue that the massacre in November was motivated by revenge for Heinrichs's murder of the militiamen. For example, David Rempel recalls that at the end of May, the occupying Red Army received "substantial reinforcements from *Bat'ko* Makhno's soldiers" in the Chortitza-Jasykowo area.[56] According to Rempel, these troops were "pretty well convinced that the earlier execution of three militia men had been the act of the settlement's *Selbstschutz* and most likely by members of the Eichenfeld unit." Furthermore, Rempel relates that "it was obvious that [the Makhnovists] had collected much intelligence during their earlier presence in our midst concerning families whose sons had been members of the once armed organization or had during the summer joined the White Army."[57] The antagonism that evolved during this period set the stage for when the Makhnovists returned in the fall.

By June 1919 Makhno's alliance with the Bolsheviks had collapsed. Over the summer, Makhno attempted to regroup his troops while being pursued westwards by the White Army. On 25 September, Makhno was surrounded at Perehonivka by White Army forces, which included a unit composed of German colonists—the First Symferopil Officers' Regiment.[58] After Makhno's breakout at Perehonivka the colonists' regiment was forced into a panicked retreat before being drowned in the Syniuka river.[59] Amidst the collapse of Denikin's rearguard the Makhnovists re-established themselves in the Mennonite colonies. Arshinov describes the Makhnovist army as it fanned out across southern Ukraine: "They literally swept through villages, towns and cities like an enormous broom, removing every vestige of exploitation and servitude. The returned *pomeshchiks*, the *kulaks*, the police, the priests . . . all these were swept out of the victorious path of the

Makhnovist movement. . . . All those known to be active enemies of the peasants and workers were condemned to death. *Pomeshchiks* and *kulaks* perished in great numbers."[60]

A large degree of violence accompanied the growth of the Makhnovist army in autumn 1919 as it swelled to as many as 100,000 men. House searches, robbery, rape, and murder characterize Mennonite descriptions of the Makhnovist occupation. In total more than 800 Mennonite men, women, and children were killed over a six-week period between late October and early December. The colonies were also economically devastated by the Makhnovists' demand for food, lodging, and clothing. Finally, at the end of the occupation in late 1919 a typhus epidemic spread across the region. By the new year the disease had ravaged the Makhnovists and colonists alike, killing untold thousands.[61]

The rapid growth of the army in autumn 1919—which was only a fifth of its size prior to Perehonivka—created enormous organizational problems. The army came to be composed largely of local forces, many of a dubious character. A large number of Reds caught behind enemy lines, Nationalist units, and independent groups all fought under Makhno's flag. Historian Michael Malet writes that at this time, "criminals entered the army for what they could get out of it, especially plunder in the towns."[62] Rempel describes Makhno's less than rigorous recruitment process in Oleksandrivsk: "One of the first acts of the Makhnovites was to release the inmates from the city prison and then blow it up."[63]

This large force of disparate groups occupied an expansive territory, which frequently resulted in the breakdown of troop discipline. Looting and drunkenness became a common complaint amongst regimental commanders. Commander Petrenko issued the following order: "Requisitioned and confiscated goods are for the use of the whole army, not just for the benefit of individuals who may have joined our army in order to sabotage it."[64] Other commanders, such as Dorosh, felt completely helpless as they watched the spread of "banditism" through the army.[65] A number of commanders were also executed for organizing Jewish pogroms.[66] Makhno issued an appeal to his troops to immediately halt all drinking, looting, and violence against civilians: "Either you and I will fight to the finish with the enemies of the people—a fight which requires the wholeheartedness and honour of each insurgent, or we'll part ways for good. I want your response—not just in words but in deeds. The Revolution we're defending demands it, and in the names of its conquests so do I."[67] On 9 October 1919, Makhno ordered the destruction of all alcohol in the army's possession due to its effect on troop discipline.[68] The Army Staff published further appeals and arrests were made, but the situation remained unmanageable.[69] The commander of the 1st Donetz Corps, A. Kalashnikov, summarized the situation in an appeal to the army: "When we arrived in Katerynoslav *gubernia*, we saw the light, but we weren't able to seize the opportunity. We've turned that light into something vulgar, disgusting."[70]

In late October, the 4th Regional Congress of Peasants, Workers, and Insurgents met in Oleksandrivsk. A "Draft Declaration of the Revolutionary Insurgent Army of Ukraine (Makhnovist) on Free Soviets" was issued. The document gave a clear ideological vision for the movement, including the following statement concerning justice within Makhnovist-controlled territories: "A system of real justice must be organized, but it must be a living, free, creative act of the community. The self-defence of the population must be a matter of free, living self-organization. And so any moribund form of justice: judicial institutions, revolutionary tribunals, codes of penalties, police institutes, Chekists, prisons—all this must collapse under its own weight."[71] Commenting on this passage, Ukrainian anarchist researcher V. Azarov remarks: "On the one hand, this is an understandable protest of the anarchist-Makhnovists against the punitive organs of the State. But on the other hand, such a formulation of the question of justice leads to the dictatorship of emotional impulses, the tyranny of momentary rage, and opens the possibility of manipulation of 'people's justice' by special-interest groups. In other words, it leads to lynch law. Furthermore, it allows any kind of abuse to flourish on the grounds of the just struggle with the exploiting classes."[72] It is in this context that the civilian section of the Makhnovist *kontrrazvedka* came to embody the worst manipulations of justice.

The civilian *kontrrazvedka* was charged with eliminating anti-Makhnovist elements. It was a ubiquitous organization that made extensive use of civilian informants. At its height, 5,000 people collaborated with the *konttrazvedka* and as many as one-in-five Makhnovists belonged to the service. According to M. Hutman, an eyewitness to the Makhnovist occupation of Katerynoslav in November 1919, "pillaging took place under the pretext of searches for hidden weaponry. A common type of pillaging [by the *kontrrazvedka*] was the looting of the quarters of Denikinist officers that had been liquidated by the Makhnovists."[73] Volin later allegedly testified under Soviet arrest that, "whole rows of people came to me with complaints which forced me to constantly interfere in the affairs of the counterintelligence . . . [they] were horrific and I was doing everything possible to stop the acts committed by them."[74] Volin further states the volume of complaints compelled the Revolutionary Military Soviet to establish a commission to mediate cases brought by the civilian population against the *kontrrazvedka*. The results of this committee, if any, are unknown. In his later writings, Makhno was defensive of the *kontrrazvedka*'s activities and described the organization as "an organ completely necessary for the struggle of the armed revolution with the armed counterrevolution." However, he simultaneously acknowledged that "during the course of the Makhnovist counterintelligence's activities, there were sometimes mistakes that deeply pained and embarrassed me, for which I was forced to apologize to the victims."[75]

Mennonite literature widely attests to the *kontrrazvedka*'s presence in the colonies and their role in hunting down *Selbstschutzler*. Three sources from Chortitza—Neufeld, Rempel, and Schroeder—refer to the *kontrrazvedka* by name and give examples of their search for weapons and *Selbstschutzler*. Rempel, who briefly billeted three *kontrrazvedka* members in Nieder Chortitza, writes, "As self-proclaimed members of the counter-intelligence . . . intent on ferreting out White Army members and other traitors to Batko Makhno and his revolutionary movement, they were the most obnoxious and ruthless of all the village's unbidden occupants. Aside from eating, they slept all day, then towards evening left for their escapades, to hunt down counter-revolutionaries, and to search houses, pilfering whatever touched their fancy or simply because they enjoyed tormenting innocent people."[76] Rempel recalled how the "Makhnovites justified their ferocious attacks as part of their relentless search for Abram Loewen [a *Selbstschutzler* at large]."[77] On 2 November, Dietrich Neufeld wrote in his diary, "It's getting more and more dangerous. Makhno has ordered his intelligence agents to finish off without mercy every person of hostile views."[78] A similar pattern emerged at Eichenfeld, in which the search for Heinrichs and his unit was used to rationalize the total destruction of the village.

Figure 23. Makhnovist unit entering Oleksandrivsk, 20 October 1919.

Schroeder writes that "the immediate excuse used by the Makhnovtsy was that the young men of the villages had during 1918–1919 formed self-defence units."[79]

In the days leading up to the massacre a series of key troop movements occurred amidst a volatile military situation. According to Belash's sequence of events, on 4 November the White Army launched an assault on Oleksandrivsk from the Dnipro's left bank. At this point a decision was made to begin transferring the army to Katerynoslav.[80] The Makhnovists had previously captured Katerynoslav on 28 October and looked to consolidate their forces there. Loewen confirms this scenario, writing, "As they marched toward Dnepropetrovsk [Katerynoslav] on October 26, 1919 [8 November, New Style] all villages of the Jasykowo Volost were overrun by the Machnovze. They pillaged and killed."[81] The evacuation of Oleksandrivsk involved marching the 1st, 2nd, and 3rd Army Corps northward through the Mennonite colonies of Chortitza and Jasykowo. Belash writes that zones of occupation were established on 9 November along the Dnipro's right bank. The 1st Army Corps was stationed between Katerynoslav and Fedorivka, and the 2nd Army Corps between Fedorivka and Chortitza.[82] Fedorivka neighboured Eichenfeld, suggesting Jasykowo straddled the two occupation zones.

According to Belash, Makhno left Oleksandrivsk on the evening of 6 November for Katerynoslav ahead of the general troop movements.[83]

At dawn on 8 November, the Makhnovists faced a serious setback when the White Army captured Katerynoslav. Makhno was forced to retreat fifteen kilometres south to the village of Sursko-Lytovske. Belash, still in Oleksandrivsk, explains that the loss of Katerynoslav "was the reason for our quick departure from Alexandrovsk, which forced us to transfer the 1st-Ekaterinoslav Regiment led by Klein and the 1st-Calvary Brigade to Ekaterinoslav, which was executed 9 November."[84] The latter units met Makhno at Sursko-Lytovske where a counterassault was launched on Katerynoslav. The city was retaken by the Makhnovists between 9 and 12 November.[85] If Belash's dates are accurate, they preclude Makhno's presence in Eichenfeld on 8 November, although it is possible occupying forces from the 1st or 2nd Army Corps participated in the massacre.

According to Julius Loewen, the first Makhnovists had appeared in Jasykowo on 24 October under the command of Simeon Pravda. Loewen recalls how in Franzfeld, Pravda threatened to kill all the villagers if they refused to hand over all weapons and a large sum of money.[86] However, Pravda is not mentioned by any source in relation to the 8 November massacre. Regardless, it is certain that Jasykowo was under Makhnovist occupation from late October and saw a large number of troops pass through its villages en route to Katerynoslav on the day of the massacre.

Exactly how and when Makhno arrived in Katerynoslav after his departure from Oleksandrivsk is unclear. Two routes were possible. The first route would have involved crossing the Dnipro to the right bank and taking the main road to Katerynoslav, which passed through Jasykowo. The second route would have involved Makhno taking an armoured train to Katerynoslav via the left bank. In either case, assuming he did not stop en route, he would have arrived in Katerynoslav, before 8 November. Makhno was known to frequently travel by armoured train. A.V. Bipetskii, a captured White officer, recalls serving Makhno on an armoured train along the Oleksandrivsk-Katerynoslav line during this period. Unfortunately, he does not specify the exact date.[87] Given Makhno's record of travelling on armoured trains and his importance to the movement, it is likely he transferred to Katerynoslav by rail on 6 November.

However, prior to leaving Oleksandrivsk Makhno wrote a citizens' address, which appeared in the Makhnovist daily *Put' k Svobode* on 5 November:

> The bourgeoisie is all laughs as it sees our failures on certain fronts. I will give them my final word: the bourgeoisie in their futile arrogance hope for our defeat and the victory of the Don and Kuban Whites. I tell you our setback in this area will be the death of the bourgeoisie. To accomplish this I have taken action. In the hands of the remaining chiefs of defense for the city of Aleksandrovsk, Kalashnikov and his adjutant Karetnik, have been invested with the task of eliminating the bourgeoisie and their minions.
>
> Death to the bourgeoisie!
> Death to all their minions!
> Long live the liberation of the working class!
> Long live the Social Revolution!
> Army Commander *Bat'ko* Makhno
>
> 4 November 1919, Alexandrovsk[88]

According to Belash, Makhno also produced a list of eighty individuals to be executed, which included Mensheviks, Socialist-Revolutionaries, industrialists, and railway unionists.[89] Belash was needed to authorize the death sentences, but he claims he refused. He describes Makhno's request as "unmotivated terror" and counterproductive to the movement's objectives. Belash also claims he released the prisoners on their word that they would not collaborate with the White Army.[90]

While Makhno's open letter was intended for Oleksandrivsk, it would have circulated amongst the rank-and-file and inflamed an already tense environment. On 30 October (17 October, Old Style) Neufeld recorded in his diary that a Makhnovist squad leader stationed in his home in Chortitza told him that a number of "Germans" had been hanged near Einlage for shooting at Makhnovists. He also told Neufeld "in confidence" that the "commanders had had a tough time preventing their troops from taking revenge against all the villages."[91] Corresponding with the publication of Makhno's letter, Neufeld wrote in his diary:

> November 4 [22 October, Old Style]: Shocking! Today the big Cossack [a commander] who was here a few days ago came back. He grandly announced that the pretended neutrality of our Mennonite villages would no longer be tolerated. The struggle had now entered a crucial

> stage and they were prepared to force the issue: it was either for or against. We must now decide whether we'd stand and fight on their side or be counted with their enemies the Whites. If the latter, then we were to be wiped out to the last man.
>
> November 5 [23 October, Old Style]: We feel as if we have been condemned to death and are now simply waiting for the executioner to come. Those who are not sunk in apathy are thinking of escape. But we have been notified that anyone caught three steps from his house will be shot without warning. Actually there are so many armed riders around that any attempt to escape would mean certain death.[92]

Neufeld's next entry reports that a massacre had occurred in Eichenfeld.[93] Makhno's open letter is not proof of his direct involvement in the massacre, but it is evidence that a strategy of terror had been embraced at the highest levels of the movement during this period. Neufeld's diary also confirms that Makhnovists at the ground level shifted their rhetoric and behaviour immediately following the publication of Makhno's letter.

Another letter from Makhno points in a different direction. According to Nikita Astakhoff, the Stundist convert present in Jasykowo during the massacre, Makhno personally granted permission to Astakhoff's tent mission to evangelize in Makhnovist-controlled territory. Astakhoff even tried to arrange a second meeting with Makhno after the massacre to secure safe passage for the surviving missionaries.[94] However, the tent missionaries in Eichenfeld were not spared despite this official "protection." According to Astakhoff, his co-religionists were killed in the afternoon prior to the massacre. According to one account, the missionaries "were asked to show their papers or vouchers, which were clearly marked 'ministers.' Makhno's men distorted this to mean 'minor officers' to suit their own evil intentions."[95] Astakhoff also writes that the Makhnovists frequently referred to the missionaries as "servants of Capital." These interactions suggest a division amongst the Makhnovists, with the leadership tolerating the missionaries' presence and the rank-and-file violently opposing them. The Makhnovists at Eichenfeld were clearly unconcerned with whatever permission Makhno may have granted the tent mission. Moreover, the perpetrators interpreted situations to suit their intents. The missionaries were identified as political and class enemies. The terms "minor officers"

Figure 24. The Stundist Tent Mission that lost five members in the Eichenfeld massacre, c. 1918–19.

and "servants of Capital" were employed to ideologically rationalize the missionaries' mistreatment and murder. The role of local forces and their use of ideology to legitimize their actions are critical to understanding the motivations behind the Eichenfeld massacre.

On the morning of 8 November a large number of Makhnovist troops passed through the villages of Jasykowo en route to Katerynoslav. An eyewitness recalls that "from 9 a.m. to 4 p.m., hundreds and thousands of the Black Ones, Machno's bandits, moved through the village [Eichenfeld] like death's shadow. It seemed as if there was no end to them."[96] At about ten in the morning their first action was to kill Heinrich Kornelius Heinrichs, the father of Eichenfeld's *Selbstschutz* leader Heinrich Heinrich Heinrichs. This incident was followed in the afternoon by the murder of six tent missionaries proselytzing in the village. The account continues: "By about 4 pm the carnage and movement of this tide of evil through the village abated. The sun set. Darkness came. Then again a large regiment rushed through the village at full gallop."[97] The village was surrounded and men were stationed at each property. In the massacre that followed, landowners and their sons over the age of sixteen were systematically executed.

The aftermath of the massacre was equally horrific. A survivor recalls how "the night that followed is simply beyond description. Mothers and daughters, new-made widows and orphans, were forced to become the playthings of the murderers. . . . Worse than anything, worse than death itself, was the horror of wholesale rape."[98] Helena Martens recounts that "women and even twelve-year-old girls were raped, manhandled in a variety of ways and infected with venereal diseases."[99] Following the massacre, peasants from the neighbouring villages descended upon Eichenfeld, taking anything of value. Raisa Gurazda, a resident of Novopetrivka, recounts her mother's story: "Later some daring people from neighbouring villages came, after everything was deserted. They took all the doors and windows. The Germans had everything of the best quality. . . . Not a single German home remained standing in the village, they were torn down. . . . It was like a 'black hole,' deserted. The bricks were scattered around. It was desolate and the cats slunk about, and the dogs."[100] The survivors fled to the neighbouring village of Adelsheim. Only after three days did they dare return to Eichenfeld to bury their relatives in twelve mass graves.

E.P. Orlov, a Red soldier attached to the Makhnovists in November 1919, passed through Nikolaipol in the massacre's immediate aftermath. He recalls, "In the evening we arrived at the German colony Nikolaipol. Not a single colonist was there, everyone had left. Sour cream stood on the tables, but the people were gone. They were afraid. We spent the night there."[101] The captured White officer Bipetskii also passed through Eichenfeld at this time, where he spoke with a survivor:

> We drove all day and finally stopped for the night in the German colony No. 4. I was struck by the fact that the village's residents were horribly intimidated. I noticed that when the owner of the home where I was staying served me coffee her hands were shaking. When I was alone with her, I asked in German, what does all this mean? She looked at me incredulously at first, but after I told her several times that I was not a Makhnovist but a prisoner, she told me the following.
>
> In September, seven horsemen arrived in the colony armed from head to toe, and began to rob the Germans and rape the residents. They had not yet heard about Makhnovists and thought it was an ordinary robber gang. The Germans armed themselves and killed all the bandits except one. This one who escaped the Germans' reprisals escaped on his horse and reported everything. Makhno dispatched 200 people who came to the colony and cruelly dealt with the Germans. Everything

> with value was taken away: cattle, horses, domestic birds, shoes, and clothes. All men between the ages 15 and 75 were shot. The colony is desolate. Children and women walked over their destroyed homes and wept over the corpses of their fathers, husbands, brothers, and sons. The violence was terrible.[102]

While Bipetskii's chronology and narrative is muddled, the details he provides indicate the survivor believed the *Selbstschutz*'s activities were a motivating factor behind the massacre. Indeed, many survivors expressed similar sentiments. For example, H.W. Klassen writes: "In Eichenfeld the people had a good self-defence group. One day a robber band came to plunder from our village. The self-defence group armed themselves and did not let the robber band into the village. Later this same band joined with Makhno to bring this village to its knees."[103]

Numerous eyewitness accounts also recall that the male population was specifically targeted and that class played a determining role in who lived and died. Klassen recalls, "Grandmother lived at the end of the village not in the farmer's row. She was an *Anwohner,* landless. Because of this, my brother and father stayed alive."[104] A female survivor also recalls how, the day after the massacre, "mothers and daughters" sought refuge "in a tiny huddle of buildings at the outskirts of the village . . . and prayed to remain unmolested." She explains that "the place had seemed too poor to arouse the cupidity of the invaders."[105] Katherina Paetkau similarily describes how she and her sister fled to "the end of the village to the Schmidts" where they were given sanctuary. Paetkau explains that the Schmidts "were not landowners and therefore were not being attacked by the Makhnovite bandits."[106]

David A. Quiring's account also confirms that the landless were spared. At the height of the massacre, Quiring was assigned the chilling task of informing each household that they were to bake bread for the Makhnovists. While performing this grim duty, Quiring was brought before the group's commander: "I prayed fervently to our gracious lord for strength and grace to endure what lay ahead. The commander placed his revolver against my temple . . . 'Who are you? Do you have any land?'" Everyone was asked that question. I answered that I had neither land nor a house, a statement verified by Mrs. Franz Klassen. I was freed and he ordered his soldier to escort me to the street."[107] Quiring met the commander again at his brother's home later that evening: "Then they interrogated my brother Klass. I came to his defence and they freed him because he possessed no material property. Then came Jacob's turn. Did he have land? He answered yes. The commander shouted for him to remove his clothing. He grew pale for he knew death was imminent."[108] Another survivor corroborates Quiring's account, writing, "The Fast family had been spared because he [*sic*] was a laborer (a smithy) and the Jakob Friesen and David Quiring families because they were renters."[109] Abram Dombrowsky saved his own life by claiming to be a worker. He recalls: "[A man] came up to me, enquired who I was and why I stood there. I must confess that the fear of a horrible death at my tender age drove me to lie. I said that I was a worker and I had been told to stand against the wall. With a snort and a strong word he told me to leave the room immediately."[110] From the surviving accounts it appears that the attackers were following orders to exclusively execute landowning males and their sons. The reasoning behind this was likely to eliminate any Mennonites' claims to ownership over the land.

As mentioned, some contemporary Mennonite histories hold Makhno personally accountable for the massacre. A number of Ukrainian oral interviews collected by Bobyleva's team also directly blame Makhno. For example, according to one interviewee, "Makhno issued the order: 'Slaughter them all!' But when evening came he said: 'Don't harm the workers, women, or children.'"[111] However, this individual was born years after the massacre and was relaying what he remembered of his mother's story. Another interviewee claims Makhno stayed in Fedorivka, although the date of this visit is unclear. In this case the witness was six years old at the time of the massacre and he was recalling these events in his late eighties. By contrast, none of the first-hand Mennonite accounts report Makhno being directly involved in the massacre.

One Mennonite source identifies Makhno as present at the Blumenort massacre (23–25 November 1919) in the Molotschna colony. However, this source is problematic for multiple reasons. Its author, Abram Berg, was seven years old at the time and writes that his childhood friend pointed out Makhno as they stared out a window. The rest of his account relies on second-hand retellings of other eyewitnesses' experiences. Berg writes that an individual named Jakob Neufeld had his horses requisitioned by

Makhno. Berg's sources are Neufeld's Ukrainian coachman who was severely beaten during the encounter and Berg's uncle who provided an oral account in 1974.[112] However, Jakob Neufeld also left an account, published in *Friedensstimme* just four days after the massacre, but makes no mention of Makhno.[113] Neither does eyewitness B.B. Janz, who specifically identifies the perpetrators as "Makhnovites from the Russian village of Troitskoye" commanded by the "Asiatic Division of Konovalov from Melitopol."[114] A Makhnovist archival document confirms the "2nd-Asiatic Regiment" was commanded by Konovalov and active along the Crimean front in November 1919. The document also reports the unit's artillery commander was arrested on Makhno's orders, although his transgressions are not described.[115] A separate order from January 1920 does however complain about the regiment's drunkenness and demands an end to its "insidious treatment of peaceful inhabitants" under the threat of execution.[116]

Furthermore, Makhnovist sources all place Makhno in Katerynoslav from 11 November onwards where he had established his headquarters and army staff. Belash describes Makhno negotiating with Nationalist commanders on 20 November and makes no mention of Makhno leaving the city at any point.[117] Belash and Volin also describe a secret Bolshevik plot to assassinate Makhno in Katerynoslav during this period.[118] Moreover, the city was effectively blockaded by the White Army for the latter half of November and into December. Historian Michael Palij writes that the Whites had "established a defensive line along the left bank of the Dnieper to prevent Makhno from crossing the river."[119] Volin, who was in Katerynoslav for the entirety of the month, writes: "Denikin's troops, who were driven out of the city, managed to dig in nearby, on the left bank of the Dnieper. Despite their efforts, the Makhnovists could not dislodge them. Daily, for a whole month, the Denikinists bombarded the city, which was within the range of the batteries on their numerous armoured trains."[120] For Makhno to have been present in Blumenort, he would have had to secretly break through the Whites' siege, cross the Dnipro through enemy lines, travel 160 kilometres south to a strategically unimportant village, and subsequently return to Katerynoslav.[121] Like Eichenfeld, the massacre at Blumenort certainly involved a Makhnovist unit, but given the military situation Makhno's physical presence is highly unlikely. While this does not absolve Makhno from the atrocities perpetrated under his name, it does point to the massacres as more local and decentralized in nature than is sometimes assumed.

The role of the local, specifically the neighbouring Ukrainian, peasants is also a recurring theme in the Eichenfeld massacre. Gerhard Schroeder writes, "Eichenfeld was a very prosperous Mennonite colony, thus constituting a highly desirable prize for looting by Makhno's men and then to be turned over for wholesale plunder to some of the neighbouring peasant villages."[122] Nikolaifeld resident Johann Neufeld emphasizes that in October 1919 "the mobs of the Russian villages joined [Makhno]," suggesting a strong overlap between the Makhnovists and local elements.[123] One Eichenfelder wrote: "Like jackals and hyenas, which follow lions and other beasts of prey and content themselves with leftovers, so, too, the Ukrainians of Ausgustinovka and [F]jodorovka and other neighbouring villages came and looted Eichenfeld completely."[124] Margaret Epp, who interviewed survivors, likewise concluded, "It must be admitted, their Russian neighbours, many of whom had long envied the prosperity of the Mennonites, had gleefully swarmed through the village, laying covetous hands on whatever caught their fancy."[125]

Looting is the most common accusation levelled at the neighbouring peasants. However, other accounts implicate them in the killings as well. One of the Ukrainian interviewees says, "In 1919 the Makhnovites and some local people from Fedorivka attacked Eichenfeld."[126] Rempel also concluded the local factor was a critical component in the tragedy's evolution:

> Eichenfeld was made to pay the price for killing the three militiamen. The act of revenge may have involved more than regular members of Makhno's army, it may have included representatives from neighboring peasant villages now finally able to even the score with a resident of Eichenfeld who had insulted or injured him in past years. . . . The virtually unanimous verdict among Mennonites was that the nightmarish experiences of Eichenfeld and the surrounding communities were part and parcel of the *Makhnovshchina*. . . . Actually it is safe to assume that many of the worst excesses in Eichenfeld, [etc.] were carried out by peasants of neighboring villages."[127]

Rempel goes on to write that survivors "had recognized among the looters and marauders familiar faces from nearby peasant villages." Rempel also writes that his cousin Cornelius Heinrichs was "of the firm opinion that responsibility for Eichenfeld's nightmarish experience rested more with the neighboring peasants than with the *Makhnovshchina* per se."[128]

Heinrich Friesen, who interviewed survivors in the 1920s, provides further insight into the nature of the tensions between Eichenfeld and the neighbouring Ukrainian villages. Friesen writes that a conflict had emerged between the communities in which "the [Ukrainians] repeatedly tried to herd their cows over Eichenfelder pastures (they did not want to make a detour) to water them in the Dnjepr."[129] One of Friesen's interviewees states the massacre was plotted in a neighbouring Ukrainian village:

> Some days before that fateful 26th of October, some friendly Russians came to Nikolaifeld from the Russian village of Lukaschowo, warned people they knew of a dreadful calamity that threatened us, especially Eichenfeld. They also advised us we should warn the Eichenfelders, at least definitely get our friends and relatives out of Eichenfeld. The Batjko Makhno band, which was only a part of this widely scattered group, was standing at the ready in the village of Lukaschowo, where the bandits, among other things, had decided on this bloody Mephistophelian act. A few of the Lukaschowo villagers knew of this diabolical decision.[130]

This passage clarifies a number of important aspects about the massacre. First, it indicates the attack was premeditated. Furthermore, it strongly suggests local peasants joined forces with the Makhnovists to execute their plan. However, it also shows that the neighbouring peasants were not united in their hatred of the Mennonites. This is confirmed in another account in which a Mennonite woman and her children were saved by a peasant family. Elizabeth Warkentin recalls, "Although it put his life on the line, the Russian father let us crawl onto the Peitsch [peasant stove] where his own children were sleeping; and he denied our presence minutes later when the bandits were out to rape the wives and daughters of the men they had murdered."[131]

Perhaps most surprising of all was the presence of German-speakers amongst the perpetrators. One of Friesen's interviewees, Katherina Penner, recalls with astonishment how "among the Machnowze, I noticed—a German, name of Schmidt. . . . Right next to Morosow, the apparent leader of the band, a name we heard frequently, stood a German—Schmidt!" Years later Penner encountered Schmidt again, writing, "How could such a scum of humanity, one who could massacre his own people, be accepted in a leading role in a Soviet governmental department."[132] David Quiring also reports encountering a German during the massacre: "Suddenly he began to speak High German. I realized he was a [German] Catholic. He cursed and hit me on the head, and asked whether I would give him money or forfeit my life."[133] Astakhoff also writes: "Some of the principal participants in the massacre of our missionaries . . . had evidently formerly belonged to a Christian church for they were heard using the language of the Bible as they spoke in the German tongue."[134]

The existence of German Makhnovists was rare but not unheard of. Makhnovists with German surnames such as Fritz, Klerfman, and Klein are mentioned in official documents.[135] Even more intriguing was a Makhnovist named Thiessen. In an order from October 1919, Thiessen is listed as the adjutant to Oleksandrivsk's garrison chief Alexander Klein. This individual may be the same Peter (Petia) Thiessen described by Rempel as a Mennonite who married a Ukrainian woman and joined the Makhnovists.[136] Rempel also recounts how he encountered a dying Makhnovist who spoke Low German.[137] Furthermore, in the Sagradowka colony, where over 200 Mennonites were killed by Makhnovists in December 1919, an eyewitness identified the leader of this massacre as "a Mennonite named Letkemann from Halbstadt."[138] Despite this aspect of Mennonite history being rarely discussed, Rempel asserts that "many residents of both the Khortitsa and Molochna settlements recall other Mennonites participating in bandit raids."[139] While the colonies as a whole were quite prosperous they also contained many landless and impoverished Mennonites, Lutherans, and Catholics. Rempel describes the execution of three Mennonites who had "presumably collaborated with a bandit gang" and had participated in raids on German and Mennonite colonies. One of the accused is described as "the son of one of the poorest *Nippaenja* [landless] families."[140] The personal details of such German and Mennonite Makhnovists are sparse, but it can be assumed Makhno's program of expropriation and redistribution was attractive to some marginalized Mennonites and Germans.[141]

The presence of Mennonites and Germans in the Makhnovist army, and their alleged participation in the massacres, subverts the notion that Makhnovist violence against Mennonites was primarily motivated by ethnic hatred.[142] There were certainly ethnic dimensions to the Makhnovist-Mennonite conflict. As previously discussed, Mennonites and Germans were disproportionately impacted by expropriation campaigns due to the concentration of land and wealth in their hands. Mennonite and German colonists were also suspected as traitors by the Makhnovists due to the *Selbstschutz*'s collaboration with the Austro-German occupation. Moreover, accounts exist of Makhnovists expressing anti-German sentiment. For example, in Franzfeld, a day before the Eichenfeld massacre, a Makhnovist is reported to have asked his victim, "German? We have orders to kill all Germans."[143] Four Mennonites were murdered, although the rest of the villagers were spared. The White Army officer Bipetskii also describes a Makhnovist who was particularly rude to a German colonist. In conversation with Bipetskii, the Makhnovist said that he considered Germans "scum" and described how his father had been hanged by the Austro-German occupation.[144]

However, if individual Makhnovists exhibited anti-German attitudes that did not differentiate an estate-owning Mennonite from a landless one, the movement at large did make that distinction. This is seen not only in Makhnovist propaganda but also in Mennonite accounts, like Neufeld's and Rempel's, which demonstrate Mennonite teachers were considered part of the working class by Makhnovists. Distinctions were also made at Eichenfeld when landless Mennonites were expressly spared. This pattern would not have been possible if the logic behind the massacre was that Germans unequivocally represented a threat to be eliminated. Reality was often far more nuanced and even contradictory. David Quiring's eyewitness account communicates the bewildering complexity of motivations on the ground. During the massacre, Quiring reports encountering in turn: an anti-German Makhnovist who yells "all the Germans should be killed"; a "murder commission" parsing out Mennonite landowners from the landless; and an ethnic German Makhnovist who robs and almost beats Quiring to death.[145]

Makhnovist perceptions of Mennonites were strongly filtered through a class-based world view that prevented Makhno and his movement from seeing Mennonites and Germans as evil without exception. Unlike an anti-Semite who is universally intolerant of Jewish people, class provided a pathway to redemption for Mennonites according to Makhnovist logic. A Mennonite could still be an exploited worker or a comrade intellectual and join the movement. This explains why the landless were spared at Eichenfeld and how German and Mennonite Makhnovists could participate in their own people's massacre.

In his biography of Nestor Makhno, the Mennonite historian Victor Peters defends Makhno against charges of anti-Semitism and Germanophobia. He also notes that the movement's membership included Jews and Germans. Drawing from his extensive correspondence with Mennonite and Ukrainian eyewitnesses, Peters concluded that "many Germans felt that Makhno was a victim of the vicious anti-German propaganda which the war had released, and that was why the German Catholic, Lutheran, and Mennonite villages were plundered and burned and the people slaughtered. There is every evidence that as far as Makhno was concerned the severe attack on the German settlements was not undertaken because they were German . . . Makhno directed those expeditions to the German volosts not out of blind hatred for the German colonists but because their villages were wealthier than the Ukrainian villages, whose turn came later."[146] David Rempel likewise attributes the Eichenfeld massacre's underlying motivation to "loot and land hunger."[147] The bitterness engendered by the unequal division of land after the peasantry's emancipation cut deeper than many Mennonites ever imagined. Situated in a fertile area, Jasykowo became very prosperous in a short period of time, and according to Rempel aroused "envy and resentment among many of the neighbouring peasantry who no longer were able to rent smaller or larger pieces of land from their former gentry landlords."[148] A contract signed in 1870 between Jasykowo's Mennonites and Ukrainian peasants from Fedorivka and Avhustynivka details a land-lease agreement and access to pastures now under Mennonite administration.[149] It is possible this contract, or ones like it, were at the root of the troubles Rempel describes.

Social tensions were further amplified by Mennonite collaboration with the Austro-German occupation and White Army. An anonymous

Figure 25. Mennonite survivors mourning victims of the Sagradowka massacre in front of a mass grave. Tiege, Sagradowka colony, 1919.

diarist who left Eichenfeld during the German occupation reflected on the massacre: "The clear understanding should have told people that it was impossible for a small heap to resist the great majority. . . . In October 1919, 85 people were hacked to pieces with sabers there, partly shot to death. A true Bartholomew-night. I do not want to sit in judgment over my own people, but I believe that one had not made the surrounding Russians into friends in the good years, but rather to enemies and this murder was the answer."[150] The majority of victims likely had nothing to do with the *Selbstschutz* or the punitive expeditions. However, the bitterness engendered through social inequalities, compounded by war and revolution, created a volatile situation where fantasies of revenge could be realized in practice.

## EICHENFELD AS REVOLUTIONARY TERROR

An alternative way to understand the events at Eichenfeld is to seek a category that communicates both the victims' experiences and the perpetrators' intentions. The concept of "revolutionary terror," or as the Makhnovists themselves referred to it, "Black Terror," captures such a balance. Revolutionary terror implicitly places more emphasis on the class element, but it does not exclude the presence of ethnic factors. It is also appropriate to the period, with "Black Terror" occurring parallel to the Red and White terrors. Terror is a term broad enough to embrace a diversity of motivating factors while still being specific enough to help conceptualize the massacres.

Terror can be defined as "a symbolic act designed to influence political behavior by extra-normal means, entailing the use or threat of violence."[151] Revolutionary terror emerges from a context of extreme reciprocal violence and is ostensibly based on the pursuit of "justice." In a revolutionary situation, this frequently occurs when the state can no longer maintain its monopoly over violence. Violence becomes decentralized and legitimated through competing local forces. Historian Arno Meyer writes, "The quantum jump of violence is both cause and effect of the breakup of a state's single sovereignty into multiple and rival power centres, which is accompanied by a radical dislocation of the security and judicial system. As a consequence, the positive legal standards for judging and circumscribing acts of political violence give way to moral and ethical criteria. In other words, in the calculus of means and ends, the principles of 'law' are superseded by those of 'justice.'"[152] Due to the disappearance of universal law as administered through the state, justice is subjectively applied according to each competing power. These competing notions of justice come into conflict, triggering, as in the case of Makhno and the Mennonites, a state of escalating violence in which each group attempts to use force and fear to compel the enemy to accept their regime. In this scenario, the moral line between justice and terror begins to blur.

This process began in fall 1918 when Makhno struggled to formulate what he considered a just policy toward the colonies. After the burning of Velyka Mykhailivka, Makhno was driven to seek vengeance through his raids on estates and colonies. According to Makhno's account, only when he realized that such a policy would descend into indiscriminate terror did he attempt to establish clear rules of engagement. However, it would prove exceedingly difficult to prevent a slip into wanton violence. Unlike Makhno's aggressive policy against anti-Semitism within the movement, any efforts to curb the murder of innocent German and Mennonite colonists were a failure.

Makhno's alleged incident with Shchus illustrates this. Shchus was guilty of executing unarmed Germans which, according to Makhno's policy, should have led to Shchus's expulsion from the movement. Makhno went further and threatened Shchus with execution. In the account, we see a confrontation between Shchus's terrorism and Makhno's attempts to uphold some sort of guiding ethical code. Terror was victorious in the end as Makhno did not follow through with his threat. Amidst the contingencies of the civil war, could Makhno have afforded to execute a commander second in popularity only to himself? Regardless, justice for the colonists was absent, and it would be increasingly so as the civil war progressed.

While there is no clear evidence Makhno participated in or directly sanctioned the massacres in 1919, his movement's behaviour was increasingly terroristic. Particularly, the activities of the *kontrrazvedka,* coupled with Makhno's public declaration of war on the bourgeoisie, helped inflame existing tensions between peasants, Makhnovists and Mennonites. At the height of Makhno's power in fall 1919, local peasant bands joined the Makhnovists to employ terror in pursuit of their own form of retribution. Embittered by land hunger and mindful of the colonists' collaboration with the Austro-German occupation, these groups vented their rage.

In the context of Eichenfeld, the *Selbstschutz*'s previous activities, particularly the murder of the local militiamen that past spring, provided further incentive to remove the village as a source of potential resistance. Tragically, the massacre at Eichenfeld was alone in neither its suffering nor its inhumanity. On 12 December 1919, another massacre was perpetrated by Makhnovist troops in the Mennonite colony of Sagradowka. According to Dietrich Neufeld, who was raised in the colony, relations with the local peasants were likewise plagued by resentments over land. As in the other colonies, the Austro-German occupation was embraced and punitive detachments were organized, along with a *Selbstschutz,* which subsequently allied itself with the White Army and came into conflict with local Ukrainian peasants. In fall 1919, these local elements united with the Makhnovists and murdered 206 colonists over three days. Unlike Eichenfeld, this massacre was far more indiscriminate, claiming men, women, and children. In an inversion of the original revolutionary impulse for justice, terror now became an end in itself, with the rhetoric of justice a convenient handmaiden for the pursuit of wholesale slaughter.[153]

# CONCLUSION

In his 1865 history of the French Revolution Edgar Quinet described the dynamics of terror as "opposing electric currents making for perpetual thunder and lightning."[1] A cyclone is an appropriate metaphor in which reprisals become progressively infused with what Quinet called a mutually reinforcing "spirit of extermination."[2] In the civil war the Makhnovshchina found itself facing an "opposing current," first in the form of the Austro-German occupation and then in the White Army. Both conducted vicious campaigns of terror against their enemies.

Many Mennonite and German colonists strongly supported these regimes and some were even complicit in the occupation's violence. From their perspective, justice was sought through the reclamation of stolen property and the protection of their families from marauding bands. But here, as in the case of the Makhnovists, the pursuit of justice gave way to terror. A White Army captain attached to a Molotschna *Selbstschutz* unit wrote in his diary about the "German colonists'" relationship with the Makhnovists: "Fine soldiers, reliable and true; but they are savages. They do not take prisoners, never bring them to the unit's staff. Formerly rich rural squires, they have now been completely ruined by the Makhnovists and take their revenge on them—deliberately, brutally and coldly. But the Makhnovists deal with them in the same manner."[3] Mennonite collaboration with the counter-revolution can also be understood as a gradual process that contributed to an evolving mutual "spirit of extermination." The embrace of the German occupation was a decisive moment. Public fraternization with the occupiers, the presence of Mennonites in punitive expeditionary units, and the military drilling of Mennonite youth under German command did nothing to ease tensions with their Ukrainian neighbours. In the eyes of Makhno's supporters, the colonies, by virtue of their wealth and collaboration, were identified as counter-revolutionary outposts.

In hindsight, Mennonite support for the Austro-German occupation is not unexpected given the threat they faced. From 1917 onward Mennonite estate owners and colonists faced a growing wave of theft, harassment, and murder. They were forced to radically alter every aspect of their pre-revolutionary lives. Former estate owners were reduced to subsistence farmers and their properties were converted to communes for the landless. Throughout the colonies, Mennonites were subjected to seemingly indiscriminate house searches, arrests, and executions. The arrival of the German army offered reprieve from the chaos, and the promise of a return to the past.

The ethnic dimension of the German occupation also played a critical role. In the developing Mennonite narrative of the civil war, the German troops were understood as brotherly saviours by many within the colonies. Their Germanic cousins were particularly romanticized by the youth, who quickly succumbed to arguments in favour of "self-defense." This ethnic component, placed in the context of the anti-German propaganda of the First World War, served only to reinforce peasant suspicions of the Mennonites as fifth columnists. Furthermore, Mennonite efforts to define themselves as Dutch (to protect themselves from the land liquidation laws) likely appeared disingenuous to their neighbours, especially after their fraternization with the Austro-Germans.

Thus far, while theft and harassment were widespread, murder had yet to take on a mass character. The first actions that constituted mass terror against the Mennonites were the Makhnovist raids in the aftermath of the burning of Velyka Mykhailivka. This event, more than any other, signalled Makhno's resolve to deal resolutely with those he considered Austro-German collaborators. Makhnovist authors narrate the ensuing raids in highly triumphant terms as a campaign of peasant liberation from the yoke of occupation. Makhno, in particular, attempts to cast himself as a voice of revolutionary justice and even restraint in the face of an immoral enemy. Rhetorically, Makhno positions himself as a liberator even of his victims, as in the case of Neu-Grüntal's destruction. These attacks also caused a large number of Schönfelders to seek refuge in the

Molotschna colony. The refugees brought with them harrowing tales of murder and rape. An immediate sense of urgency was brought to bear on the question of self-defence. With fear in the air, and the Germans on the verge of withdrawing from Ukraine, the *Selbstschutz* was allowed to flourish in the majority of Mennonite villages with minimal opposition. Prior to the German army's withdrawal, the *Selbstschutz* made overtures to the White Army for munitions and operational advice. While the *Selbstschutz* leadership ensured its operational autonomy from the Whites, from the Makhnovist perspective the Mennonites had once more militarily aligned themselves with the counter-revolution. Even these technical distinctions were eliminated when many *Selbstschutzler* later joined the White Army's ethnic German battalions.

It is at this juncture that the conflict became truly Manichean and exponentially susceptible to the logic of terror. The narrative on both sides of the field hardened. Individual actors were increasingly subsumed by caricatures of the enemy so as to psychologically rationalize the violence they deemed necessary. The Makhnovist was perceived as a murderous rapist and the Mennonite kulak as a scheming counter-revolutionary agent. Such stereotypes commonly acted as rhetorical devices to justify personal vendettas and community grievances. Typically, this was achieved by invoking deeply ingrained cultural narratives of the enemy. In the language of the Mennonites, the Makhnovists are spiritually demonic and the events accompanying them are apocalyptic. Makhno functions as an Antichrist and his hordes of plague-infested troops as fallen angels. Defilement and the spread of disorder and pestilence are themes against which the *Selbstschutzler* act as guardians. The *Selbstschutzler* are portrayed as reluctant warriors who maintain their morality in the face of battle.[4] Yet, there is a sense that they too are fallen in their inability to embrace the fate of the suffering martyr. Seemingly contradictory narratives can be encountered. For example, *Selbstschutz* member Henry Regehr believed that God disapproved of the *Selbstschutz* but also protected them in battle.[5]

A common interpretation is that the *Selbstschutz* was a tragic misjudgement that carries the burden of having contributed to provoking the massacres. One cannot help but contrast this interpretation with other cultures in which armed resistance to a perceived evil is considered honourable. The historical memory of the *Selbstschutz* is not one of defiant glory, but one of tragedy linked to the near loss of a crucial part of Mennonite identity. As Dietrich Neufeld reflected, "A Mennonite who surrenders the fundamental idea of peace and affirms war has judged himself. He is henceforth no longer a Mennonite."[6] In an attempt to prevent the outward destruction of the colonies, an equally serious internal process of destruction was provoked by embracing armed self-defence. Still, *Selbstschutz* members rightfully considered their actions a desperate response to the brutal realities of civil war, namely to protect their communities from theft, murder, and rape.[7]

In the final analysis, while the *Selbstschutz* was able to hold off the Makhnovists at various moments, the sum effect was to confirm in the eyes of Makhno's supporters the colonies as a source of staunch resistance to their revolution. The *Selbstschutz* provided evidence for the stereotyped image of the Mennonite as a German or White collaborator, which proved a convenient rationalization for the increased terrorization of the colonies. House searches were justified on the basis of searching for weapons and hiding counter-revolutionaries. This is not to argue that the colonies would have escaped persecution—indeed, a massacre at the Borosenko colony appears to have not involved the *Selbstschutz* in any way.[8] However, the presence of the *Selbstschutz* and their ties to the German and White armies were important factors in the escalating cycle of violence.

The legacy of the *Selbstschutz* would continue to haunt the Mennonites, as when the Soviet chairman for the Ukrainian Committee for National Minorities toured the colonies in 1922. The chairman concluded that "the Mennonites represented a segment of the counter-revolutionary elements previously active in the south, particularly in view of the activities of the *Selbstschutz*." He further criticized the Mennonites for their "religious hypocrisy."[9] In the longer term, as historian John B. Toews concludes, "the fatal suspicion" aroused by the *Selbstschutz* negatively "affected the status of the Mennonites and Germans during the 1930s and again in World War II."[10]

A second Mennonite narrative representing a majority of emigré literature is the pacifist one, in which Makhno plays the role of God's punishing hand. According to this narrative, the terror is a consequence of the Mennonites' lack of faith and their attachment to materialism. For many, the massacres were interpreted as "a judgment upon the constituency for its disregard of a sacred principle."[11] The image of God is of one who metes out punishments and rewards based on the observance of certain strictures. Anton Sawatsky interpreted Eichenfeld from such a position: "The day of reckoning came for Eichenfeld because God could not leave their offence unpunished. But in his great mercy, God, who does not want the death of sinners but that they turn to Him and live, sent tent missionaries to Eichenfeld two days before this terrible night, giving them a chance in the last minute to repent and make right what they had wronged. . . . But those who died were not martyrs, but victims of God's judgment."[12] The terror is presented as a "purification" of the community, through which God intends to shepherd his flock back to the enclosure of the true faith. For Sawatsky and other pacifists, the *Selbstschutz* and Mennonite materialism were seen as roadblocks to the successful revival of the suffering church. The acceptance of a passive martyrdom would achieve God's forgiveness and ensure the community's survival. It is an extreme interpretation by today's secular standards, but it is one that carried significant weight at the time, as evidenced in the *Friedensstimme* editorials and its prevalence in many private reflections.

One might expect the pacifist narrative to have been sympathetic towards impoverished peasants given its close identification with the persecuted. Certainly, pacifists condemned the more excessive instances of abuse and exploitation and were known for their charity amongst the poor, but their critique of Mennonite society often remained highly metaphysical without interrogating the broader political and socio-economic forces at play. The writings of Dietrich Neufeld and David G. Rempel are important exceptions to the latter, displaying a deep knowledge and compassion for the peasants' socio-economic plights.

While most Mennonites did not physically oppose the revolutionary peasantry, the colonies' and estates' social organization remained inimical to the world of the peasant. As colonists, Mennonites were dependent on an imperial power for their special status, reliant on a master-servant economy, and in general culturally insular. To the more vengeful segments of the region's population, wealthy landowning Mennonites represented a privileged caste that prevented the peasants from accessing land they regarded as theirs.

Mennonite accounts from the period often seem unaware of the violence employed during the Russian Empire's eighteenth-century expansion into southern Ukraine or the socio-economic roots behind the hostilities they faced. Catherine the Great's invitation to the Mennonites seemed like a godsend in the face of Prussian persecution. In New Russia, an "empty" frontier was found where separation from the world could be maintained. However, in this very drive to avoid the secular world and create a peaceable community, the Mennonites found themselves embedded inside an imperial system that had imposed serfdom in the region and perpetuated stark socio-economic inequalities. The wealth and land acquired by Mennonites over the eighteenth and nineteenth centuries uniquely positioned them to draw the enmity of the neighbouring land-hungry peasant population. This was especially the situation after the serfs' emancipation, which brought wealthier Mennonites and Ukrainian peasants into direct economic relations. Mennonite economic success without cultural integration only quickened resentments as the widespread employment of peasant labourers acquired characteristics of a master-servant relationship. Largely unaware of the coming storm, the Mennonites built their commonwealth as an oasis in the dry steppe: a city on a hill for all to envy.

In the context of these systemic resentments and frustrations, violence found expression amidst the breakdown of civil society. For southern Ukraine's impoverished peasantry, the landowning Mennonite was both an immediate face of economic exploitation and an embodiment of a cultural "outsider." War and revolution facilitated the dissolution of law, and the revolutionary pursuit of justice through expropriation frequently gave way to vengeance and terror. In the absence of effective restraints, as was the case in late 1919, any action was possible, and even deemed necessary, to purge the enemy. The exterminationist rhetoric of Makhno against class enemies just days before the Eichenfeld massacre is illustrative of the degree to which Makhnovists had embraced terror as a legitimate tool to achieve their revolutionary objectives.

The Ukrainian tent missionary Astakhoff provides insight into the psychology of those possessed by a "logic" of terror. After a Makhnovist describes in detail how he and his comrades massacred a German family, Astakhoff asks in desperation: "Pray tell me what was the reason for all this horrible violence and bloodshed? What were your feelings when you mercilessly hacked to pieces men, women and innocent children?" The Makhnovist responds:

> The most ferocious beasts could not have acted worse; but we never realized what we did. Afterwards some feelings of pity and sorrow came into our hearts, but it was then too late! If there had been someone amongst us at those moments to have spoken a few quiet, reasonable words to calm us, it might have been different! For instance: I do not know what possesses me (and others will tell you the same) but in those moments of bloodshed there is neither pity, nor thought of consequences, but only the thirst for blood, and still more blood; although now I can speak, and think and reason.[13]

Unfortunately, it is often only in a state of mutual brokenness that intractable enemies are able to rehumanize each other. The pressure to make crude abstractions of the enemy is confronted by the reality of human suffering and, if for a moment, mutual understanding and even forgiveness is sometimes possible. During both the typhus outbreak of 1920 and the famine of 1921–22, many Mennonites practised forgiveness as they attended to ailing Makhnovists in the hospitals and relief committees. The memoirs of an anonymous *Selbstschutzler* serve as a poignant example. Following the typhus outbreak of 1920 he found himself under Red occupation and enlisted as a medic in the Red Army. He was posted to a hospital in Mykolaiv where, he writes, "Many Makhnovtse were brought in. It was an opportunity to practice love to my enemies. Many died."[14] Later he recounts how he was mistaken for a Makhnovist and sent to a camp in Siberia. In the camp he became the "best of friends" with a former Makhnovist named Ivan, with whom he successfully planned an escape.[15] The former *Selbstschutzler* eventually escaped the Soviet Union and made his way to Canada, as thousands of other Mennonites did throughout the 1920s.

The famous Zaporizhian oak tree is an apt symbol for both Ukrainians and Mennonites. Seven centuries old, the tree provided shelter for both the early Cossacks and the first Mennonite colonists. In the 1930s, when the Soviets decided to dam the Dnipro River, the process caused an abrupt rise in the water table, condemning the oak to a slow death through drowning. Today the tree is nearly dead, its largely leafless limbs supported by wired anchors. Yet, new beginnings are evident. Acorns of the old oak have been

Figure 26. Memorial to the Eichenfeld Massacre.

Figure 27. Memorial statue of Nestor Makhno in Huliaipole.

planted in many locations across North America, and in Ukraine shoots from the original oak are carefully tended in the hopes of growing a new tree for a new history.

In southern Ukraine today there is a growing awareness of the region's Mennonite heritage. Numerous memorials now dot the landscape, including one that is dedicated to the Eichenfeld massacre and maintained by Ukrainian residents from Novopetrivka. In Zaporizhia, as part of the decommunization process, the city council renamed five streets after Mennonites in 2016. Even in Huliaipole, amidst the bronze statues of Makhno, a plaque was recently installed on the former home of Jakob Kroeger, the owner of the agricultural machinery factory where Makhno worked as a youth.

By engaging with Makhno and his movement, I have attempted to decentre his role, to give him his due but nothing more. The interlocking and overlapping narratives of Makhnovists and Mennonites have been allowed to commingle and present a differently narrated landscape. Throughout my investigation I have come to see that more often than not the memories of Makhno are not the historical Makhno. Rather, they are the stories carried by us. Makhno certainly played his role in instigating a mass peasant insurgency that brought Makhnovists and Mennonites into a deadly conflict, but Makhno also frequently serves as a metonym through which cultural narratives are told, be it the revolutionary justice sought by anarchists or the suffering experienced by Mennonites. However, the conflict's roots extended far beyond Makhno's life, or even the immediacy of the civil war. Reflection on Makhnovist-Mennonite violence compels us to meditate not only upon the Russian colonization of southern Ukraine and the socioeconomic tensions it created, but also on how different peoples became entangled in this system and constructed powerful cultural narratives around it. These narratives—the stories through which Ukrainians and Mennonites lived—played a pivotal role in how events were understood and how violence was rationalized.

# ACKNOWLEDGEMENTS

This book could not have been accomplished without the many people who have assisted me over the years. Foremost I want to thank the University of Manitoba Press for their guidance and patience throughout the publishing process. I also want to acknowlege the generous support of the Canadian Foundation for Ukrainian Studies, which provided assistance in the form of a publishing grant.

I want to acknowledge Guy Lalande and Oleh Gerus for first setting me on the path of this book's subject matter. Likewise, I am especially grateful to Royden Loewen, Hans Werner, Kathleen Venema, Andriy Zayarnyuk, Heather Coleman, Nataliya Venger, Colin Neufeldt, Colin Darch, and two anonymous peer-reviewers for offering critical feedback and encouraging me in new directions.

Much of this book would not have been possible without help from the staff at the archives of the International Institute of Social History, the Mennonite Heritage Centre, the University of Toronto, the University of Michigan, and Harvard University. Invaluable sources were additionally provided by Marianne Janzen, Margie Koop, and Yuriy Kravetz. Ludmilla Karyaka, my Zaporizhian guide, also deserves a heartfelt thank you, as does the staff at the Huliaipole Local History Museum.

This book involved working with sources in French, German, Russian, and Ukrainian. I want to especially acknowledge Malcolm Archibald of Black Cat Press. He has generously helped me with many translations and drawn my attention to a wide range of sources. I met Malcolm early in my research on Makhno, and his passion for and extensive knowledge of anarchist history has proven a constant inspiration.

I also want to acknowledge Eldon Heinrichs and Marilyn Heidebrecht for sharing their families' stories with me. I wish to thank my father who first motivated me to write, seek all sides of a story, and pursue a life committed to peace and compassion. Finally, my wife Kelly Ruth deserves special mention for her ceaseless patience, inspirational conversations, and infectious creativity.

# NOTES

## A NOTE ON THE TEXT

1 For an extensive discussion of the use of the term Ukraine in the early modern period, see Ostras', "Zvidky pishla nazva 'Ukraina,'" 109–18.

2 Plokhy, *The Gates of Europe*, 38–39; Kappeler, "Great Russians and Little Russians," 14.

## INTRODUCTION

1 For more on this myth, see Skrypnyk, *Za zolotom Nestor Makhna*. The early Soviet historian M. Kubanin also mentions Makhno's buried gold, Kubanin, *Makhnovshchina*, 173.

2 Kropotkin, "Some of the Resources of Canada," 494–514. Kropotkin praised Mennonites for their cooperative and anti-statist tendencies, but criticised them for their embrace of private property. See also, Ivanov, *Kropotkin and Canada*.

3 The label "pacifist" for Mennonites who refused to take up arms is somewhat anachronistic. The word "pacifism" was first coined by Émile Artaud and adopted as an official term by the secular peace movement in 1901. However, the term is widely used in academic literature to describe Mennonite adherence to *Wehrlosigkeit*—sometimes translated as "defencelessness" or "nonresistance." In my use of the label "pacifist" I follow such Mennonite historians as John B. Toews, Lawrence Klippenstein, and Benjamin Goosen.

4 Makhno, "Mon Autobiographie," *Le Libertaire*, no. 61, June 4, 1926, 3; Berkman, *Bolshevik Myth*, 190–91. For an account of Huliaipole's Union of Poor Peasants that makes use of trial documents, see Novopolin, "Makhno i guliai-pol'skaia gruppa anarkhistov," 131–36.

5 Kropotkin, "Anarchist Communism," 46.

6 Kropotkin, "Preface to Bakunin's The Paris Commune and the Idea of the State," 237.

7 Kropotkin, "The Lyon Anarchist Trial of 1883," 207.

8 Kropotkin, "Anarchism," 287.

9 Ibid., 236.

10 For a discussion of the Anarchist-Communist tradition, see Turcato, "Anarchist Communism," 237–47. For Kropotkin's philosophy, see Kropotkin, *Mutual Aid*; Kropotkin, *The Conquest of Bread*. For commentary on Kropotkin, see Avrich,

*The Russian Anarchists*, 26–32; McKay, *Direct Struggle Against Capital*, 13–132. For commentary on Kropotkin's agrarian socialism, see Brian Morris, *Kropotkin*, 89–102. For the Russian debates over the revolutionary role of peasants and workers in the revolution, see Philip Pomper, *The Russian Revolutionary Intelligentsia*, 146–57

11 Makhno, "Mon Autobiographie," *Le Libertaire*, no. 64, 2 July 1926, 3.

12 Makhno, *Under the Blows of the Counterrevolution*, 113.

13 Makhno, *The Russian Revolution in Ukraine*, xi. For an archived letter dated May 1919 from Makhno to Kropotkin, see Makhno, *Under the Blows of the Counterrevolution*, 179.

14 Avrich, *The Russian Anarchists*, 215; Arshinov, *History of the Makhnovist Movement*, 241; *Rezoliutsii pervogo s'ezda Konfederatsii anarkhistiskikh organizatsii Ukrainy "Nabat,"* 18.

15 For the protocols of the second and fourth Makhnovist congresses, see Danilov and Shanin ed., *Nestor Makhno*, 70–91, 231–35; For the Makhnovist position on free soviets, see Skirda, *Nestor Makhno*, 371–72, 390–92. For commentary on the congresses see: Volin, *The Unknown Revolution*, 576–78, 594–95, 633–48; Arshinov, *History of the Makhnovist Movement*, 93–96, 152–153. For a Mennonite account of elections within Makhnovist-controlled territory, see Schroeder, *Miracles of Grace and Judgement*, 105–9.

16 Makhno, *The Russian Revolution*, 183–91; Arshinov, *History of the Makhnovist Movement*, 92–93; Volin, *The Unknown Revolution*, 574–75. The Soviet author Kubanin confirms, "This commune was created not only on paper, but existed in reality." He writes that the commune was previously an estate owned by a Mennonite named Klassen. It had 285 members in May 1919 and sowed 125 acres of land. Kubanin, *Makhnovshchina*, 60.

17 Skirda, *Nestor Makhno*, 374–75.

18 "Draft Declaration of the (Makhnovist) Revolutionary Insurgent Army of the Ukraine" in Skirda, *Nestor Makhno*, 368–80. Translated from a Bulgarian copy held at the International Institute for Social History in Amsterdam. A partial Russian copy is available in Verstiuk, ed., *Nestor Ivanovich Makhno*, 156–63. See also Makhnovist proclamations in Arshinov, *History of the Makhnovist Movement*, 257–75. For the original copies, see Ugo Fedeli Papers, Inventory No. 914, International Institute of Social History, Amsterdam. For extensive analyses on the Makhnovists' social and political activities, see Michael Malet, *Nestor Makhno*; Michael Palij, *The Anarchism of Nestor Makhno*; A. Shubin, *Anarkhistskii sotsialnyi eksperiment*; Skirda, *Nestor Makhno*.

19 Adams, "The Great Ukrainian Jacquerie," 253.

20 The Russian suffix *-shchina* does not have an English equivalent. It sometimes has a slightly negative connotation, but it roughly refers to a "movement" centred on a person or idea. I employ *Makhnovshchina* as a neutral term to indicate the movement formed by Nestor Makhno.

21 For literature on the Greens, see Radkey, *The Unknown Civil War*; Landis, *Bandits and Partisans*; Landis, "Who Were the 'Greens'?," 30–46.

22 See Dubovik and Rublev, *After Makhno*; Savchenko, "The Anarchist Movement in Ukraine at the Height of the New Economic Policy."

23 Nomad, *Apostles of Revolution*, 302–42.

24 For studies on the Mennonite *Selbstschutz*, see: Toews, "Origins and Activities of the Mennonite *Selbstschutz*," 5–39; Klippenstein, "*The Selbstschutz*"; Chipman, "Mennonite *Selbstschutz*."

25 Letkemann, "Mennonite Victims of Revolution," 2.

26 For example, Danilov and Shanin's 1,000-page collection of Makhnovist archival documents does not contain any references to the massacres.

27 Friesen, "Bartholomew Night," 5.

28 Volin's pseudonym roughly translates to "free man."

29 Volin, "Contribution aux études sur l'énigme de la personalité," 15–16.

30 Ricoeur, "The Human Experience of Time and Narrative," 106.

31 White, "The Historical Text as Literary Artifact," 223.

32 For example, see Skirda, *Nestor Makhno*, 337.

33 Makhno, "Zapiski Nestora Makhno," 28.

34 For works that address Imperial Russia's relationship to southern Ukraine from a post-colonial perspective see, Willard Sunderland, *Taming the Wild Field*; and Alexander Morrison, "Russian Settler Colonialism."

35 For an analysis of Mennonite social and economic development in Imperial Russia, see: Urry, *Mennonites, Politics, and Peoplehood*, chp. 4; Brandes, "German Colonists in Southern Ukraine," 10–28. Friesen presents a convincing argument that Mennonite economic success was premised on a combination of privileges granted by the Imperial authorities, Mennonite land tenure, and village size. Friesen, *Rural Revolutions*, 54–59.

36 For Mennonite and German land acquisition, see Friesen, *Rural Revolutions*, 129–35.

37 Kappeler, "Ukrainians and Germans," 45–68; James Urry, "Through the Eye of a Needle," 7–35.

38 Kappeler, "Ukrainians and Germans," 56; Friesen, *Rural Revolutions*, 221–22.

39 Kappeler, "Ukrainians and Germans," 56.

40 For works that address Imperial Russia's relationship to Ukraine from a post-colonial perspective see, Sutherland, *Taming the Wild Field*; Morrison, "Russian Settler Colonialism."

41 Kubanin, *Makhnovshchina*, 161, 182.

42 Belash, *Dorogi Nestora Makhno*, 346.

43 Danilov and Shanin, ed., *Nestor Makhno*, 90–91.

44 Skirda, *Nestor Makhno*, 374.

## CHAPTER 1 THROUGH MAKHNOVIST EYES

1 Makhno, "Mon Autobiographie," *Le Libertaire*, no. 71, 27 August 1926, 3.

2 Makhno, *Under the Blows*, 142.

3 Makhno, *Russian Revolution*, xii. Makhno's native language was most likely a Ukrainian steppe dialect; however, he learned to read and write Russian. One source claims Makhno said, "In that damn prison I completely forgot my native tongue." Cited in Palij, *Nestor Makhno*, 76.

4 Makhno, "A Few Words on the National Question in Ukraine," 24–27.

5 Sysyn, "Nestor Makhno," 303. For a discussion of Makhno's self-identity, see Masnenko, "Nestor Makhno: Ukraina."

6 Makhno, *Russian Revolution*, 103–4.

7 Makhno, *Under the Blows*, 166.

8 Makhno, *Russian Revolution*, 194–207.

9 In September 1919, a formal truce with the nationalists lasted four days during which the Makhnovists spread anti-nationalist propaganda and conspired to assassinate the nationalist leader Symon Petliura. Sysyn, "Nestor Makhno," 290–91; Arshinov, *Makhnovist Movement*, 143–44. Palij and Kubanin argue Makhno converted to nationalism in 1921. Palij, *Nestor Makhno*, 79; Kubanin, *Makhnovshchina*, 165–66. Makhno vehemently dismissed these charges in an extended rebuttal to Kubanin. Makhno, "Makhnovshchina i ee vcherashnie soiuzniki," 114–15. Sysyn also concludes "there is considerable cause to doubt Kubanin's charge." Sysyn, "Nestor Makhno," 292.

10 Danilov and Shanin, ed., *Nestor Makhno*, 88–89.

11 Volin, *The Unknown Revolution*, 701. The same proclamation is reproduced and provided an archival citation in Belash, *Dorogi Nestora Makhno*, 196–97.

12 Verstiuk, ed., *Nestor Ivanovich Makhno*, 155.

13 Skirda, *Nestor Makhno*, 377–78.

14 Roger, "Makhno: The Impressions of a French Journalist." In his article, Roger uses the Ukrainian toponym Molochansk for Halbstadt.

15 Toews, "Biography," 34–35.

16 For example, Rempel describes a Bolshevik Mennonite named Wall who Ukrainianized his name to Vallenko. He led an expropriation campaign in 1917 with other landless Mennonites in the Chortitza colony. Rempel, *Mennonite Family*, 187–88.

17 Friesen, "Bartholomew Night," 12.

18 Rempel, *Mennonite Family*, 185.

19 Ibid., 223.

20 Danilov and Shanin, ed., *Nestor Makhno*, 112.

21 Assotsiatsiia Rossiiskaia politicheskaia entsiklopediia, ed., *Anarkhisty*, 388.

22 Ibid., 388–89.

23 Skirda, *Facing the Enemy*, 121. For Arshinov's early memoirs, see Arshinov, *Dva pobega*.

24 Skirda, *Facing the Enemy*, 123; Avrich, *Russian Anarchists*, 204–9.

25 Avrich, *Russian Anarchists*, 205–6; Palij, *The Anarchism of Nestor Makhno*, 258–59.

26 For an English translation of the *Platform*, see Skirda, *Facing the Enemy*, 192–214.

27 Ibid., 136–49.

28 Malet, *Nestor Makhno,* 191; "Interview de Léo Voline," 24.

29 Avrich, *Russian Anarchists,* 241–43; Skirda, *Facing the Enemy,* 140–41; Rublev, "Russkiye anarkhisty v Ispanskoy grazhdanskoy voyne (1936–1939 gg.)," 226.

30 Arshinov, *History of the Makhnovist Movement,* 33.

31 Ibid.

32 Arshinov, *History of the Makhnovist Movement,* 34–35.

33 Arshinov briefly criticizes Makhno for tending towards "carelessness." He also states Makhno and the movement as a whole were underdeveloped in their grasp on political theory. Ibid., 221, 223, 235–36.

34 Avrich, *Anarchist Portraits,* 125–37. Paul Avrich provides a detailed biography of Volin, from which this brief sketch is derived.

35 Gorelik, Komov, and Volin, *Goneniia na anarkhizm v Sovetskoi Rossii.*

36 Volin, *Le Fascisme Rouge.*

37 Volin, "Contribution aux etudes sur l'énigme de la personnalité," 20–27. Volin's unpublished writings further explore Makhno's darker side, but they do not provide any verifiable accusations. Volin also discusses Makhno's close relationship with Kuzmenko in exile.

38 Makhno, *Miatezhnaia Iunost',* 11–67; Makhno, "Jeunesse," 23–71. Skirda's versions differ from the original texts. He appears to have created his own rendition by combining elements from the various versions. For this book, I have consulted the original French and German versions in full, and an incomplete copy of the original Russian in *Rassvet.* I footnote to the French version published in *Le Libertaire.*

39 Makhno also published a booklet entitled *Makhnovshchina i ee vchorashnie soiuzniki-Bol'sheviki,* which contains limited commentary on the years 1919 to 1921. It was written as a response to M. Kubanin's book *Makhnovshchina.* I employ it as a minor supplementary source.

40 Savchenko, *Makhno,* 401. Savchenko claims the German courts conducted a thorough investigation and Makhno was indicted for "pogroms and banditism," but no footnotes are provided. Skirda may be the first to have made this claim. He writes that Makhno was "arrested on charges of having persecuted German settlers in Ukraine." Skirda, *Nestor Makhno,* 408. I previously proposed such a scenario but have since reconsidered the evidence. Patterson, "The Eichenfeld Massacre,"151.

41 Group of Russian Anarchists Abroad, "Auf zum Protest," *Der Syndikalist,* No. 9, 28 February 1925, 1; Peters, *Nestor Makhno,* 90. Mennnonite historian Victor Peters interviewed Makhno's nurse, Sister Frieda Franz. Franz confirms Makhno was ill with tuberculosis, but she could not speak with him as he did not know German. Franz also says she was unaware of Makhno's notorious reputation until she later heard stories from Mennonite refugees.

42 Makhno, "Po povudu 'raz'iasneniia' Volina," 145–46.

43 Ibid., 146.

44 The letter is reproduced in Rublev, "Zhdu vizy, kakoi-libo vizy, s neterpeniem," 53–54.

45 Ibid., 54.

46 Letter from Alexander Berkman to Dr. M. Cohn, 16 September 1924.

47 Cited in Skirda, *Nestor Makhno*, 270–71.

48 Group of Russian Anarchists Abroad, "Auf zum Protest," *Der Syndikalist*, No. 9, 28 February 1925, 1.

49 Letter from Alexander Berkman to Dr. M. Cohn,16 September 1924.

50 S.N. Semanov, "Pod chernym znamenem," 32.

51 Cited in Malinovs'kii, "Zahin N. Makhna u druhii polovyni zhovtnia," 359.

52 Arshinov, *History of the Makhnovist Movement*, 68, 69–70.

53 Ialans'kyi and Ver'ovka, *Nestor i Halyna*, 431.

54 For Halyna's autobiographical account, see Semanov, "Pod chernym znamenem," 32–33.

55 Volin, "Contribution aux études sur l'énigme de la personalité," 17–18. According to Volin, on their first meeting Makhno scared Kuzmenko so much she hid in a closet before reluctantly accepting his advances.

56 Sukhorgorskaia, "Agafia Andreevna," in Verstiuk, ed., *Nestor Ivanovich Makhno*, 107; Semanov, "Pod chernym znamenem," 33. Sukhogorskaia mistakenly believed both parents were killed by the Whites.

57 Ibid., 106; Tsebry, *Memoirs of a Makhnovist Partisan*, 5.

58 Volin, "Contribution aux études sur l'énigme de la personalité," 20–26.

59 Semanov, "Pod chernym znamenem," 32–37.

60 Eideman, *Bor'ba s kulatskim*, 46–49.

61 Litvinov, "An Unsolved Mystery – The 'Diary of Makhno's Wife,'" 6–9.

62 Makhno, "Makhnovshchina i ee vcherashnie soyuzniki," 115–19; Arshinov, *History of the Makhnovist Movement*, 221.

63 Semanov, "Pod chernym znamenem," 24.

64 Ibid.

65 Ialans'kyi and Ver'kova, *Nestor i Halyna*, 374.

66 Ibid., 384; Eideman, *Bor'ba s kulatskim*, 48. Danilov and Shanin also suggest this entry was altered by Eideman. Danilov and Shanin, ed., *Nestor Makhno*, 34, footnote 30.

67 Eideman, *Bor'ba s kulakim*, 47.

68 Kuzmenko, "Shchodennyk Halyny Kuz'menko druzhyny Nestora Makhna," 612. The Russian translation found in Danilov and Shanin's document collection uses the equivalent vocabulary: *podvypil* and *nakhal'no*. Kuzmenko, "Dnevnik zheny N.I. Makhno Galiny Kuz'menko," 832.

69 For biographical information on Belash, see Arshinov, *History of the Makhnovist Movement*, 226.

70 Archibald, "Anarchist Renegade."

71 Danilov and Shanin, ed., *Nestor Makhno*, 716–24.

72 Chubenko, "Vospominaniia," 731–67. A translated English excerpt is found in Makhno, *The Ukrainian Revolution*, 196–205.

73 Danilov and Shanin, ed., *Nestor Makhno*, 601.

74 Ibid.

75 Chubenko, "Vospominaniia," 739.

76 Malynov'skyi, "Zahin N. Makhna u druhii polovyni zhovtnia," 357.

77 Sukhogorskaia, "Guliai-Pole v 1918 godu," 41.

78 Ibid.

79 Nestor's parents were Ivan Mikhnenko (later Makhno) and Evdokia Perederi. Ivan died when Makhno was an infant. His siblings were Polikarp, Omelian, Sava, and Hryhorii. Skirda, *Nestor Makhno*, 17; Semanov, "Pod chernym znamenem," 4.

80 Makhno, "Mon Autobiographie," *Le Libertaire*, no. 50, 19 March 1926, 2. Huliaipole was the capital of its own *volost* with a population of 16,151 in 1913. It was situated roughly ninety kilometres east of Oleksandrivsk. It had two orthodox churches, a synagogue, three schools, two flourmills, and two agricultural implement factories. The town was serviced by the Haichur railway station located seven kilometres west. Throughout the civil war Huliaipole exchanged hands some eighteen times. Malet, *Nestor Makhno*, xix; Peters, *Nestor Makhno*, 16–18.

81 Makhno, "Mon Autobiographie," *Le Libertaire*, no. 50, 19 March 1926, 2.

82 Ibid.

83 Ibid.

84 Arshinov, *History of the Makhnovist Movement*, 57.

85 Makhno, "Mon Autobiographie," *Le Libertaire*, no. 51, 21 March 1926, 2.

86 Ialans'kyi and Ver'ovka, *Nestor i Halyna*, 293–94.

87 Skirda's version of the text reads: "I had no other choice but to return to Janzen." Makhno, "Jeunesse," 27. This line appears to be Skirda's personal interpretation. It does not appear in any of the original texts. Makhno, "Mon Autobiographie," *Le Libertaire*, no. 51, 21 March 1926, 2.

88 Makhno, "Mon Autobiographie," *Le Libertaire* no. 51, 21 March 1926.

89 Ibid.

90 Ibid.

91 Makhno, "Mon Autobiographie," *Le Libertaire*, no. 52, 2 April 1926, 3.

92 Kappeler, "Ukrainians and Germans in Southern Ukraine," 55–56; Martin, "The Empire's New Frontiers," 184.

93 Urry, "Through the Eye of a Needle," 8.

94 For a detailed history of the Schönfeld settlement by one of its inhabitants, see Toews, *Schönfeld*.

95 Schapansky, "Origins of Mennonite Estates," 37; Reger and Plett, *Diese Steine*, 348.

96 A dessiatine was the most commonly used unit of area in Russia during this period. One dessiatine is equivalent to 2.7 acres or 1.1 hectares.

97 Huebert, *Mennonite Estates,* 188–89. Prior to the estate's division its average income was 100,000 rubles.

98 Urry, "Through the Eye of a Needle," 11.

99 Toews, *Schönfeld,* 24–26.

100 Ibid., 8.

101 Ibid., 13.

102 Darch, *The Makhnovshchina,* 144.

103 Ibid., 147.

104 Palij, *The Anarchism of Nestor Makhno,* 49.

105 Kappeler, "Ukrainians and Germans in Southern Ukraine," 54; Friesen, "Mennonites and their Peasant Neighbours," 60.

106 Kappeler, "Ukrainians and Germans in Southern Ukraine," 59.

107 Friesen, "Mennonites and their Peasant Neighbours," 63.

108 Urry, "Through the Eye of a Needle," 26–27.

109 Kappeler, "Ukrainians and Germans in Southern Ukraine," 60.

110 Ibid.

111 Urry, *Mennonites, Politics, and Peoplehood,* 116.

112 Palij, *The Anarchism of Nestor Makhno,* 50.

113 Ibid.

114 Ibid.

115 Makhno, "Mon Autobiographie," *Le Libertaire,* no. 52, 2 April 1926, 3.

116 Ibid.

117 Belash, *Dorogi Nestora Makhno,* 578, footnote 10.

118 Makhno, "Mon Autobiographie," *Le Libertaire,* no. 52, 2 April 1926, 3.

119 Makhno, "Mon Autobiographie," *Le Libertaire,* no. 53, 9 April 1926, 3. Belash also recalls these events. Belash, *Dorogi Nestora Makhno,* 13.

120 Makhno, "Mon Autobiographie," *Le Libertaire,* no. 53, 9 April 1926, 3.

121 Hosking, *Russia and the Russians,* 371; Pomper, *The Russian Revolutionary Intelligentsia,* 189.

122 Goosen, *Daydreams and Nightmares,* 21–26.

123 Kushnirenko and Zhylins'kyi, *Nestor Makhno i "Soiuz bidnykh khliborobiv,"* 56. The original document is held in the Huliaipole Local Museum's archives.

124 Belash, *Dorogi Nestora Makhno,* 19.

125 For Makhno's account of prison life, see Makhno, "Mon Autobiographie," *Le Libertaire,* nos. 62, 64–66, 68, 70–71, 73–75.

126 Makhno, *Russian Revolution in Ukraine*, 5.

127 Ibid., 5–6.

128 Ibid., 8.

129 Ibid., 30.

130 Ibid., 30, 31.

131 Ibid., 40.

132 Arshinov, *History of the Makhnovist Movement*, 60. According to Arshinov, peasant congresses in the Katerynoslav, Tavriia, Poltava, and Kharkiv provinces followed the example set by Huliaipole.

133 Makhno, *Russian Revolution in Ukraine*, 68.

134 Arshinov, *History of the Makhnovist Movement*, 60.

135 Malet, *Nestor Makhno in the Russian Civil War*, 120. The Klassen estate was located near Silberfeld. In early 1919, part of the Klassen estate was renamed the "Rosa Luxembourg Commune" in honour of the murdered German revolutionary. For more on the communes, see Belash, *Dorogi Nestora Makhno*, 21.

136 Makhno, *Russian Revolution in Ukraine*, 183.

137 Ibid., 184.

138 Ibid., 187.

139 Hunczak, "Ukraine Under Hetman Pavlo Skoropadskyi." For a focused study of the Ukrainian peasant rebellion and its various manifestations, see Adams, "The Great Ukrainian Jacquerie," 247–70.

140 Makhno, *The Ukrainian Revolution*, 18–22.

141 Arshinov, *History of the Makhnovist Movement*, 65.

142 Ibid., 67.

143 Makhno, *The Ukrainian Revolution*, 92–98. *Batko* is a traditional Ukrainian title indicating paternalistic respect and authority. In the context of the civil war it was a title commonly given to local military leaders. There is no direct English translation that communicates the title's full meaning, but it is most frequently translated as "little father." For a Mennonite description of the battle at Dibrivka, see J. Doerksen, "Aus deutschen Ansiedelungen," *Friedensstimme*, no. 71, 23 November 1918, 7–8.

144 Ibid., 111.

145 Ibid., 105.

146 Ibid., 112.

147 Ibid., 113.

148 Ibid.

149 According to an official report, a total of eighteen colonists were killed in the attack. The population at the time of the attack was seventy-five. Malynov'skyi, "Zahin N. Makhna u druhii polovyni zhovtnia," 357. Belash describes a similar attack on

"German colony no. 2," although chronologically places it before the burning of Velyka Mykhailivka. Belash, *Dorogi Nestora Makhno*, 36.

150 Makhno, *The Ukrainian Revolution*, 121.

151 Ibid., 132.

152 Ibid., 134–35. The same order is reproduced in an earlier writing published in 1923. Makhno, "Zapiski Nestora Makhno," 26.

153 Danilov and Shanin, ed., *Nestor Makhno*, 286–87.

154 Ibid., 52.

155 Makhno does not give colony #4's German or Russian name, but based upon his description in relation to other villages it can be determined he was describing the German Lutheran colony of Eigenheim [modern-day Lystivka].

156 Makhno, *The Ukrainian Revolution*, 172.

157 Ibid.

158 Ibid., 173. *Tachankas* were spring-loaded wagons often stolen from Mennonite farmers. The Makhnovists loaded machine guns on them to create improvised mobile artillery units.

159 Ibid., 174.

160 Arshinov, *History of the Makhnovist Movement*, 64.

161 Makhno, *The Ukrainian Revolution*, 98.

162 Alternative narratives of the battle of Dibrivka are present in Makhnovist literature. Arshinov presents a highly romanticized version of events, which excises the tension between vengeance and justice found in Makhno's narrative. See Arshinov, *History of the Makhnovist Movement*, 65–68. By contrast, Belash accuses Makhno of celebrating the destruction of Velyka Mykhailivka in the belief that it would encourage the peasantry to join his insurgency. See Belash, *Dorogi Nestora Makhno*, 38. This incident is also described by a peasant delegate from Velyka Mykhailivka in the protocols of the Makhnovists' second congress. He describes "German punitive units" carrying out a massacre and setting his village on fire. He states the village is in "dire need of financial assistance." Danilov and Shanin, ed., 75–76

163 Letkemann, "Mennonite Victims of Revolution," 2. Letkemann uses the Old Style calendar dates 26 October to 5 December.

164 Klippenstein, "The *Selbstschutz*," 61.

165 Arshinov, *History of the Makhnovist Movement*, 91.

166 Ibid., 99. For the White Army's relationship with anti-Semitism and pogroms, see Peter Kenez, "Pogroms and White Ideology in the Russian Civil War," 293–313.

167 For an analysis of the White-*Selbstschutz* relationship, see Klippenstein, "The *Selbstschutz*," 67–81.

168 Arshinov, *History of the Makhnovist Movement*, 98.

169 Ibid., 91.

170 Belash, *Dorogi Nestora Makhno*, 26.

171 Ibid.

172 Ibid., 27.

173 Belash, *Dorogi Nestora Makhno*, 110. Chubenko, "Vospominaniia," 739–40.

174 Belash, *Dorogi Nestora Makhno*, 189.

175 Chubenko, "Vospominaniia", 740.

176 Belash, *Dorogi Nestora Makhno*, 317.

177 Ibid., 188; Makhno, "Makhnovshchina i ee vcherashnie soiuzniki," 112–13.

178 Belash, *Dorogi Nestora Makhno*, 189.

179 Volin, *The Unknown Revolution*, 703.

180 Arshinov, *History of the Makhnovist Movement*, 147–48.

181 Belash, *Dorogi Nestora Makhno*, 349.

182 Makhno, "Makhnovshchina i ee vcherashnie soiuzniki,"124.

183 Arshinov writes that the RMS was established at the Second Regional Congress of Peasants, Workers, and Insurgents in February 1919. Its delegates represented thirty-two districts of the Katerynoslav and Tauride provinces and was to "carry out all the economic, political, social and military decisions made at the Congress, and thus was in a sense, the supreme executive organ of the movement." Arshinov, *History of the Makhnovist Movement*, 96.

184 Belash, *Dorogi Nestora Makhno*, 322.

185 Volin, *The Unknown Revolution*, 705.

186 Volin, "Contribution aux études sur l'énigme de la personalité," 13.

187 Letter from Ida Mett to Victor Peters, 1967.

188 Kuzmenko, "An Answer to the Article 'Pomer Makhno' in *Nova Pora*, September 9, 1934, Detroit, MI," 120–23.

189 Tsebry, *Memoirs of a Makhnovist Partisan*, 5.

190 Letter from Mark Mratchnyi to Peter Arshinov, 13 September 1925. Responses from Arshinov and Makhno are contained in the same collection, in which they refute Mratchnyi's charges.

191 Yelensky, "In the Social Tempest: Memoirs of the Russian Revolution."

192 Kuzmenko, "Shchodennyk Halyny Kuz'menko druzhyny Nestora Makhna," 612.

193 Ibid., 614–15.

194 Ibid., 615.

195 Volin, *The Unknown Revolution*, 571.

196 Belash, *Dorogi Nestora Makhno*, 607.

## CHAPTER 2 THROUGH MENNONITE EYES

1 This excerpt is from the description accompanying the clock at the Mennonite Heritage Centre in Winnipeg, MB.

2 Peters, *Nestor Makhno,* 53. In the German version of Peters's book the passage is also cited differently, although Wiens's details are excised rather than altered: "Als am 21. Januar die Nachtricht kam, dass der Selbstschutz der deutschen Siedler heranrücke, trafen Prawda und seine Gefolgschaft grosse Vorbereitungen zur Flucht. Alle Häuser wurden ausgeräumt. Es began die Abfahrt. Auch Frauen und Kinder waren dabei. Doch der Selbstschutz wurde geschlagen, worauf die ganze Bande zurückkehrte." Victor Peters, *Nestor Machno,* 43.

3 Letter from H.B. Wiens to Victor Peters, 7 November 1963, 5.

4 Klippenstein, "*The Selbstschutz,*" 61; Toews, "Origins and Activities of the Mennonite *Selbstschutz,*" 38–40.

5 Schroeder, *Miracles of Grace and Judgment,* 105.

6 For example, Malet notes his "sympathy with Makhno and his ideals." Malet, *Nestor Makhno,* ix. Palij's monograph is also largely uncritical of the movement.

7 Skirda, *Nestor Makhno,* 351.

8 Roden and Koop, "Janzens: From Tragedy in Russia to a New Life in Canada," 26–27.

9 Kroeker, "Wherein Lies Our Fault," 171–75; Kroeker, "Mennonites and Nonresistance," 177–78.

10 For more background on *Friedensstimme* see: Toews, "A Voice of Peace in Troubled Times," 93–94; Toews, "The Beginnings of *Friedensstimme,*" 1–2.

11 Urry, *Mennonites, Politics, and Peoplehood,* 3–4.

12 Ibid., 4.

13 For a full English translation of the decree, see March, *Cossacks of the Brotherhood,* 243–50.

14 Palij, *The Anarchism of Nestor Makhno,* 4.

15 Ibid., 47.

16 Friesen, *Rural Revolutions,* 30–31.

17 Martin, "The Empire's New Frontiers," 185.

18 Plokhy, *Gates of Europe,* 485–86.

19 For an exhaustive work on this period, see Friesen, *Rural Revolutions.*

20 Martin, "The Empire's New Frontiers," 187.

21 Krahn and Sawatzky, "Old Colony Mennonites."

22 Rempel, "The Mennonite Commonwealth in Russia," 259–308.

23 Lohrenz, *The Fateful Years,* 27.

24 For an English copy of the *Privilegium,* see Rempel, *A Mennonite Family,* 263–65.

25 Brandes, "German Colonists in Southern Ukraine", 17; Toews, *The Russian Mennonite Story,* 27.

26 Friesen, *Rural Revolutions*, 51–52, 57.

27 Ibid., 91.

28 Ibid.

29 Urry, *Mennonites, Politics, Peoplehood*, 88.

30 Urry, "Through the Eye of a Needle," 15–16.

31 Friesen, *Rural Revolutions*, 180–82.

32 Staples, "On Civilizing the Nogai," 229–56; Huebert, *Mennonite Estates*, 294; Urry, *Mennonites, Politics, and Peoplehood*, 93.

33 Lohrenz, *Storm Tossed*, 17.

34 Neufeldt, "'We are Aware of Our Contradictions,'" 132.

35 Urry, "Through the Eye of a Needle," 17.

36 For an account of the civil war through the eyes of a young Mennonite female servant, see Baerg, *Diary of Anna Baerg*.

37 Friesen, *Rural Revolutions*, 57–58.

38 Darch notes that unlike the Russian peasant commune, the most common land tenure practices in southern Ukraine were neither fully communal nor private but hybrid in practice. Only 14 percent of peasant villages followed a fully communal model. However, under both systems allotments were divided as families grew, which resulted in diminishing landholdings. Darch, "Makhnovshchina," 131–32, 134.

39 Friesen, *Rural Revolutions*, 129–33; Urry, *Mennonites, Politics, and People*, 96, 104.

40 Loewen, *Jasykowo*, 9; Derzhavnyi arkhiv Zaporiz'koi oblast' (DAZO), f. 1, op. 1, spr. 59, ark. 160.

41 Neufeld, *Russian Dance of Death*, 77.

42 Lohrenz, *Storm Tossed*, 50.

43 Numerous examples of workers saving their Mennonite employers' lives are recounted in "Ueber die schaurige Mordgeschichte bei Schönfeld," *Friedenstimme*, no. 74, 4 December 1918, 7; Toews, "Biography," 14.

44 Toews, "Biography," 8.

45 Ibid., 12–13.

46 Ibid.

47 "Unsere Anarchisten," *Friedensstimme*, no. 18, 4 May 1918, 5.

48 Toews, "Biography," 9.

49 Lohrenz, *Storm Tossed*, 53.

50 Letter from H.B. Wiens to Victor Peters, 7 November 1963, 1.

51 Neufeld, *Russian Dance of Death*, 78.

52 Kappeler, *The Russian Empire*, 238–42.

53 Urry, *Mennonites, Politics, and Peoplehood*, 96–100.

54 Ibid., 83.

55 Ibid., 107–9.

56 Martin, "The Empire's New Frontiers," 190–93; Urry, *Mennonites, Politics, and Peoplehood*, 106–7.

57 Ibid., 131.

58 Neufeld, *Russian Dance of Death*, 78.

59 Lohr, "Patriotic Violence and the State: The Moscow Riots of May 1915," 607–26.

60 Dyck, *Troubles and Triumphs*, 13.

61 J. Friesen, "Bestrafung wegen Deutschsprechens," *Molotschnaer Flugblatt*, 12 August 1917, 7; Kroeker, *Unsere Brüder in Not*, 40–44.

62 Dyck, *Troubles and Triumphs*, 23.

63 Lohrenz, *Stormed Tossed*, 55–56.

64 Neufeld, *Russian Dance of Death*, 78.

65 Toews, "Biography of Jacob Cornelius Toews," 15.

66 Ibid.

67 Urry, *Mennonites, Politics, and Peoplehood*, 132.

68 For a detailed study of the *Hollanderei* debate, see Friesen, *In Defense of Privilege*, 192–250, 271–302.

69 Dyck, *Troubles and Triumphs*, 22.

70 Loewen, *Jasykowo*, 58.

71 Cited in Toews, "Origins and Activities of the Mennonite *Selbstschutz*," 15, footnote 1.

72 Reimer, "How Did it Happen?," 163.

73 Citied in Friesen, *Defense of Privilege*, 466.

74 For example, see "Die Bande Machno," *Friedensstimme*, no. 70, 19 November 1918, 4; "Über die schaurige Mordgeschichte bei Schönfeld," *Friedensstimme*, no. 75, 4 December 1918, 7; "Wie man sich bettet, so liegt man," *Friedenstimme*, no. 75, 7 December 1918, 7. Sixty-eight murders in total were ascribed to the autumn Makhnovist raids. "Aus deutschen Ansiedlungen," *Friedensstimme*, no. 21, 12 July 1919, 7.

75 "Ein bewaffneter Überfall und ein grauenhafter Mord," *Friedensstimme*, no. 65, 2 November, 1918, 7; J. Doerksen, "Aus deutschen Ansiedlungen," *Friedensstimme*, no. 71, 23 November 1918, 7.

76 "Von der Bande Machno," *Friedensstimme*, no. 71, 23 November 1918, 7.

77 For one of the first reports of rape by Makhnovists, see "Das Räuberwesen in dem Alexandrowsker Kreise setzt sich fort," *Friedensstimme*, no. 78, 18 December 1918, 8. Another report mentions the murder of a Russian noble and the rape of his wife and daughter. "Neue Opfer des Räuberunwesens im Alexandrowsker Kreis," *Friedensstimme*, no. 74, 4 December 1918, 7.

78 Cited in Toews, *Czars, Mennonites and Soviets*, 84.

79 Lohrenz, *Fire Over Zagradovka*, 33.

80 Ibid.

81 Ibid., 33–34.

82 Inal, "The Production of Rape as a Weapon," 3–4.

83 Ibid., 4.

84 Klippenstein, "The *Selbstschutz*," 8.

85 "Nachruf," *Volksfreund*, no. 20, 18 May 1918, 2. *Friedensstimme* was renamed *Volksfreund* during the Austro-German occupation.

86 Cited in Toews, "Origins and Activities of the Mennonite *Selbstschutz*," 15.

87 Toews, "Biography of Jacob Cornelius Toews," 26. Toews witnessed the execution of this entire unit during the Bolshevik retreat from the Austro-Germans in April 1918.

88 See "Lichtenau Conference June 30, July 1, 2, 1918," in Toews, ed., *The Mennonites in Russia*, 404–27.

89 *Friedensstimme*, 27 July 1918, 4–6. The newspaper reports of "compulsory military service" for German colonists and the establishment of armed self-defence units in Sagradovka.

90 "Was du säst, sollst du ernten," *Friedensstimme*, 18 December 1919, 7.

91 "Aus deutschen Ansiedelungen," *Friedensstimme*, 2 July 1918, 6.

92 Makhno, *The Ukrainian Revolution*, 19–20.

93 Toews, *Czars, Mennonites and Soviets*, 82.

94 Toews, "Biography," 27.

95 Ibid.

96 Ibid.

97 Urry and Loewen, "Protecting Mammon," 45.

98 Dueck, "Breaking Bread in a Barn," 14. This may not have been the author's intent, but as a literary effect, "the Makhno" evokes images of a dark, impersonal force.

99 Konrad, *Red Quarter Moon*, 116.

100 Bender, "Theology of Martyrdom."

101 Stauffer, "The Anabaptist Theology," 187.

102 Ibid., 180.

103 Ibid.

104 Ibid., 199.

105 Ibid., 189.

106 Ibid., 184.

107 Ibid., 205.

108 "Die Diktatur des Proletariats," *Friedensstimme*, no 34, 14 September 1919, 7.

109 C. Orosander, "Warum geschieht uns solches?" *Friedensstimme*, no. 42, 14 December 1919, 1.

110 A. Kroeker, "Unsere Befreiung," *Friedensstimme*, 27 April 1918, 1.

111 Reimer, "How Did it Happen?" 166.

112 Pacifists employed this same argument of collective sinfulness provoking divine punishment during the 1870s military service crisis. See Urry, *Mennonites, Politics, Peoplehood*, 97.

113 "Ihr sollt euch nicht Schätze sammeln," *Friedensstimme*, 2 November 1918, 2.

114 Hermann Neufeld, "Die Zeit der Heimsuchung," *Friedensstimme*, no. 31, 4 August 1919, 3.

115 C. Orosander, "Warum geschieht uns solches?" *Friedensstimme*, no. 43, 21 December 1919, 1.

116 Neufeld, *Russian Dance of Death*, 79–80.

117 Reimer, "How Did it Happen?," 166–67.

118 A notable exception is Dietrich Neufeld, who offers insightful commentary on the socio-economic roots of the 1919 massacres. See Neufeld's analysis of the Sagradovka massacre in Neufeld, *Russian Dance of Death*, 65–88.

119 Lohrenz, *Storm Tossed*, 22.

120 Kroeker, "Ein mennonitischer Revolutionär," *Friedensstimme*, no. 5, 24 January 1918, 8.

121 Neufeldt, "'We are Aware of Our Contradictions,'" 134–35.

122 Neufeld, *Russian Dance of Death*, 18.

123 Epp, "A Time of Darkness," 46; Toews, *Mennonite Marytrs*, 142.

124 Schroeder, *Miracles of Grace and Judgment*, 71.

125 Roden and Koop, "Janzens," 26–27.

126 Genealogical Registry and Database of Mennonite Ancestry, "Abram J. Janzen #365724," California Mennonite Historical Society; Khniaz'kov, *Zaporiz'ka oblast*, 179–80; Huebert, *Mennonite Estates*, 188–89.

127 Ibid.

128 *Friedenstimme*, 3 August 1918, 9.

129 Makhno, *The Russian Revolution*, 181.

130 Roden and Koop, "Janzens," 26.

131 Ibid.

132 Peters, *Nestor Makhno*, 32; Letter from Anna Goerz to Victor Peters, n.d., 2–3.

133 Ibid. In 1912 Ebenfeld is listed as jointly owned by Jakob Neufeld and G. Klassen. Huebert, *Mennonite Estates*, 37.

134 Schroeder, *Miracles of Grace and Judgment*, 40. A raid on the Ebenfeld estate is described in *Friedensstimme*, no. 65, 2 November 1918, 7. Chubenko's memoir also briefly mentions a raid on a "very wealthy German, Neufeld (a deaf man)." Chubenko, "Vospominaniia," 734.

135 Schroeder, *Miracles of Grace and Judgment*, 45–46.

136 Neufeld, *Russian Dance of Death*, 31.

137 Letter from H.B. Wiens to Victor Peters, 7 November 1963, 9–10; Schroeder, *Miracles of Grace and Judgment*, 118–21.

138 Neufeld, *Russian Dance of Death*, 45.

139 Makhno, *Ukrainian Revolution*, 154. The passage notes the Makhnovist Army Staff's intention to hand over the front near Orikhiv to Pravda.

140 Belash, *Dorogi Nestora Makhno*, 48.

141 Letter from H.B. Wiens to Victor Peters, 7 November 1963, 11.

142 Ibid., 3.

143 Ibid., 4.

144 Ibid., 11.

145 Schroeder, *Miracles of Grace and Judgment*, 93.

146 Ibid., 101. This incident is also described in Rempel, *A Mennonite Family*, 221.

147 Peters, "Petersdorf," 160.

148 Ibid., 161–62.

149 Dyck, "Breaking the Silence," 98.

150 Arshinov, *History of the Makhnovist Movement*, 147–48.

## CHAPTER 3 THE EICHENFELD MASSACRE

1 For a full list of victims, see Dyck, Staples, and Toews, eds., *Nestor Makhno and the Eichenfeld Massacre*, 105–12.

2 Ibid., 33.

3 Skirda, *Nestor Makhno*, 337.

4 Dyck, Staples, and Toews, eds., *Nestor Makhno and the Eichenfeld Massacre*, 79, 80.

5 For a typical Soviet perspective on Makhno, see Iaroslavskii, *History of Anarchism in Russia*, Chapter 5.

6 The memorial at Eichenfeld also uses the Old Style date of 26 October. Dyck, Staples, and Toews, eds., *Nestor Makhno and the Eichenfeld Massacre*, 113.

7 Belash, *Dorogi Nestora Makhno*, 317.

8 Venger, "Nestor Makhno ta "nimets'ke pytannia" na ukrains'kykh zemliakh,"49. Beznosov likewise dates the massacre to 26 October without clarifying the calendar issue. He attributes the attack to a "reconnaissance unit" retreating south from Katerynoslav. Although how Beznosov arrives at this scenario is unclear. Beznosov, "Die Nikolaipoler Mennonitensiedlungen," 11.

9 Belash, *Dorogi Nestora Makhno*, 313.

10 Neufeld, *Russian Dance of Death*, 12, 14.

11 Ibid., 25. Rempel's account of the same events also gives the date September 21. The guards were Rempel's former classmates named Andres and Kroeger. Andres survived and later emigrated to Canada. Rempel, *A Mennonite Family*, 221–22; Rempel, "I Too Was There," 4.

12 Krahn, "Yazykovo Mennonite Settlement"; Loewen, *Jasykowo*, 9.

13 Beznosov, "Die Nikolaipoler Mennonitensiedlungen," 2.

14 DAZO, f. F-59, op. 1, spr. 10.

15 Beznosov, "Die Nikolaipoler Mennonitensiedlungen," 2.

16 Nikolaifeld/Nikolaipol (#1); Franzfeld/Varvarovka (#2); Adelsheim/Dolinovka (#3); Eichenfeld/Dubovka (#4); Hochfeld/Morosovo (#5). Mennonite estates included Petersdorf, Reinfeld, and Paulheim. Toews, ed., *Mennonites in Ukraine*, 151.

17 Vogt, "Liste der Mennonitischen Industrie- und Handelsunternehmen in Russland."

18 Rempel, *A Mennonite Family*, 72, 294.

19 Ibid., 157.

20 Beznosov, "Die Nikolaipoler Mennonitensiedlungen," 3–4.

21 Malynov'skyi and Malynov'skaya, "Nemtsy-zemlevladel'tsy v sotsial'nyn konflitakh," 136–37.

22 Beznosov, "Die Nikolaipoler Mennonitensiedlungen," 4.

23 Ibid., 5–6.

24 Dyck, "One Who Was There," 147; Letter from Cornelius Heinrichs to Marianne Janzen, n.d. Sawatsky, "Reminiscences," 151; Beznosov, "Die Nikolaipoler Mennonitensiedlungen," 6; "Chortitzer Gebiet, August 1919," *Friedensstimme*, no. 32, 7 September 1919, 3.

25 Dyck, "One Who Was There," 147.

26 Letter from Cornelius Heinrichs to Marianne Janzen, n.d.

27 "Chortitzer Gebiet, August 1919," *Friedensstimme*, no. 35, 18 September 1919, 3.

28 Loewen, *Jasykowo*, 61.

29 Heinrichs, "From the Diary of Heinrich Heinrichs," 1.

30 Sawatsky, "Reminiscences," 152. While Sawatsky was not an eyewitness to the massacre, he was intermittently present in Jasykowo and was in close contact with the wife of Peter van Kampen.

31 "Die Bande Machno," *Friedensstimme*, no. 70, 19 November 1918, 4.

32 Penner, "Report on Adelsheim," 149.

33 Belash, *Dorogi Nestor Makhno*, 340.

34 Beznosov, "Die Nikolaipoler Mennonitensiedlungen," 7.

35 Loewen, *Jasykowo*, 63.

36 Dyck, "One Who Was There," 147.

37 Letter from Cornelius Heinrichs to Marianne Janzen, n.d.

38 Beznosov, "Die Nikolaipoler Mennonitensiedlungen," 7–8.

39 Ibid., 8.

40 Loewen, Dyck, and Heinrichs recall this event as occurring in July 1919. However, according to Beznosov the Nikolaipol district was under White occupation during this period. Archived Soviet reports date the incident to mid-February 1919. Rempel also

notes that there "must be a confusion of dates" as the attack could not have occurred in the summer. Rempel, "I Too Was There," 4.

41 Letter from Cornelius to Marianne Janzen, n.d. Dyck claims *no Selbstschutzler* were lost. Dyck, "One Who Was There," 147.

42 Ibid.

43 Letter from Cornelius Heinrichs to Marianne Janzen, n.d.

44 Ibid.

45 Ibid.

46 Beznosov, "Die Nikolaipoler Mennonitensiedlungen," 8.

47 Dyck, "One Who Was There," 147.

48 Letter from Cornelius Heinrichs to Marianne Janzen, n.d.

49 Klippenstein, "Recollections," 2.

50 Letter from Cornelius Heinrichs to Marianne Janzen, n.d.; Dyck, "One Who Was There," 149; Beznosov, "Die Nikolaipoler Mennonitensiedlungen," 10. David Rempel, the cousin of H.H. Heinrichs, also writes that "rumours about Eichenfeld's self-defence units complicity in this act of revenge were true." Rempel, "I Too Was There," 3.

51 Epp, *But God Hath Chosen*, 10–11.

52 Beznosov, "Die Nikolaipoler Mennonitensiedlungen," 10.

53 Rempel writes that Heinrichs hid at his grandmother's and uncle's home in Rosenthal, Chortitza. Rempel, "I Too Was There," 3; Heinrichs, "From the Diary of Heinrich Heinrichs," 1. Heinrichs joined the White Army after his flight from Eichenfeld. In 1921 he immigrated to the United States, where he worked for the Ford Motor Company. He died in Detroit in 1941.

54 Penner, "Report on Adelsheim," 150.

55 Loewen, *Jasykowo*, 64.

56 Rempel, "I Too Was There," 3.

57 Ibid., 4.

58 For a first-hand account of this regiment, see Al'mendinger, "Simferopol'skii ofetserskii polk v boiakh protiv makhnotsev," 72–76.

59 Palij, *The Anarchism of Nestor Makhno*, 195; A.V. Bipetskii, "Bor'ba s Makhno v raione Aleksandrovska," 773.

60 Arshinov, *History of the Makhnovist Movement*, 148.

61 Belash, *Dorogi Nestora Makhno*, 342; Loewen, *Jasykowo*, 69–70. According to Belash, Makhno himself was delirious with typhus by early January 1920. Volin was captured by the Red Army while sick with the disease. Volin, "Volin raz'iasnenie," 135–36.

62 Malet, *Nestor Makhno*, 91–92.

63 Rempel, *A Mennonite Family*, 222.

64 Danilov and Shanin, eds., *Nestor Makhno*, 257.

65 Cited in Koval'chuk, *Bez peremozhtsiv*, 148.

66 Azarov, *Kontrrazvedka*, 24.

67 Cited in Kovalchuk, "Borot'ba povstankoi armii N. Makhna," 30.

68 Skirda, ed., *Mémoires et Écrits*, 484.

69 Koval'chuk, *Bez permozhtsiv*, 148. See also Makhno's orders on army discipline between 9 October and 18 November 1919 in Skirda, ed., *Mémoires et Écrits*, 484–86.

70 Danilov and Shanin, eds., *Nestor Makhno*, 261–62.

71 Azarov, *Kontrrazvedka*, 25; Verstiuk, ed., *Nestor Makhno*, 161.

72 Ibid.

73 Cited in Azarov, *Kontrrazvedka*, 27.

74 Kubanin, *Makhnovshchina*, 116. Both Makhno and Volin challenged the testimonial's authenticity. Makhno, "Makhnovshchina i ee vchorashnie soiuzniki," 123; Volin, "Volin raz'iasnenie,"139.

75 Makhno, "Makhnovshchina i ee vchorashnie soiuzniki", 124.

76 Rempel, *A Mennonite Family*, 230–31.

77 Ibid., 229.

78 Neufeld, *Russian Dance of Death*, 38.

79 Schroeder, *Miracles of Grace and Judgment*, 115.

80 Belash, *Dorogi Nestora Makhno*, 330.

81 Loewen, *Jasykowo*, 66. See also Rempel, "I Too was There," 5.

82 Belash, *Dorogi Nestora Makhno*, 334.

83 Ibid., 331.

84 Belash, *Dorogi Nestora Makhno*, 333. The 1st Calvary Brigade was commanded by Feodir Shchus according to Makhnovist documents from February 1920. Danilov and Shanin, ed., *Nestor Makhno*, 305–6. Belash's account is corroborated by an order from 9 November, which emphasizes the importance of recapturing Katerynoslav and dispatches a cavalry unit along the road passing through Jasykowo. Danilov and Shanin, ed., *Nestor Makhno*, 255–56.

85 Belash dates Kayternoslav's recapture to 11–12 November. Belash, *Dorogi Nestora Makhno*, 336–39. Historian Volkovinskii, using Soviet newspapers, gives the date 9–10 November. Volkovinskii, *Makhno i ego krakh*, 138. A Soviet report states the city was retaken 9 November and held by Makhno until 9 December. Konovets, "1919 god v Ekaterinoslave i Aleksandrovske," 90.

86 Loewen, *Jasykowo*, 44. Loewen describes "an invalid with wooden legs" as the unit's leader.

87 Bipetskii, "Bor'ba s Makhno," 794.

88 Belash, *Dorogi Nestora Makhno*, 331.

89 Ibid.

90 Ibid, 331–32.

91 Neufeld, *Russian Dance of Death*, 38.

92 Ibid., 43.

93 Neufeld's diary dates the massacre to 24 October (6 November, New Style). This suggests he either initially entered the wrong date or retroactively added it incorrectly. Regardless, Neufeld's description of the massacre corresponds with other reports. Ibid., 44–46.

94 Astakhoff, *Interesting Facts*, 103.

95 Hildebrand, "Eichenfeld," 1.

96 Ibid.

97 Ibid.

98 Epp, *God Hath Chosen*, 13.

99 Martens, "A Night of Horror," 68.

100 Dyck, Staples, and Toews, ed., *Nestor Makhno*, 82–83.

101 Cited in Golovanov, *Nestor Makhno*, 357.

102 Bipetskii, "Bor'ba s Makhno v raione Aleksandrovska," 79

103 Klassen, "Remembrances of Eichenfeld," 1.

104 Ibid.

105 Epp, *God Hath Chosen*, 14.

106 Martens, "A Night of Horror," 70.

107 Quiring, "The Days of Terror," 144.

108 Ibid., 145.

109 Friesen, "Bartholomew Night," 8.

110 Dombrowsky, "Something Out of My Life," 1.

111 Dyck, Staples, and Toews, ed., *Nestor Makhno*, 84.

112 Berg, "Reflections and Recollections on Blumenort," 117–18.

113 Neufeld, "The Days of Terror in Blumenort, Halbstadt Volost," 112.

114 Janz, "We Have Sinned," 118. J.N. Wittenberg also identifies Konovalov as the perpetrator of a massacre the previous month in Altonau, Molotschna colony. Wittenberg, "Some Highlights on the Murderous Day in Altonau," 123.

115 Danilov and Shanin, ed., *Nestor Makhno*, 272–73.

116 Ibid., 299–300.

117 Belash, *Dorogi Nestora Makhno*, 339. The existing archival trail likewise gives no indication Makhno left Katerynoslav during this period. Minutes from a meeting of the Revolutionary Military Soviet confirm Makhno's presence in Katerynoslav on 20 November. A detailed order signed by Makhno in Katerynoslav on 2 December also references a resolution signed by himself and the Revolutionary Military Soviet on 30 November. Danilov and Shanin, ed., *Nestor Makhno*, 279; 274. See also two Bolshevik

reports that describe Makhno's occupation of Katerynoslav. Konovets, "1919 god v Ekaterinoslave i Aleksandrovske," 89–103.

118 Belash, *Dorogi Nestora Makhno*, 360–64; Volin, *Unknown Revolution*, 632.

119 Palij, *The Anarchism of Nestor Makhno*, 202.

120 Volin, *The Unknown Revolution*, 648.

121 An archived White Army leaflet states Makhno was forced to evacuate Katerynoslav on 25 November (Old Style)/7 December (New Style). Danilov and Shanin, ed., *Nestor Makhno*, 244. Volin writes that the evacuation occurred at the end of November (New Style). He is either mistaken, or his statement suggests the withdrawal began late in the month and continued over a number of days. Volin, *The Unknown Revolution*, 632.

122 Schroeder, *Miracles of Grace and Judgment*, 116.

123 Neufeld, "Eichenfeld Massacre," 1.

124 Friesen, "Bartholomew Night," 11.

125 Epp, *God Hath Chosen*, 15.

126 Schroeder, *Miracles of Grace and Judgment*, 86.

127 Rempel, "I Too Was There," 5, 6.

128 Ibid., 15.

129 Friesen, "Bartholomew Night," 26.

130 Ibid., 12.

131 Warkentin, "Eichenfeld," 1.

132 Friesen, "Bartholomew Night," 13.

133 Quiring, "The Days of Terror," 146.

134 Astakhoff, *Interesting Facts*, 117. The Russian version of Astakhoff's text specifically identifies these German-speakers as "from Mennonite communities" (ot menonitskikh obshchin). Astakhoff, *Palatochnaia missiia*, 66–67.

135 Beznosov, "Kolonistskoe naselenie i vooruzhennaia bor'ba na iuge Ukrainy," 73.

136 DAZO, f. P-337, op. 1, spr. 74, ark. 181; Rempel, *A Mennonite Family*, 228, 242, 248.

137 Ibid., 242.

138 Goosen, "The Makhno Bands in Zagradovka," 140.

139 Rempel, *A Mennonite Family*, 242.

140 Ibid. Rempel defines *Nippaenja* as a slightly derogatory term for those that lived at the end of the village that housed the landless (*Anwohner*) and renters (*Einwohner*). Ibid., 121.

141 See also Rempel, "Mennonite Revolutionaries in the Khortitza Settlement."

142 For an argument that the massacres should be considered ethnic pogroms, see Venger, "Nestor Makhno ta 'nimets'ke pytannia'"; Venger, "Yevreis' kit a menonits' ki pohromy na pivdni ukrayini." By contrast for a thesis that agrees with the one articulated in this book, see Mikhail Akulov, "Playground of Violence: Mennonites and Makhnovites in the Time of War and Revolution."

143 Epp, "A Time of Darkness," 47.

144 Bipetskii, "Bor'ba s Makhno," 781–82.

145 Quiring, "The Days of Terror," 144–46.

146 Peters, *Nestor Makhno*, 106–7. Beznosov comes to a similar conclusion noting that at Eichenfeld "fatalities, for the most part, came from wealthy families." He also argues the Makhnovists' primary motivation was to deter the *Selbstschutz* and collectively punish the colony's collaboration with the Austro-German occupation and White Army. Beznosov, "Die Nikolaipoler Mennonitensiedlungen," 12.

147 This assessment mirrors Neufeld's conclusions regarding the local context of the Sagradowka massacre. Neufeld, *Russian Dance of Death*, 77–78.

148 Rempel, "I Too Was There," 1.

149 DAZO, f. 59, op. 1, spr. 1, ark. 160,

150 Unpublished Eichenfelder's Diary. Name withheld at the request of the family. Copy in author's possession.

151 Thornton, "Terror as a Weapon of Political Agitation," 73.

152 Mayer, *The Furies*, 87.

153 A systematic investigation of the Sagradowka massacre is needed but these broad conclusions can be stated with confidence based on the currently available sources. Neufeld, *Russian Dance of Death*, 65–88; Toews, ed., *Mennonites in Ukraine*, 126–39; Lohrenz, *Zagradowka*, 89–101.

## CONCLUSION

1 Mayer, *The Furies*, 102.

2 Ibid.

3 Cited in Beznosov, "Za 'Heimatland,'" 15.

4 See in particular Gerhard Lohrenz's semi-fictional novel *The Fateful Years*.

5 Interview with Henry J. Regehr, Oral History Russian Mennonite Migration 1920s, Inventory No. 170, Mennonite Archives of Ontario.

6 Neufeld, *Russian Dance of Death*, 80.

7 Also see interviews with *Selbstschutzler* and pacifists in *And When They Shall Ask* [1983].

8 "Report from the Makhnovile Era," 155–57.

9 Cited in Toews, *Tsars, Mennonites and Soviets*, 104–5; 202.

10 Ibid., 93.

11 Ibid., 95.

12 Sawatsky, "*Selbstschutz* or Self-Defence," 3.

13 Astakhoff, *Interesting Facts*, 115–16.

14 Unpublished *Selbstschutzler* memoir. Name withheld at request of the family. Copy in author's possession.

15 Ibid.

# BIBLIOGRAPHY


### ARCHIVES AND PERSONAL FILES

Alexander Berkman Papers. International Institute of Social History. Amsterdam, Netherlands.

Boris Yelensky Papers. International Institute of Social History. Amsterdam, Netherlands.

David G. Rempel Papers. Thomas Fisher Rare Book Library, University of Toronto. Toronto, ON.

Derzhavnyi arkhiv Zaporiz'koi oblast' (DAZO), Zaporizhia, Ukraine.

*Friedensstimme* Newspaper, 1917–1920. Centre for Mennonite Brethren Studies. Winnipeg, MB.

Marianne Janzen Collection. Personal files. Winnipeg, MB.

Mark Mratchnyi Papers. Special Collections, University of Michigan. Ann Arbour, MI.

Oral History Russian Mennonite Migration 1920s. Mennonite Archives of Ontario, Conrad Grebel University. Waterloo, ON.

Ugo Fedeli Papers. International Institute of Social History. Amsterdam, Netherlands.

Vernon Richards Papers. International Institute of Social History. Amsterdam, Netherlands.

Victor Peters Papers. Ukrainian Research Institute, Harvard University. Cambridge, MA.

Volin Papers. International Institute of Social History. Amsterdam, Netherlands.

### PRIMARY SOURCES

Al'mendinger, V. "Simferopol'skii ofetserskii polk v boiakh protiv makhnotsev (avgust-sentiabr' 1919 g)." In *Nestor Ivanovich Makhno. Vospominaniia, materialy i dokumenty,* edited by V.F. Verstiuk, 72–76. Kyiv: RIF "Dzin," 1991.

Arshinov, Peter. *History of the Makhnovist Movement 1918–1921*. Translated by Lorraine and Fredy Perlman. Detroit: Black and Red, 1974.

———. *Dva pobega: Iz vospominanii anarkhista 1906–9 gg.* Paris: Delo Truda, 1929.

———. *Organizatsionnaia platforma vseobschego soiuza anarkhistov (proekt).* In *Anarkhisty. Dokumenty i materialy. Tom 2, 1917–1935 gg.*, edited by V.V. Kriven'kii, et al., 471–93. Moscow: ROSSPEN, 1999.

Baerg, Anna. *Diary of Anna Baerg: 1916–1924*. Translated and edited by Gerald Nicolas Peters. Winnipeg: CMBC Publications, 1985.

Belash, Viktor. *Dorogi Nestora Makhno*. Kyiv: REC "Proza," 1993.

Berg, Abram. "Reflections and Recollections on Blumenort." In *Mennonites in Ukraine Amid Civil War and Anarchy (1917–1920): A Documentary Collection*, translated and edited by John B. Toews, 113–18. Fresno: Center for Mennonite Brethren Studies, 2013.

Berkman, Alexander. *The Bolshevik Myth (Diary 1920–1922)*. New York: Boni and Liveright, 1925.

Bipetskii, A.V. "Bor'ba s Makhno v raione Aleksandrovska." In *Nestor Makhno. Krest'ianskoe dvizhenie na Ukraine*. 1918—1921, edited by V. Danilov and T. Shanin, 772–822. Moscow: ROSSPEN, 2006.

Chubenko, Aleksei. "Vospominaniia o N.I. Makhno. Dnevnik Alekseia Chubenko (ad'iutanta Makhno)." In *Nestor Makhno. Krest'ianskoe dvizhenie na Ukraine. 1918—1921*, edited by V. Danilov and T. Shanin, 731–67. Moscow: ROSSPEN, 2006.

Danilov, V., and Teodor Shanin, eds. *Nestor Makhno: Krest'ianskoe dvizhenie na Ukraine. 1918–1921, Dokumenty i materialy*. Moscow: ROSSPEN, 2006.

Dombrowsky, Abram. "Something Out of My Life." Translated by Marianne Janzen. Marianne Janzen Collection. Copy in author's possession.

Dueck, Jack. "Breaking Bread in a Barn." *Canadian Mennonite* 13, no. 9 (27 April 2009): 14.

Dyck, Jacob A. "One Who Was There." In *Mennonites in Ukraine Amid Civil War and Anarchy (1917–1920)*, translated and edited by John B. Toews, 147–48. Fresno: Center for Mennonite Brethren Studies, 2013.

Dyck, Peter J. *Troubles and Triumphs, 1914–1924: Excerpts from the Diary of Peter J. Dyck. Ladekopp, Molotschna Colony, Ukraine*. Edited by John P. Dyck. Springstein, MB: Self-published, 1981.

Eideman, R.P. *Bor'ba s kulatskim povstanchestom i banditizmom*. Kharkiv, 1921.

Konovets (Grishuta). "1919 god v Ekaterinoslave Aleksandrovske." *Letopis' Revoliutsii* 4 (1925): 74–103.

Epp, Issac. "A Time of Darkness." In *Nestor Makhno and the Eichenfeld Massacre*, translated and edited by Harvey L. Dyck, John R. Staples, and John B. Toews, 45–52. Kitchener, ON: Pandora Press, 2004.

Friesen, Heinrich. "Bartholomew Night in Eichenfeld." Translated by Arthur Toews. Volume 645, file 7, Mennonite Heritage Archives, Winnipeg, MB, Canada.

Goosen Friesen, Helena. *Daydreams and Nightmares: Life on the Wintergruen Estate*. Winnipeg: CMBC Publications, 1990.

Goosen, P. "The Makhno Bands in Zagradovka." In *Mennonites in Ukraine Amid Civil War and Anarchy*, translated and edited by John B. Toews, 139–40. Fresno: Center for Mennonite Studies, 2013.

Group of Russian Anarchists Abroad. "Auf zum Protest gegen die Inhaftierung Machnos." *Der Syndykalist*, No. 9, 28 February 1925.

Heinrichs, Heinrich H. "From the Diary of Heinrich Heinrichs." Marianne Janzen Collection. Copy in author's possession.

Hildebrand, Katherina. "Eichenfeld—The Diary of Katherina Hildebrand." Translated and edited by Jacob Rempel and Veralyn Warkentin. Marianne Janzen Collection. Copy in author's possession.

Interview with Henry J. Regehr. Oral History Russian Mennonite Migration 1920s, Inventory No. 170. Mennonite Archives of Ontario, Conrad Grebel College. Waterloo, ON, Canada.

Janz, B.B. "We Have Sinned." In *Mennonites in Ukraine Amid Civil War and Anarchy (1917–1920): A Documentary Collection*, translated and edited by John B. Toews, 118–22. Fresno: Center for Mennonite Brethren Studies, 2013.

Klassen, H.W. "Remembrances of Eichenfeld-Dubovka Jasykovo 1919." Translated by Marianne Janzen. Marianne Janzen Collection. Copy in author's possession.

Klippenstein, Susanna Warkentin. "Recollections." Marianne Janzen Collection. Copy in author's possession.

Kriven'kii, V.V., et al., ed. *Anarkhisty: dokumenty i materialy. Tom 2, 1917–1935 gg.* Moscow: ROSSPEN, 1999.

Kroeker, Abraham. "Mennonites and Nonresistance." In *Mennonites in Ukraine Amid Civil War and Anarchy (1917–1920)*, translated and edited by John B. Toews, 177–78. Fresno: Center for Mennonite Brethren Studies, 2013.

———. "Wherein Lies Our Fault?" In *Mennonites in Ukraine Amid Civil War and Anarchy (1917–1920)*, translated and edited by John B. Toews, 171–75. Fresno: Center for Mennonite Brethren Studies, 2013.

Kuzmenko, Halyna. "An Answer to the Article 'Pomer Makhno' in *Nova Pora*, September 9, 1934, Detroit, MI." In *Nestor Makhno: The Life of an Anarchist*, translated by Victor Peters, 120–23. Winnipeg: Echo Books, 1970.

———. "Shchodennyk Halyny Kuz'menko druzhyny Nestora Makhna." In *Nestor Makhno. Spovid' anarkhista*, edited by Mykola Holovatyi, 606–22. Kyiv: TOV "Knyha Rodu", 2008.

Letter from Alexander Berkman to Dr. M. Cohn, 16 September 1924, folder 14, Alexander Berkman Papers, International Institute of Social History, Amsterdam, Netherlands.

Letter from Anna Goerz to Victor Peters, n.d., series 2, Victor Peters Papers, Ukrainian Research Institute, Harvard University. Cambridge, MA.

Letter from Cornelius Heinrichs to Marianne Janzen, n.d., Marianne Janzen Collection. Copy in author's possession.

Letter from H.B. Wiens to Victor Peters, 7 November 1963, series 2, Victor Peters Papers, Ukrainian Research Institute, Harvard University. Cambridge, MA.

Letter from Ida Mett to Victor Peters, 1967, series 1, Victor Peters Papers, Ukrainian Research Institute, Harvard University. Cambridge, MA.

Letter from Mark Mratchnyi to Peter Arshinov, 13 September 1925, box 1, folder 1, Mark Mratchnyi Papers, Special Collections, University of Michigan. Ann Arbour, MI.

Lohrenz, Gerhard. *Storm Tossed: The Personal Story of a Mennonite From Russia.* Winnipeg: Lohrenz, 1976.

Makhno, Nestor. *Mémoires et Écrits: 1917–1932.* Translated and edited by Alexandre Skirda. Paris: Ivrea, 2009.

———. "A Few Words on the National Question in the Ukraine." In *The Struggle Against the State and Other Essays,* edited by Alexandre Skirda, 24–27. San Francisco: AK Press, 1996.

———. "Jeunesse." In *Mémoire et Écrits, 1917–1932,* edited by Alexandre Skirda, 23–71. Paris: Éditions Ivrea, 2009.

———. *Miatezhnaia iunost'.* Translated and edited by Alexandre Skirda. Paris: Hromada, 2006.

———. "Makhnovshchina i ee vcherashnie soiuzniki—Bolsheviki." In *Na Chuzhbine 1923–1934 gg. Zapiski i stat'i,* edited by Alexandre Skirda, 102–33. Paris: Hromada, 2004.

———. "Meine Autobiographie." *Der freie Arbeiter* (Berlin), nos. 34–48 (1927).

———. "Mon autobiographie." *Le Libertaire* (Paris), nos. 50–59, 61–62, 64–66, 68, 70–71 (1926).

———. "Moia avtobiografiia." *Rassvet* (New York), no. 493–502 (1926).

———. "Po povudu 'raz'iasneniia' Volina," In *Na Chuzhbine 1923–1934 gg. Zapiski i stat'i,* edited by Alexandre Skirda, 140–46.

———. *Nestor Makhno. Spovid' anarkhista,* edited by Mykola Holovatyi. Kyiv: TOV "Knyha Rodu," 2008.

———. *The Struggle Against the State and Other Essays.* Translated and edited by Alexandre Skirda. San Francisco: AK Press, 1996.

———. *The Russian Revolution in Ukraine.* Translated by Malcolm Archibald. Edmonton: Black Cat Press, 2009.

———. *The Ukrainian Revolution.* Translation by Will Firth and Malcolm Archibald. Edmonton: Black Cat Press, 2011.

———. *Under the Blows of the Counterrevolution: April–June 1918.* Translated by Malcolm Archibald. Edmonton: Black Cat Press, 2009.

———. "Zapiski Nestora Makhno." In *Na Chuzhbine 1923–1934 gg. Zapiski i stat'i,* edited by Alexandre Skirda, 9–30. Paris: Hromada, 2004.

Makhnovist Proclamations, Inventory No. 914, Ugo Fedeli Papers. International Institute of Social History, Amsterdam.

Martens, Helena Harder, and Katherina Harder Paetkau. "A Night of Horror, as told by Two Sisters." In *Nestor Makhno and the Eichenfeld Massacre,* edited by Harvey L. Dyck, John R. Staples, and John B. Toews, 67–71.

Neufeld, Dietrich. *A Russian Dance of Death: Revolution and Civil War in the Ukraine.* Translated and edited by Al Reimer. Winnipeg: Hyperion Press, 1977.

Neufeld, Jakob. "The Days of Terror in Blumenort, Halbstadt Volost." In *Mennonites in Ukraine Amid Civil War and Anarchy (1917–1920): A Documentary Collection,* translated and edited by John B. Toews, 155–57. Fresno: Center for Mennonite Brethren Studies, 2013.

Penner, David. "Report on Adelsheim." In *Mennonites in Ukraine Amid Civil War and Anarchy (1917–1920)*, translated and edited by John B. Toews, 149–51. Fresno: Center for Mennonite Brethren Studies, 2013.

Peters, Maria. "Petersdorf." In *Jasykowo: Mennonite Colony on the Dnieper*, translated by Jakob B. Klassen, 155–63. Beausejour, MB: The Standard Press, 1995.

*Proekt-Deklaratsiia na revoliutsionno-vuzstanicheskata armiia v ukraina (makhnovtsi)*. Sofia: Edison, 1921. Copy held at the International Insitute of Social History, Amsterdam, Netherlands.

Quiring, David. "The Days of Terror in the Village of Eichenfeld, South Russia, in October 1919." In *Mennonites in Ukraine Amid Civil War and Anarchy (1917–1920)*, translated and edited by John B. Toews, 140–47. Fresno: Center for Mennonite Brethern Studies, 2013.

Reimer, Adolf A. "How Did it Happen?" In *Mennonites in Ukraine Amid Civil War and Anarchy (1917–1920)*, translated and edited by John B. Toews, 160–71. Fresno: Center for Mennonite Brethren Studies, 2013.

Rempel, David G. "I Too Was There, And Mead I Drank: An Analysis and Commentary on the Mennonite Film 'And When They Shall Ask.'" Box 22, Folder 10–12, David G. Rempel Papers, Thomas Fisher Rare Book Library, University of Toronto. An edited version is published in *Preservings* 21 (December 2002): 25–27.

———. *A Mennonite Family in Tsarist Russia and the Soviet Union, 1789–1923*. Edited by Cornelia Rempel Carlson. Toronto: University of Toronto Press, 2011.

"Report from the Makhnovite Era by One Who Was There." In *Mennonites in Ukraine Amid Civil War and Anarchy (1917–1920): A Documentary Collection*, translated and edited by John B. Toews, 110–13. Fresno: Center for Mennonite Brethren Studies, 2013.

*Rezoliutsii pervogo s'ezda Konfederatsii anarkhistiskikh organizatsii Ukrainy "Nabat" (sostoiavshegosia v g. Elisavetgrade 2-7 aprelia 1919 g.)*. Rabochei gruppy v Resp. Argentine, 1923. Copy held at the International Institute of Social History, Amsterdam, Netherlands.

Roger, Stéphane. "Makhno. Vpechatleniya odnogo frantsuzskogo publitsista." In *Nestor Makhno. Krest'yanskoye dvizheniye na Ukraine. 1918–1921: Dokumenty i materialy*, edited by V. Danilov and T. Shanin, 142–43. Moscow: ROSSPEN, 2006. Available online: "Makhno: The Impressions of a French Journalist." 1919. Translated by Malcolm Archibald. *Libcom.org*. http://libcom.org/history/makhno-impressions-french-journalist-st%C3%A9phane-roger (accessed 2019).

Rublev, D.I., ed. "'Zhdu vizy, kakoi-libo vizy, s neterpeniem!' Pis'ma Nestora Makhno, 1924–1925 gg." *Istoricheskii Arkhiv* 4 (2016): 51–66.

Sawatsky, Anton. "Reminiscences." In *Mennonites in Ukraine Amid Civil War and Anarchy (1917–1920)*, translated and edited by John B. Toews, 151–55. Fresno: Center for Mennonite Brethren Studies, 2013.

———. "Selbstschutz or Self-Defence or A Black Spot on Our History." Translated by Peter J. Dyck. Marianne Janzen Collection. Copy in author's possession.

Saloff-Astakhoff, N.I. *Interesting Facts of the Russian Revolution, or In the Flame of Russia's Revolution with God and the Bible*. New York: 164 Second Ave, 1931.

———. *Palatochnaia missiia*. Kyiv: Tsentr khrystyians'koi spivpratsi, 2000.

Schroeder, Gerhard P. *Miracles of Grace and Judgment*. Edited by David G. Rempel, Gordon Ginn, and Joan P. Rowe. Lodi, CA: Gerhard P. Schroeder, 1974.

Toews, Aron A., ed., *Mennonite Martyrs: People Who Suffered for Their Faith, 1920–1940*. Translated by John B. Toews. Winnipeg: Kindred Press, 1990.

Toews, Gerhard. *Schönfeld: Werde- und Opfergang einer deutschen Siedlung in der Ukraine*. Winnipeg: Rundschau Publishing House, 1939.

Toews, Heinrich. *Eichenfeld-Dubowka, ein Tatsachenbericht aus der Tragödie des Deutschtums in der Ukraine*. Karlsruhe: H. Schneider, 1938.

Toews, Jacob. "Biography of Jacob Cornelius Toews 1882–1968." Translated by Frieda Toews. EKMHA Collections, Essex-Kent Mennonite Historical Association, Leamington, ON, Canada.

Verstiuk, V., ed. *Nestor Ivanovich Makhno. Vospominaniya, materialy i dokumenty*. Kyiv: RIF "Dzvin," 1991.

Volin.*The Unknown Revolution 1917–1921*. Translated by Holley Cantine and Fredy Perlman. Montreal: Black Rose Books, 1975.

———. "Contribution aux études sur l'énigme de la personalité." Inventory no. 166, Vernon Richards Papers, International Institute of Social History, Amsterdam, Netherlands.

Warkentin, Elizabeth Harder. "Eichenfeld." Marianne Janzen Collection. Copy in author's possession.

Wittenberg, J.N. "Some Highlights on the Murderous Day in Altonau in October, 1919." In *Mennonites in Ukraine Amid Civil War and Anarchy (1917–1920): A Documentary Collection*, translated and edited by John B. Toews, 122–23. Fresno: Center for Mennonite Brethren Studies, 2013.

Yelensky, Boris. "In the Social Tempest: Memoirs of the Russian Revolution," folder 100–101, Boris Yelensky Papers, International Institute of Social History, Amsterdam, Netherlands. https://libcom.org/library/memoirs-russian-revolution-boris-yelensky (accessed 2019).

## SECONDARY SOURCES

Adams, Arthur E. "The Great Ukrainian Jacquerie." In *The Ukraine, 1917–1921: A Study in Revolution*, edited by Taras Hunczak, 247–70. Cambridge: Harvard University Press, 1977.

Akulov, Mikhail. "Playground of Violence: Mennonites and Makhnovites in the Time of War and Revolution." *International Relations and Diplomacy* 3, no. 7 (July 2015): 439–47.

*And When They Shall Ask*. Directed by John Morrow and produced by David Dueck. Winnipeg: David Dueck Film Productions, 1984. DVD.

Archibald, Malcolm. "Anarchist Renegade: Victor Belash in Tashkent." Kate Sharpley Library, February 2015. http://www.katesharpleylibrary.net/31zdp5 (accessed 2019).

Avrich, Paul. *Anarchist Portraits*. Princeton: Princeton University Press, 1988.

———. *The Russian Anarchists*. Oakland: AK Press, 2005.

Azarov, V. *Kontrrazvedka: The Story of the Makhnovist Intelligence Unit*. Edmonton: Black Cat Press, 2008.

Bender, Harold S. "Theology of Martyrdom." *Global Anabaptist Mennonite Encyclopedia Online*. 1959. http://www.gameo.org/encyclopedia/contents/T546.html (accessed 2019).

Beznosov, A.I. "Die Nikolaipoler Mennonitensiedlungen in den Jahren des Bürgerkriegs (1918–1920)." Translated by Lars Nehrhoff. Nord-Ost Institut. 2019. https://www.ikgn.de/cms/index.php/uebersetzte-geschichte/beitraege/beznosov-die-nikolaipoler-mennonitensiedlungen (accessed 2019).

———. "Kolonistskoe naselenie i vooruzhennaia bor'ba na iuge Ukrainy (konets 1918 – osen' 1919 gg.)." In *Voprosy germanskoy istorii*, edited by Svetlana Bobyleva, 71–96. Dnepropetrovsk: RVV DNU, 2005.

Beznosov, O. "Za 'Heimatland': zbroini formuvannia nimets'kykh kolonistiv ta menonitiv Pivdnya Ukrayiny (1918–1921 rr.)." *Viis'kovo-istorychnyi al'manakh* 22 (2011): 7–23.

Brandes, Detlef. "German Colonists in Southern Ukraine Up to the Repeal of the Colonial Statute." In *German-Ukrainian Relations in Historical Perspective*, edited by Hans-Joachim Torke and John-Paul Himka, 10–28. Edmonton: Canadian Institute of Ukrainian Studies, 1994.

Chipman, Josephine. "The Mennonite *Selbstschutz* in the Ukraine: 1918–1919." Master's thesis, University of Manitoba, 1988.

Darch, Colin Major. "The Makhnovshchina, 1917–1921: Ideology, Nationalism, and Peasant Insurgency in Early Twentieth Century Ukraine." PhD diss., University of Bradford, 1994.

Dubovik, Anatoly V., and D.I. Rublev. *After Makhno: Hidden Histories of Anarchism in the Ukraine*. Translated by Szarapow. London: Kate Sharpley Library, 2009.

Dyck, Harvey L. "Breaking the Silence: *Aussiedler* Images of the Soviet Mennonite Tragedy." *Journal of Mennonite Studies* 16 (January 1998): 97–100.

Dyck, Harvey L., John R. Staples, and John B. Toews, eds. *Nestor Makhno and the Eichenfeld Massacre: A Civil War Tragedy in a Ukrainian Mennonite Village*. Kitchener: Pandora Press, 2004.

Epp, Margaret. *But God Hath Chosen . . . : The Story of John and Mary Dyck*. North Newton, KS: Mennonite Press, 1963.

Friesen, Abraham. *In Defense of Privilege: Russian Mennonites and the State Before and During World War I*. Winnipeg: Kindred Productions, 2006.

Friesen, Leonard. *Rural Revolutions in Southern Ukraine: Peasants, Nobles and Colonists, 1774–1905*. Cambridge: Harvard University Press, 2008.

———. "Mennonites and their Peasant Neighbours in Ukraine Before 1900." *Journal of Mennonite Studies* 10 (1992): 56–69.

Golovanov, Vasilii. *Nestor Makhno*. Moscow: Molodaia gvardiia, 2013.

Gorelik, A., A. Komov, and Volin. *Goneniia na anarkhizm v Sovetskoi Rossii*. Berlin: Gruppy russkikh anarkhistov v Germanii, 1922.

Hosking, Geoffrey. *Russia and the Russians: A History*. Cambridge: Harvard University Press, 2011.

Huebert, Helmut. *Mennonite Estates in Imperial Russia*. Winnipeg: Springfield Publishers, 2005.

Hunczak, Taras, ed. "Ukraine Under Hetman Pavlo Skoropadskyi." In *The Ukraine, 1917–1921: A Study in Revolution*, edited by Taras Hunczak, 71–75. Cambridge: Harvard University Press, 1977.

Ialans'kyi, Viktor, and Larysa Ver'ovka. *Nestor i Halyna: rozpovidaiut' fotokartky*. Kyiv: Vydannia zhurnalu "Iarmarok," 1999.

Iaroslavskii, Emel'ian. *History of Anarchism in Russia*. New York: International Publishers, 1937.

Inal, Tuba. "The Production of Rape as a Weapon in the Making of 'Just' Wars." In *Rape Cultures and Survivors: An International Perspective*, volume two, edited by Tuba Inal and Merril D. Smith, 1–24. Santa Barbara: Praeger, 2018.

"Interview de Léo Voline," *Itinéraire* 13 (1996): 21–24.

Ivanov, Alexey G. *Kropotkin and Canada*. Translated by Malcolm Archibald. Edmonton: Black Cat Press, 2020.

Janzen, Marianne. "The Story of Eichenfeld." Unpublished manuscript. Term Paper, University of Winnipeg, 1991. Copy in author's possession. The paper was published in an edited version as "The Eichenfeld Massacre – October 26, 1919," *Preservings* 18 (2001): 25–31.

Kappeler, Andreas. "Ukrainians and Germans in Southern Ukraine, 1870s to 1914." In *German-Ukrainian Relations in Historical Perspective*, edited by Hans-Joachim Torke and John-Paul Himka, 45–68. Edmonton: Canadian Institute of Ukrainian Studies Press, 1994.

———. *'Great Russians' and 'Little Russians': Russian-Ukrainian Relations and Perceptions in Historical Perspective*. Seattle: University of Washington, 2003.

Kenez, Peter. "Pogroms and White Ideology in the Russian Civil War." In *Pogroms: Anti-Jewish Violence in Modern Russian History*, edited by John D. Klier and Shlomo Lambroza, 293–313. New York: Cambridge University Press, 2004.

Klippenstein, Lawrence. "The *Selbstschutz*: A Mennonite Army in Ukraine: 1918–1919." In *History and Mission in Europe: Continuing the Conversation*, edited by Mary Raber and Peter Penner, 49–106. Schwarzenfeld: Neufeld Verlag, 2011.

Kniaz'kov, Iurii Petrovych. *Zaporiz'ka oblast:istoryko-heohrafichnyi i toponimichnyi slovnyk*. Zaporizhia: Tandem, 2004.

Konrad, Anne. *Red Quarter Moon: A Search for Family in the Shadow of Stalin*. Toronto: University of Toronto Press, 2012.

Koval'chuk, Mykhailo. *Bez peremozhtsiv. Povstans'kyi rukh v Ukraini proty bilohvardiis'kykh viis'k henerala A. Denikina (cherven' 1919 r. – liutyi 1920 r.)*. Kyiv: Stylius, 2012.

———. "Borot'ba povstankoi armii N. Makhna proty bilohrafdiis'kykh viis'k generala A. Denikina v lystopadi – hrudni 1919 r.," *Kyivska starovyna* 4 (2010): 79–95.

Krahn, Cornelius. "Yazykovo Mennonite Settlement (Zaporizhia Oblast, Ukraine)." *Global Anabaptist Mennonite Encyclopedia Online*. 1959. https://www.gameo.org/index.php?title=Yazykovo_Mennonite_Settlement_(Zaporizhia_Oblast,_Ukraine), (accessed 2019).

Krahn, Cornelius, and H. Leonard Sawatzky. "Old Colony Mennonites." 1990. *Global Anabaptist Mennonite Encyclopedia Online*, http://www.gameo.org/encyclopedia/contents/O533ME.html (accessed 2019).

Kroeker, Abraham. *Unsere Brüder in Not: Bilder vom Leidensweg der Deutschen Kolonisten in Russland*. Striegau: Verlag von Theodor Urban, 1930.

———. *Bilder aus Sowjet-Russland*. Striegau: Verlag von Theodor Urban, 1930.

Kropotkin, Peter. "Anarchism." In *Direct Struggle Against Capital: A Peter Kropotkin Anthology*, edited by Iain McKay, 287–306. Oakland: AK Press, 2014.

———. "Anarchist Communism." In *Kropotkin's Revolutionary Pamphlets*, edited by Roger N. Baldwin, 44–78. New York: Dover Publications, 1970.

———. *Mutual Aid: A Factor of Evolution*. New York: Dover Publications, 2006.

———. "Preface to Bakunin's The Paris Commune and the Idea of the State." In *Direct Struggle Against Capital: A Peter Kropotkin Anthology*, edited by Iain McKay, 231–42. Oakland: AK Press, 2014.

———. "Some of the Resources of Canada." *The Nineteenth Century*, March 1898.

———. *The Conquest of Bread*. London: Penguin Books, 2015.

———. "The Lyon Anarchist Trial of 1883." In *Direct Struggle Against Capital: A Peter Kropotkin Anthology*, edited by Iain McKay, 201–8. Oakland: AK Press, 2014.

Kubanin, M. *Makhnovshchina. Krest'ianskoe dvizhenie v stepnoi Ukraine v gody grazhdanskoi voiny*. Leningrad: Priboi, 1927.

Kushnirenko, Ivan, and Volodymyr Zhylins'kyi. *Nestor Makhno i "Soiuz bidnykh khliborobiv."* Zaporizhia: "Dniprovs'kyi Metalurh," 2010.

Landis, Erik c. *Bandits and Partisans: The Antonov Movement in the Russian Civil War*. Pittsburgh: University of Pittsburgh, 2008.

———. "Who Were the 'Greens'? Rumor and Collective Identity in the Russian Civil War." *Russian Review* 69, no.1 (2010): 30–46.

Letkemann, Peter. "Mennonite Victims of Revolution, Anarchy, Civil War, Disease and Famine, 1917–1923." *Mennonite Historian* 24, no. 2 (1998): 1–2, 9.

Litvinov, V.N. "Neraskrytaia taina 'dnevnika zheny Makhno," *Obshchina* 43 (1990): 6–9. Available online: "An Unsolved Mystery – The 'Diary of Makhno's Wife.'" Translated by Malcolm Archibald. *Nestor Makhno Archive*. http://www.nestormakhno.info/english/litvinov-diary.htm (accessed 2019).

Loewen, Harry H., and James Urry. "Protecting Mammon: Some Dilemmas of Mennonite Nonresistance in Late Imperial Russia and the Origins of the *Selbstschutz*." *Journal of Mennonite Studies* 9 (1991): 34–53.

Loewen, J.A., and W.J. Prieb. "The Abuse of Power Among Mennonites in South Russia 1789–1919." *Journal of Mennonite Studies* 14 (1996): 17–44.

Loewen, Julius. *Jasykowo: Mennonite Colony on the Dnieper*. Translated by Jakob B. Klassen, Beausejour, MB: The Standard Press, 1995.

Lohr, Eric. "Patriotic Violence and the State: The Moscow Riots of May 1915." *Kritika: Explorations in Russian and Eurasian History* 4.3 (2003): 607–26.

Lohrenz, Gerhard. *The Fateful Years, 1913–1923: The Story of a Young Mennonite of Southern Russia, in the Forestry Service, in a Red Cross Unit, and in the Selbstschutz (Self-Defence) Movement*. Winnipeg: Lohrenz, 1970.

———. *Fire over Zagradovka*. Steinbach: Lohrenz, 1983.

Malet, Michael. *Nestor Makhno in the Russian Civil War*. London: Macmillan Press, 1982.

Malynov'skyi, B. "Zahin N. Makhna u druhii polovyni zhovtnia – na pochatku lystopada 1918 r." *Hurzhiivs'ki istorychni chytannia. Vypusk* 3 (2009): 354–58.

Malynov'skyi, B.V., and T.V. Malynov'skaya. "Nemtsy-zemlevladel'tsy v sotsial'nyn konflitakh perioda ukrainskoi narodnoi respubliki i ukrainskoi derzhavy getmana P.P Skoropadskogo (1918 g.)." In *Voprosy germanskoi istori*, edited by Svetlana Bobyleva, 136–37. Dnipropetrovsk: RVV DNY, 2007.

March, G.P. *Cossacks of Brotherhood: The Zaporog Kosh of the Dniepr River*. New York: P. Lang, 1990.

Martin, Terry. "The Empire's New Frontiers: New Russia's Path from Frontier to 'Okraina.'" *Russian History* 19, no. 1/4 (1992): 181–201.

Masnenko, V.V. "Nestor Makhno i Ukraina: do problemy samoidentyfikatsii 'selians'koho bat'ka.'" *Ukrains'ka Selianyn* 21 (2019): 21–33.

Mayer, Arno J. *The Furies: Violence and Terror in the French and Russian Revolutions*. Princeton: Princeton University Press, 2000.

Morris, Brian. *Kropotkin: The Politics of Community*. Oakland: PM Press, 2018.

Morrison, Alexander. "Russian Settler Colonialism." In *The Routledge Handbook of the History of Settler Colonialism*, edited by Lorenzo Veracini and Ed Cavanaugh, 313–26. Abingdon: Routledge, 2017.

Neufeldt, Reina c. "'We Are Aware of Our Contradictions': Russlaender Mennonite Narratives of Loss and the Reconstruction of Peoplehood, 1914–1923." *Journal of Mennonite Studies* 27 (2009): 129–54.

Nomad, Max. *Apostles of Revolution*. Boston: Little, Brown and Company, 1939.

Novopolin, G. "Makhno i guliai-pol'skaia gruppa anarkhistov." In *Nestor Ivanovich Makhno. Vospominaniia materialy i dokumenty*, edited by V.F. Verstiuk, 131–36. Kyiv: RIF Dzvin, 1991.

Ostras,' E.S. "Zvidky pishla nazva Ukraina." *Visnyk Donets'koho natsional'noho universytetu* 1 (2008): 109–18.

Palij, Michael. *The Anarchism of Nestor Makhno, 1918–1921: An Aspect of the Ukrainian Revolution*. Seattle: University of Washington Press, 1976.

Patterson, Sean. "The Eichenfeld Massacre: Recontextualizing Mennonite and Makhnovist Narratives." *Journal of Mennonite Studies* 32 (2014): 151–74.

Peters, Victor. *Nestor Makhno: The Life of an Anarchist*. Translated by Victor Peters. Winnipeg: Echo Books, 1971.

Plokhy, Serhii. *The Gates of Europe: A History of Ukraine*. New York: Basic Books, 2015.

Pomper, Philip. *The Russian Revolutionary Intelligentsia*. Arlington Heights, IL: H. Davidson, 1993.

Rempel, Johann G. "Mennonite Revolutionaries in the Khortitza Settlement Under the Tsarist Regime." *Journal of Mennonite Studies* 10 (1992): 72–86.

Ricoeur, Paul. "The Human Experience of Time and Narrative." In *The Ricoeur Reader: Reflection and Imagination*, edited by Mario J. Valdés, 99–116. Toronto: University of Toronto Press, 1991.

Roden, Evelyn, and Margie Koop. "Janzens: From Tragedy in Russia to a New Life in Canada." *Saskatchewan Mennonite Historian* 16 no. 3 (October 2010): 26–27.

Rublev, D. I. "Russkiie anarkhisty v Ispanskoi grazhdanskoi voine (1936–1939 gg.)." In *Grazhdanskaia voina v Ispanii: Izvestnoe i neizvestnoe*, edited by A. Iu. Fedorov and Iu. V. Fetisov, 201–29. Moscow: URSS, 2017.

Savchenko, V.A. *Makhno*. Kharkiv: Folio, 2005.

———. "The Anarchist Movement in Ukraine at the Height of the New Economic Policy (1924–25)." Translated by Malcolm Archibald. *East/West: Journal of Ukrainian Studies* 4, no. 2 (2017): 173–86.

Schapansky, Henry. "On the Origins of the Mennonite Estates in Russia," *Preservings* 27 (2007): 34–38.

Semanov, S.N. "Pod chernym znamenem, ili zhizn' i smert' Nestora Makhno" *Roman-Gazeta* 4 (1993): 1–37.

Shubin, A. *Anarkhistskii sotsialnyi eksperiment: Ukraina i Ispaniia, 1917–1939 gg.* Moscow: Institut vseobshchei istorii RAN, 1998.

Skirda, Alexandre. *Facing the Enemy: A History of Anarchist Organization from Proudhon to May 1968*. Translated by Paul Sharkey. Oakland: AK Press, 2002.

———. *Nestor Makhno – Anarchy's Cossack: The Struggle for Free Soviets in the Ukraine, 1917–1921*. Translated by Paul Sharkey. Oakland: AK Press, 2004.

Skrypnyk, Oleksandr. *Za zolotom Nestora Makhna*. Kyiv: Iaroslaviv Val, 2011.

Staples, John R. "On Civilizing the Nogais': Mennonite-Nogai Economic Relations, 1825–1860." *Mennonite Quarterly Review* 74.2 (April 2000): 229–56.

Stauffer, Ethelbert. "The Anabaptist Theology of Martyrdom." *Mennonite Quarterly Review* 19 (1945): 179–214.

Sutherland, Willard. *Taming the Wild Field: Colonization and Empire on the Russian Steppe.* Ithaca, NY: Cornell University Press, 2004.

Sysyn, Frank. "Nestor Makhno and the Ukrainian Revolution." In *The Ukraine: 1917–1921, A Study in Revolution*, edited by Taras Hunczak, 271–304. Cambridge: Harvard University Press, 1977.

Thornton, Thomas Perry. "Terror as a Weapon of Political Agitation." In *Internal War: Problems and Approaches*, edited by Harry Eckstein, 71–99. New York: Free Press of Glencoe, 1964.

Toews, John B. "The Beginnings of *Friedensstimme*." *Mennonite Historian* 24, no. 3 (September 2000): 1–2.

———. *Czars, Soviets and Mennonites.* Newton, KS: Faith and Life Press, 1982.

———. "The Origins and Activities of the Mennonite *Selbstschutz* in the Ukraine (1918–1919)." *Mennonite Quarterly Review* 46 (1972): 5–40.

———. "A Voice of Peace in Troubled Times." *Mennonite Life* (September 1972): 93–94.

Towes, John B., ed. *The Mennonites in Russia from 1917 to 1930: Selected Documents.* Winnipeg: Christian Press, 1975.

Toews, Paul, with Aileen Friesen. *The Russian Mennonite Story: The Heritage Cruise Lectures.* Winnipeg: Centre for Transnational Mennonite Studies, 2018.

Timoshchuk, A. *Anarkho-kommunisticheskie formirovaniia N. Makhno: sentiabr' 1917-avgust 1921 r.* Simferopol: "Tavriia," 1996.

Tsebry, Osip. *Memoirs of a Makhnovist Partisan*. London: Kate Sharpley Library, 1993.

Turcato, Davide. "Anarchist Communism." In *The Palgrave Handbook of Anarchism*, edited by Carly Levy and Matthew S. Adams, 237–47. Cham, Switzerland: Palgrave Macmillan, 2019.

Urry, James. *Mennonites, Politics, and Peoplehood: Europe, Russia, Canada, 1525–1980.* Winnipeg: University of Manitoba Press, 2006.

———. "Through the Eye of a Needle: Wealth and the Mennonite Experience in Imperial Russia." *Journal of Mennonite Studies* 3 (1985): 7–35.

Venger, N.V. "Nestor Makhno ta "nemets'ke pytannia" na ukrains'kykh zemliakh." In *Persha svitova viina i revoliutsii vektory sotsiukul'turnykh transformatsii*, edited by C.C. Troiana, 30–62. Kyiv: Kondor, 2017.

———. "Yevreis' kit a menonits' ki pohromy na pivdni ukrayini: do pytannya pro typologiyu ta semantyku podii 1919 r." *Humanitarnyi zhurnal* 3–4 (lito-osin' 2011): 138–47.

Vogt, Willi. "Liste der Mennonitischen Industrie- und Handelsunternehmen in Russland." *Mennonitische Geschichte und Ahnenforschung Chortitza*, https://chort.square7.ch/Pis/Indust.pdf (accessed 2019).

Volkovinskii, V.N. *Makhno i ego krakh.* Moscow: VZPI, 1991.

# INDEX


A

anarcho-communism, 4–5, 66

anti-semitism, 21, 25, 66, 70, 140, 142

Antoni, Voldemar, 49

Arshinov, Peter: accused of covering up for Makhno, 70; biography, 26–28; denies Soviet version of Kuzmenko diary, 37; describes Makhnovist army in fall 1919, 123–24; on Dibrivka, 166n162; on formation of Selbstschutz, 56; and hatred of privileged class, 63, 64; and *History of the Makhnovist Movement*, 28; on Makhno, 42, 107; on Makhnovist-White Army fighting, 68; and *The Unknown Revolution*, 31; view of seizure of land by Peasant Union, 54; on violent reprisals by Makhnovists, 62

Astakhoff, Nikita Saloff, 112, 130, 138, 150–51

Austro-German troops: fight with Makhnovists, 7, 34, 55–59, 63; Mennonite embrace of, 56, 90–91, 117, 145–46; occupation of Ukraine, 7, 64–65; and punitive detachments, 117; treatment of peasants, 96; withdraw from Ukraine, 8, 34, 118

B

Baron, Aron, 70

Belash, Viktor: attitude towards violence, 66; biography, 38–39; on German colonists change of alliance, 72; on German occupation, 64–65; on *kontrrazvedka*, 69; on Makhno's execution list, 129; on Makhnovist membership, 15; on Makhnovists battles, 127, 166n162, 176n84, 176n85; memoir described, 39; on N. Makhno's movements at time of massacre, 127, 128, 135; on S. Pravda, 105; on Velyka Mykhailivka, 166n162; use of New Style calendar dates, 113–15

Berg, Abram, 134

Berkman, Alexander, 33

Bipetskii, A.V., 111, 128, 132–33, 139

Blumenort massacre, 134–36

Bolsheviks: alliance with Makhnovists, 8–9; extract goods from Mennonites, 122; fight White Army, 8; fighting at Katerynoslav, 120; plot to assassinate Makhno, 135; seize power, 7; and Volin, 30, 31

Borosenko massacre, 148

C

Catherine the Great, 14, 79, 150
Chortitza colony, 63, 81, 106, 115–16, 160n16
Chubenko, Aleksei, 39–40, 65–66
Cornies, Johann, 82
Cossacks, 7, 79, 96, 117, 151

D

Denikin, Anton, 8, 9, 63, 68, 69, 123
Dibrivka, Battle of, 56, 166n162
Dombrowsky, Abram, 134
Doubinsky, Jacques, 31
Doukhobors, 79
Dyck, Jakob, 117, 120, 121, 122, 174n40
Dyck, John, 122
Dyck, Peter J., 76, 88, 89–90

E

Eichenfeld, village of, 116
Eichenfeld massacre: confusion arising from new and old dating systems, 113–15; described, 109–10, 131–32; first hand accounts, 132–34; killing of landowners and not workers during, 133–34; memorial for, 152, 154; motivation for, 132–33, 140–41, 143; rape and plunder during, 132; as religious reckoning, 149; as retribution for killing of militia men, 123; role of local peasantry in, 110, 112, 136–37; significance of Makhno's citizens' address to, 130; sources for, 110–13
Eichenfelder Selbstschutz, 122–23
Eideman, R.P., 36–38
emplotment, 12
Epp, Margaret, 136

F

Feldman, Leah, 70
*Friedensstime* (newspaper): assessed as source, 77–78; coverage of Makhnovist murder and robbery, 91; and Makhno's fall 1918 raids, 23; and Mennonite-peasantry relationship, 84, 85; questions Mennonite religious faith, 98–99; reports of punitive detachments, 94; reports on *Selbstschutz*, 93–94, 118
Friesen, Heinrich, 137
Friesen, Peter, 87–88

G

Gaenko, Feodora, 36, 37, 38
German colonists: face anti-German sentiment during First World War, 88–90; land received from Tsar, 81; Makhno's view of, 53; Makhnovists view of, 10–11, 24, 25, 26, 65; relations with Makhnovists, 145; and retribution for burning Velyka Mykhailivka, 57; support for Austro-German troops, 56; and Russian nationalism, 87–88; working for Makhnovists, 72, 137–39
Gladchenko, T. F., 120
Goerz, Anna, 102, 104
Goosen family, 50
Greens, 8
Gurazda, Raisa, 132

H

Heinrichs, Cornelius, 116, 117–18, 120, 121, 137, 174n40
Heinrichs, Heinrich H.: and the Eichenfeld *Selbstschutz*, 118–19; flees Eichenfeld, 123, 175n50, 175n53; as friend of D. Rempel, 116; photos, 117, 119; relation of M. Janzen, 112
Heinrichs, Heinrich Kornelius, 116, 131

Hetmanate, 34
Hiebert, Daniel, 122, 123
Hollanderei, 89–90
Huliaipole Anarcho-Communist Group, 54
Huliaipole Peasant Union, 51–55
Hutman, H., 125–26

I
Iudenich, Nikolai, 8
Ivanchenko (Bolshevik commander), 121

J
Janz, B.B., 135
Janzen, Abram Jakob, 101–2, 103
Janzen, Heinrich Peter, 43, 46
Janzen, Maria Friesen, 102, 103
Janzen family, 77, 101
Jews, 48, 63, 124. *See also* anti-semitism

K
Kaethler, Heinrich, 102
Kalashnikov, A., 125, 129
Karetnik (Adjutant), 129
Klassen, H.W., 133
Klassen estate, 54, 104, 158n16, 165n135
Klein, Alexander, 128, 138
Klippenstein, Susanna, 122
Kolchak, Aleksander, 8
Kolesnik, Kornei, 43–44
Konovalov (Commander), 135, 177n114
*kontrrazvedka*, 69–70, 75, 123, 125–27
Kornilov, Lavr, 53
Kroeger, Arthur, 73, 77–78
Kroeger, Jakob, 154
Kroeker, Abraham, 77–78, 98–99, 100
Kropotkin, Peter, 2, 4–6, 157n2
Kuzmenko, Halyna: biography, 35–36; description of diary, 36–38; and Makhno's arrest, 32, 34–35; on Makhno's erratic behaviour, 71–72; on Mariental massacre, 71; meets Makhno, 162n55; and Volin, 32, 70

L
Lenin, 20, 30
Lentz (estate owner), 60
Levadnyi, Paraska, 50
Lichtenau Conference, 94
Loewen, Abram, 126
Loewen, Julius, 90, 118, 120, 123, 127, 128
Lohrenz, Gerhard: on anti-German sentiment during First World War, 88–89; assessed as source, 76–77; on Mennonite village in 19th century, 80; on Mennonite-peasantry relationship, 84, 85–86; on Mennonites as successful farmers, 82; on rape of Mennonite women, 91–92; on what constitutes a sin, 100

M
Makhno, Elena, 37
Makhno, Nestor: accused of banditry and anti-semitism, 25; arrest in Danzig, 32–35, 161n40; alliance with Red Army, 9, 120, 123; asked to protect tent missionaries, 130; and the Blumenort massacre, 134–36; break out at Perehonivka, 68, 123; and burning of Velyka Mykhailivka, 57–58, 91; as child labourer, 42–45; claims of atrocities by, 13, 23, 70, 91; defends *kontrrazvedka*, 126; description of his memoirs, 32; details of life pre-civil war, 3–4; early involvement in revolutionary politics, 49, 50, 51–52; effect his raids had on growth of *Selbstschutz*, 91, 97; erratic behaviour of, 70, 71–72; ethical position on use of violence, 24, 41, 55, 58–59, 62, 66–67; evidence for

his movements at time of Eichenfeld massacre, 127, 128, 135; and F. Shchus, 65–66, 67, 142–43; failure to stop violence, 142–43; family of, 163n79; fighting White Russians, 68, 113–15, 123, 127–28, 178n121; given title of Bat'ko, 56; hatred for the rich, 44–45, 55; and Ukrainian ethnicity, 19–20, 160n3; indicted by Soviets in 1922, 39; influence of Kropotkin on, 5–6; land redistribution by, 52–55, 59–60; local lore about, 1, 41–42; and Makhnovist violence, 25–26, 124–25; memorial statue, 153; Mennonite encounters with, 42, 101–7; Mennonite view of, 1–2, 3, 11, 97, 101, 147; opposition to political nationalism, 20, 21, 160n9; organizes insurgency against Austro-German troops, 7, 55–56, 63; photos, 49, 51, 57, 61; assassination plan, 56, 65, 135; relations with P. Arshinov, 27; relations with Volin, 30, 32; relationship with H. Kuzmenko, 36, 162n55; return to Ukraine after release from prison, 51; role in Eichenfeld massacre, 109–10, 134, 177n117; Soviet propaganda on, 111; view of German colonists, 53; view of Mennonites, 55; Volin on, 11–12, 70; citizens' address, 128–29, 130. *See also* Makhnovists/Makhnovshchina

Makhno, Omelian, 55

Makhnovists/Makhnovshchina: alliance with Bolsheviks, 8–9; and anti-semitism, 66, 70; and Blumenort massacre, 135–36; claims of atrocities by, 13, 91–93, 129–30; class and ethnicity, 10, 19–22, 24, 139–40; Draft Declaration, 21–22, 125; emergence of, 7, 8; *kontrrazvedka*, 69–70, 123, 125–26; fight against Austro-German troops, 7, 34, 55–59, 63; fight against White Army, 8, 9, 63–64, 68–69, 123, 135; G. Schroeder on, 101; German Makhnovists, 137–39; hatred for colonies, 24; and Jewish pogroms, 124; killing of tent missionaries, 130–31; terror, 141–43, 147, 150–51; and Mariental massacre, 71; Mennonite sources view of, 75–76; Mennonite Makhnovists, 138–39; moral decline of, 67–68; and October 1919 election, 75; problem of violence within, 25–26, 91, 123–25, 139–40; raids of Mennonites, 23, 60–62, 91–93, 97, 146–47; redistribution of land by, 6, 9–10, 15–16; role in Eichenfeld massacre, 109, 110–11, 131–32; strength and violence of army in fall 1919, 63, 123–25; view of German colonists, 10–11, 24, 25, 26, 65; view of Mennonites, 3, 10; view of peasants, 15; violence on Mennonites by, 7, 62–63, 124, 128, 146–47; written sources for, 28–40. *See also* Makhno, Nestor

Mariental colony, 71

Martens, Helena, 132

Marxism, 5

Mennonites: and Anabaptist martyrdom, 97–100; and anti-German sentiment during First World War, 88–90; assessment of sources, 74–75, 76–78; attacked by Soviets, 121, 122; and the Austro-German occupation, 56, 90–91, 117, 145–46; criticized for materialism, 98–99; early years in Russia, 79–88; economic success of, 13–14, 46, 81–82, 98, 159n35; effect of *Selbstschutz* on identity, 96, 147–48; emigration to N. America, 87; encounters with N. Makhno, 42, 101–7; Hollanderei, 89–90, 146; and killing of tent missionaries, 130–31; and land tenure, 82–84; in the Makhnovist army, 138–39; and Makhnovist occupation, 9–10; organization of *Selbstschutz*, 9; and pacifism, 78, 148–49, 157n3; and *Privilegium*, 80–81; and punitive detachments, 94–96, 116–17; rape of, 10, 91–92; relationship with peasantry, 48, 82–86, 137, 146, 150, 169n38; in S. Roger report, 22–23; social insularity of, 80; and Russian nationalism, 87–88; sources on Eichenfeld massacre, 112–13; sources on *kontrrazvedka*, 75, 126–27; pacifism and self-defence, 91, 92, 99–100, 147–48; and the Tsar, 87–88; and Velyka Mykhailivka, 57, 58; view of Makhnovists, 11, 75–76, 147; view of N. Makhno, 1–2, 3, 97, 101; view of peasants, 15, 149; and Makhnovist violence, 7, 62–63, 124, 146–47; and the White Army, 63; who joined revolutionary groups, 23. *See also* Eichenfeld massacre; *Selbstschutz*

Mett, Ida, 70

Molotschna colony: arrival of Austro-German troops in, 90; and Blumenort massacre, 134; effect of First World War on, 88; overrun by Makhnovists, 23, 64, 69; and *Selbstschutz*, 63–64, 93, 94; takes in fleeing colonists, 34, 61, 63, 97, 146–47

Mratchnyi, Mark, 70, 71

N

Nabat anarchists, 25

Nabat Confederation, 27

Neu Grüntal, 58, 146, 165n149

Neufeld, Dietrich: on abandoning pacifism, 99–100; on anti-German feeling during First World War, 88, 89; asked to write poem to Makhno, 105; assessed as source, 77; comparing dates of with Belash's, 114–15; knowledge of peasants' plight, 149; on *kontrrazvedka*, 126; on local peasants' conditions, 84; on Makhno, 101; and Makhnovist atrocities, 129–30; on Mennonite-peasantry relationship, 86; and Mennonites loss of identity, 148; and Sagradowka massacre, 143

Neufeld, Jakob (Blumenort), 134–35

Neufeld, Jakob (Ebenfeld), 102–3, 104

Neufeld, Johann, 136

New Russia, 79–80

Niebuhr, Jakob, 117

O

Orlov, E. P., 111, 132

P

Paetkau, Katherina, 133

peasants: Austro-German troops treatment of, 96; campaign of black terror, 49–50; envy and resentment of Mennonites, 140–41; identifying, 14–15; raids on Mennonite property, 116; reaction to Mennonites' support of Austro-German troops, 91; relationship with Mennonites, 48, 82–86, 137, 146, 150, 169n38; resistance to Austro-German troops, 55–59; revolts, 47–49; role in Eichenfeld massacre, 110, 112, 136–37; view of Makhnovists, 16

Penner, David, 119, 123

Penner, Katherina, 137–38

Peters, Maria, 106–7

Petliura, Symon, 8, 160n9

Petrenko (Commander), 124

Pravda, Simeon, 105–6, 128

*Privilegium*, 80–81, 87

Provisional government, 51, 53

Q

Quiring, David A., 133–34, 138, 139

R

Rada (Ukrainian nationalists), 7, 20

rape: during Eichenfeld massacre, 109, 132; Makhno accused of, 70; in Mennonite reports, 75, 147, 170n77; of Mennonite women, 10, 63, 91–92; at Velyka Mykhailivka, 56; as weapon of war, 92–93, 124

Regehr, Henry, 147

Reimer, Adolf, 90–91, 93–94, 99

Rempel, David: as friend of H. Heinrichs, 116, 175n50, 175n53; on German-speaking Makhnovists, 138; on kontrrazvedka, 126; and Makhnovist hatred of colonies, 24; on Mennonite insularity, 80; and Mennonites joining revolutionary groups, 23; on motivation for Eichenfeld massacre, 140; on peasantry's role in Eichenfeld massacre, 136–37

Revolutionary Military Soviet (RMS), 6, 30, 126, 167n183

*Roads of Nestor Makhno* (Belash), 39

Roger, Stéphane, 22–23

Russian Revolution, 7–9, 31

S

Sagradowka massacre, 138, 141, 143

Sawatsky, Anton, 118, 149, 174n30

Schönfeld colony, 23, 46, 60, 61, 104–5

Schroeder, Gerhard: assessed as source, 77; encounter with Makhno, 104–5; on kontrrazvedka, 127; on Makhnovist philosophy, 101; and October 1919 election, 75; and role of peasantry in Eichenfeld massacre, 136; and Wiens, 105–6

Selbstschutz: defends Jasykowo, 119–20, 121; effect of on Mennonite identity, 96, 147–48; in Eichenfeld, 117–19; formation of, 56, 93–94, 171n87; gives up weapons to Soviets, 121, 174n40; growth of due to Makhnovist raids, 91, 97; H. B. Wiens on, 74–75; joins White Army, 9–10, 147; kontrrazvedka's role in hunting down, 126; and Mariental massacre, 71; organization of, 9–10, 117–18, 147; as protector of Molotschna, 23; punitive detachments role in growth of, 94–96; rape as motive for joining, 91, 93; role in Eichenfeld massacre, 110, 112, 122–23, 132–33; White Army training of, 63

self-censorship, 26

Semeniuta, Prokop, 49

Shchus, Fedir, 56, 57, 65–66, 67, 142–43, 176n84

Silberfeld estate, 47, 101–2, 103

Silbertal, 65, 66

Skirda, Alexandre, 32, 76, 110, 161n38, 161n40, 163n87

Skoropadskyi, Pavlo, 7

Snissnarenko (Soviet militia chief), 122

Soviet Union, 33, 36–38, 39, 111, 116

Stolypin, P.A., 50

Stundist tent mission, 130–31

T

Taranovskii (Makhnovist commander), 114

Thiessen, Peter, 138

Toews, Jacob, 23, 84–85, 89, 94, 96, 171n87

Tsarist government, 50, 87–88

typhus epidemic, 124, 151, 175n61

U

Ukraine, 7, 14–15, 46–49, 55–56
Ukrainian Civil War, 13–14
Ukrainian peasantry. *See* peasantry
Ukrainian People's Army, 8, 120
Ukrainian People's Republic, 7
Union of Poor Peasants, 49–50

V

Van Kampen, Peter, 117, 118, 119
Velyka Mykhailivka, burning of, 56–57, 91, 146, 166n162
Victor Peters collection, 76
Volin (Vsevolod Eikhenbaum): biography, 28–31; and H. Kuzmenko, 36, 70; and influence of counter-intelligence, 70; on Makhno, 11–12, 70; on Makhno-Kuzmenko relationship, 162n55; on Makhno's evacuation from Katerynoslav, 178n121; Makhno's letters to, 33; on Makhnovist-White Army fight, 135; on moral decline of Makhnovists, 67, 71; relations with Arshinov, 27; and *The Unknown Revolution*, 31–32; view of kontrrazvedka, 126

W

Warkentin, Elizabeth, 137
White Army: fight against Makhnovists, 8, 9, 63–64, 68–69, 123, 135; launches assault on Oleksandrivsk, 127; and Selbstschutz, 9–10, 147; tie to Mennonites, 9–10, 93
Wiens, H.B., 74–75, 86, 105–6
Wintergruen estate, 47, 50
First Wold War, 88–91

Y

Yazykov (Russian noble), 115

Z

Zadov, Lev, 37
Zaporizhian oak tree, 151, 154
Zaporizhian Sich, 79